T0368024

CHINA'S DESTINY
AND CHINESE ECONOMIC THEORY

CHINA'S DESTINY
AND CHINESE ECONOMIC
THEORY

CHIANG KAI-SHEK

With Notes and Commentary
by
PHILIP JAFFE

GLOBAL
ORIENTAL
LEIDEN • BOSTON
2013

Global Oriental Classic Reprints No.12

CHINA'S DESTINY AND CHINESE ECONOMIC THEORY

By Chiang Kai-shek

First published in Great Britain in 1947 by Dennis Dobson Limited, London

ISBN 978-19-05-24681-6

CONTENTS

5

"THE SECRET OF CHINA'S DESTINY"

By Philip Jaffe

THE SECRET OF "CHINA'S DESTINY"

NEARLY fifty years ago, an American Secretary of State declared that "the world's peace rests with China, and whoever understands China . . . holds the key to world politics during the next five centuries." John Hay's appraisal of China's role in world affairs can be made with even greater validity today. For the first time in more than a century, the four hundred and fifty million people of China have a chance to become real masters of their own destiny. The renunciation of the "unequal treaties" by the United States and Great Britain in 1942 officially ended China's humiliating semicolonial status and marked her emergence as a potential political equal among the other great powers. But whether China succeeds in converting her hard-won formal independence into actual freedom from foreign domination is certain to exercise a profound influence on the future history of Asia and the world.

It is easy enough to demonstrate that what happens to China is of vital importance to world peace and prosperity, but it is not so easy to evaluate the conflicting forces and contradictory trends in present-day China, or to predict the path that China will follow in the future. Invariably certain pertinent questions readily come to mind. How are we to reconcile the courage and endurance displayed by the Chinese people during more than eight years of devastating war with the existence in China of one of the most corrupt governments of modern times? What weight can we give to that government's claim that it intends to introduce democracy, when in practice it has followed a policy of bloody suppression of civil liberties and has made extensive use of secret police and concentration camps to enforce its system of "thought control?" Can we accept at

11

their face value the ambitious plans for China's future industrial development put forward by the Central Government when that same government has shown itself strongly
opposed to the basic agrarian reforms that alone can create
a sound economic foundation for such industrialization?

Admittedly, the situation in China is confusing and complex. For every hopeful and progressive trend, it is possible
to cite an example of extreme reaction and social demoralization. How, then, can we hope to understand China? What
standard or guide shall we use to interpret conflicting reports
of the state of affairs in a country that was our valued ally
in war and that must of necessity play an important role in
the winning of the peace?

One essential key to such understanding is to recognize
that China is a nation in revolution—a revolution precipitated more than a century ago by the impact of the West
on China's ancient civilization. The Chinese people fought
an exhausting war for national survival for more than eight
years. But for a far longer period, they have been struggling
to free themselves from the fetters of an outmoded and oppressive political and economic system, and to build a sound
foundation for national freedom and economic progress. In
this second phase of their revolution, the people of China
have been opposed not only by the foreign interests that
have sought to keep them in semicolonial subjection, but
also by their own officials, warlords, and landed gentry,
who have frequently sided with the foreign powers against
their own people. Even today, when China is well on the
way to winning permanent freedom from foreign domination, this same bureaucratic hierarchy, fearful of losing its
privileges and power, is again seeking foreign aid in order
to retain that power.

The many seemingly contradictory aspects of the current
situation in China are reflections of this continuing struggle
between those that are working to build a new and independent China based on a democratic system of government

and modern methods of production, and those that have a vested interest in preserving the semicolonial and traditional social structure of ancient China with its system of rule by a privileged bureaucracy and its preindustrial economy supported by the hand labor of millions of peasants living in a status of virtual serfdom. This struggle has shaped the course of Chinese political history during the past twenty-five years; it explains the acute internal strains and tensions that developed during the war; it is responsible for the existence of two sharply differing schools of thought regarding China's future political, economic, and cultural structure. It is a conflict between old and new philosophies of government and human rights, and it is being waged not only between the Kuomintang and opposition parties and groups, but also within the Kuomintang itself. Only in the light of this conflict is it possible to understand the real nature of the internal struggle in China.

The agents of reaction in the China of today are distinguished by their championing of China's ancient culture, particularly the political and social concepts embodied in the Confucian feudal philosophy of life. They maintain that these concepts are far superior to the doctrines of Western liberal thought and that they must remain the basis of Chinese society. They paint a highly idealized and romanticized picture of the beauty and harmony that arise from a faithful adherence to the "ancient virtues" of a paternalistic, agrarian society. They write rapturously of the moral precepts of Confucianism which for more than two thousand years enabled the emperors and mandarins of China to keep the people in subjection and enforce unquestioning obedience to the rule of the "scholar-gentry." They understand fully that the Confucian theory of personal government by "gentlemen" justifies the monopoly of power by a privileged elite. They know only too well that the Confucian doctrine of "social status," with its emphasis on authority and subservience, provides the perfect dogma with which those that have acquired a monopoly of power may oppose popular demands for democracy and equal civil rights for all.

Indoctrination in Confucian ethical principles has replaced independent thought and teaching in the schools and colleges of Kuomintang China. The educational principle of "training the people to be leaders of the nation" has been supplanted by the rules laid down by the Kuomintang, one of which reads: "Obedience is the basic spirit of responsibility. . . . The people must obey absolutely the orders of the Government and the commands of the Leader." Agents of the Kuomintang's secret police keep close supervision over the activities and "thoughts" of both students and teachers, and those that dare to disobey the dictates of the Party's Ministry of Education do so at the risk of their careers, if not their lives.

A similar philosophic outlook characterizes the official Kuomintang attitude toward economic reconstruction. The comprador-landlord-merchant-usurer class, which today holds political power in China, is naturally in favor of preserving the semicolonial semifeudal land and tax system that is the basis of their wealth and power. These successors to the mandarins and landed gentry of imperial China do not want a program of genuine economic modernization and industrial development that would free millions of peasants from the land and necessitate basic reforms in the present system of landlord-tenant and semicolonial relations. Though ambitious plans have been outlined for the establishment of modern industries under state supervision, in none of these is there any mention of measures to raise the living standards of the people by freeing them from the burdens of extortionate rents, usurious interest charges and insupportable taxation, so that they may constitute a prosperous market for the products of these new industries. Instead, the peasants of Kuomintang China are offered lofty moral disquisitions on the Confucian virtues of obedience to authority, righteousness, harmony, frugality, and the simple life.

These reactionary forces are the living symbol of the old China—the China that revered tradition and abhorred experiment and innovation; the China that identified literacy and a knowledge of the classics with governing ability and the right to power; the China of the ancient family system that made protection of the family's interests the highest virtue, encouraged nepotism and official corruption in the name of "filial piety," and thus discouraged the growth of social responsibility and national consciousness; the China of Confucius, who said that "courtesy is not extended to the commoners and punishment is not served up to the lords," and of Mencius, who argued that "without the gentleman there would be no one to rule the common people, and without the common people there would be no one to feed the gentleman." As the dominant political power in Kuomintang China, these representatives of the old China have enforced their reactionary philosophy in the fields of education, government, and economic administration, in a determined effort to counteract the increasingly powerful forward drive of the new China—the China that believes in democracy, in full independence, and in basic political and economic rights for all citizens.

The spokesmen for this new China include most intellectuals in Kuomintang China, the members of the Democratic League, many younger army officers, students, small businessmen, the more progressive-minded industrialists and bankers who recognize the necessity for national independence and thorough-going agrarian reforms, and the Communists and their supporters. These forward-looking groups do not contemplate a complete break with China's past, or the indiscriminate adoption of foreign concepts of political and social organization. But they are convinced that the "ancient virtues" of feudalism cannot form the basis of a strong and democratic nation; that China can achieve unity, independence, and prosperity only on the basis of a political system that guarantees the people a real voice in their government and on the basis of an economic system that can make full use of modern methods of industrial and agricultural production with the welfare of the people as a whole as its main goal. These forward-looking groups see no reason why China should remain "unique" in the sense of rejecting what is best in Western thought and science. While fully agreed that the new structure of Chinese society should retain all that is sound and valuable in Chinese culture and tradition, they are determined that it shall discard the oppressive features of a political and economic system that made the old China a symbol of "supreme changeless magnificence" for the few, based upon supreme changeless poverty and ignorance for the many.

A vivid illustration of the war of ideas that is raging in present-day China is provided by comments on Confucianism made by Madame Sun Yat-sen, widow of China's great revolutionary leader, and her brother-in-law, Generalissimo Chiang Kai-shek. In Madame Sun's opinion, "the structure of our present society is radically changing and it is difficult to solve the many problems that arise from great changes. Confucianism cannot help to solve these problems; it has lost every practical value. . . . Confucian teachings are feudalistic and autocratic from beginning to end. . . . We must make great efforts to uproot Confucian ideas from every nook and corner of our life and thought." Chiang Kai-shek, on the other hand, pays the following tribute to the Confucian way of life in his book, *China's Destiny:* "China's own philosophy of life, developed by Confucius, amplified and propagated by Mencius, and further explained by the Han scholars, automatically became a lofty system that is superior to any other philosophy in the world. . . . The glories and scope of our ancient Chinese learning cannot be equaled in the history of any of the strong Western nations of today."

Viewed in terms of a conflict between the new and the old, recent Chinese history seems at first glance to represent a victory for the old. The suppression of civil liberties and

the persecution of opposition groups; the unbridled speculation in land and commodities while industrial production
is neglected; a rapacious and inequitable taxation system
that serves chiefly to line the pockets of local warlords and
officials—all these and many other equally ugly features of
the Chinese scene can be cited to prove that the reactionary
forces are strongly in the saddle in the Chinese Government.

But the philosophy of these reactionaries no longer has
any deep roots in present-day China. The core of the old
Chinese social structure was the feudal family system, but
today millions are homeless, families have been broken up,
and the new concepts of individual initiative, patriotism,
national unity, and collective action have replaced the old
pattern of isolated family units, following obediently in the
paths prescribed by the elders of the clan. The leaders of the
Kuomintang may dwell on the beauties of the old agrarian
society and the virtues of a "pure and frugal life." But millions
of peasants know at bitter cost that this system condemns
them to abject poverty and leaves them at the mercy of the
landlord, tax collector, and usurer. The Kuomintang sponsored "New Life Movement" urges the Chinese people to
button their shirts, keep their houses clean, and lead a
righteous life. But the peasants of China have no shirts and
no cleaning materials, and their lives are little more than a
desperate struggle for mere existence. They are in no mood
to accept moralizing as a substitute for constructive reforms.

It is true that China today is ruled by a feudal-minded
oligarchy of compradors, landlords, merchants, and usurers,
but that oligarchy has been obliged to use the most severe
repressive measures to remain in power and even so its
control over the country has steadily weakened. This in
itself is evidence that the Chinese people do not willingly
support semicolonialism and the traditional structure of
Chinese society. Millions of Chinese men and women outside
the sacred circle of the upper bureaucracy know that they
cannot find a solution for their problems by adhering to an

autocratic, semifeudal and semicolonial social structure, and an outmoded and stagnant economic system. These millions are the true representatives of the Chinese Revolution. It is they who since the fateful day of July 7, 1937, have been the real fighting soldiers in the struggle for national survival and who at the same time have kept the flames of freedom within China from being completely extinguished by the Kuomintang hierarchy.

In this struggle between the old and the new China, Chiang Kai-shek occupies a position both unique and contradictory. On the one hand, he is the symbol to the world of China's unbroken resistance to Japan, the man under whose government China threw off the fetters of the unequal treaties, and thus the logical candidate for the leadership of post-war China. Yet it is difficult to envisage Chiang as the leader of a new China, in view of his actions and writings in which he has consistently aligned himself with the old. His feudal and antidemocratic political and economic philosophy is given its fullest expression in the two books, *China's Destiny* and *Chinese Economic Theory*, both shrouded in mystery and secrecy as far as the American people are concerned, and now made available for the first time in English in this volume.

It is interesting to consider why two such importan books have been kept from the American people. For example, in January, 1946, at the height of a Congressional controversy over China, the request of six Congressmen to see the State Department's translation of *China's Destiny* was refused by the Secretary of State on the ground that it was a "top secret" document and that it was not a propitious moment at which to make this document public. This was a strange comment on a book that has sold over a million copies in China and that since 1944 has been on public sale in this country in the Chinese language edition, to be translated and published by anyone who cared to do so.

Why was the State Department so "cautious" about a book that, though a "secret" to the American people, is no

secret to its millions of Chinese readers? One can only speculate as to the reasons, but it is a fact that one of the most
effective sections of *China's Destiny* is its accurate description
and vigorous denunciation of Western imperialist penetration
of China, and of the crippling effects of the "unequal treaties"
on China's development. It may well be that inasmuch as
the State Department has been playing a very big part in
directing the economic, military, and political life of China
since V-J Day, it wished to avoid any unflattering comparisons
between the earlier days of Western intervention in China
and the post-war policy of the United States. But more than
this, *China's Destiny* clearly reveals the antidemocratic views
and opposition to all concepts of Western liberalism, not
only of the author but of the entire Kuomintang hierarchy
that has directed the affairs of the Chinese Government for
many years. This is a truth that the State Department may
not have wished to publicize in view of the fact that it has
been throwing its full weight behind that Government. But
whatever the State Department's reasons may have been,
the fact remains that *China's Destiny* gives clear expression
to the political philosophy of China's ruling clique—in fact,
it is widely known as the *Mein Kampf* of China—and as such
is a document of great import to the American people.

China's Destiny was first published on March 10, 1943, in
Chungking by the Chung Cheng Publishing House, the
official publishing house of the Kuomintang Party. Despite
an acute paper shortage, the first printing consisted of two
hundred thousand copies, and to insure a wide circulation,
this 213-page book was priced at approximately ten cents
U. S. In the extensive advance publicity given the book, it
was described as the most important book written since the
Three People's Principles of Sun Yat-sen. By the end of 1943,
more than two hundred printings had been issued, many of
these through the facilities of other publishing houses. A
catechism, synopsis, and a book of notes were also published.
When *China's Destiny* was first issued, it was officially an-

nounced that it would be used in Chinese schools and colleges "as the most important extra-curricular reading matter." Since then, thousands of students have had to pass examinations on it. It is required reading for all civil servants, all army officers, all members of the Kuomintang Youth Corps, and all students at the Central Political Training Institute, who must not only read the book but must also submit their notes to group leaders for checking. It is thus fair to describe *China's Destiny* as the political bible of the Kuomintang, and to state that intensive efforts have been made to indoctrinate the potential leaders of China with its ideology.

The writing of *China's Destiny* was begun in November, 1942, and it is pertinent here to recall the events of the previous months. In the summer and fall of 1942, the Nazi armies were driving forward toward Stalingrad and Alexandria, and Japan was continuing her virtually unchecked advance in Southeast Asia and the Southern Pacific. The British had been driven out of Burma, and the Burma Road, China's last means of contact with the outside world, had been cut off. The position of China's Western Allies appeared gloomy, to say the least. The "CC" clique, the most reactionary and one of the most powerful groups within the Kuomintang hierarchy, which had always been more concerned with suppressing any popular challenge to its power than in promoting a united war effort against the Japanese, took advantage of this situation to encourage anti-Western and anti-Communist sentiment in China. It was no secret that the "CC" clique was preparing the ground for collaboration with the Axis Powers had they emerged victorious. And it is widely believed that the views of this clique greatly influenced Chiang Kai-shek in the writing of *China's Destiny*.

There has been considerable controversy as to how much of the actual writing of *China's Destiny* was done by Chiang Kai-shek himself. Some claim that all the writing was actually done by Tao Hsi-sheng, who only showed Chiang the results for purposes of checking. Others contend that Chiang spent three hours a day dictating and discussing the contents of the book, and that Tao was merely the ghost writer. Whichever version is closer to the truth, it is certain that Tao Hsi-sheng played a prominent part in the compiling of the book. Formerly a professor at Peiping National University, Tao was educated in Japan and is generally regarded as hostile to Western political and economic concepts. Although in the 1928 period, Tao was secretary to Chiang Kai-shek, he later became a follower of Wang Ching-wei with whom he fled to Shanghai to join the Japanese, but broke with him in January, 1940, and escaped to Hong Kong with the text of a secret treaty between Wang and the Japanese. The text of this treaty was published in full in a Chinese newspaper in Hong Kong and Tao was reinstated in the good graces of the Kuomintang. In Chungking, Tao lived with Chen Pu-lei, the Generalissimo's personal secretary, and was reported to be on extremely friendly terms with Chiang. Though most Chinese believe that Tao was really a traitor, he was eventually appointed Chairman of the Cultural Branch of the Second Department of the Generalissimo's Personal Headquarters, the Chinese name for which is the "Office to Serve and to Obey." In this capacity, Tao was a leading figure in the cultural and propaganda activities of the Kuomintang, and either wrote or edited the majority of editorials in the *Central Daily News*, the chief organ of the Central Executive Committee of the Kuomintang.

Shortly after the publication of *China's Destiny*, it was officially announced that an English-language version was being prepared under the editorship of Dr. Wang Chung-hui, then Foreign Minister, and that this would be published in April or May of 1943. No such version, however, was forthcoming, and it may be that the adverse criticism of the book voiced in many American newspaper editorials and a number of important radio broadcasts caused this project to be abandoned. Another possible explanation is that the Chinese Government considered the publication in the United

States of Lin Yutang's *Between Tears and Laughter* as an adequate substitute. For this book, with its strongly anti-foreign tone and its emphasis on ancient Confucian ethics as the ideal basis for China's future social structure, faithfully echoed the philosophic outlook of *China's Destiny*. Not only did Lin Yutang indulge in bitter diatribes against war-time American and British policy toward China, but he also delivered a sweeping indictment of all Western thought and science, reserving particular venom for the "swine and slop" economists of the West and their concern for the material conditions of life. He argued that China's traditional culture would be debased by preoccupation with such material considerations, and showed only contempt for the struggles and aspirations of the Chinese people to achieve the very things, i.e., rising living standards, adequate housing, public health measures, etc., that he so curtly dismissed as "swine and slop" economics. As an alternative to a materialist Western world, he advocated the teachings of Confucianism, with its emphasis on "government by music and courtesy," and sketched an idyllic picture of Chinese peasants living "harmoniously" in mud huts, while steadfastly resisting corruption by "European standards of ease and idleness." It is easy to see why Lin Yutang was regarded as a fully qualified spokesman by those in China that were interested in preserving the "ancient virtues" of an oppressive social order, and that were entirely willing to place the entire blame for China's trials and tribulations on the West. In the United States, however, *Between Tears and Laughter* received severe criticism, and this may well have been an additional reason why no official English version of *China's Destiny* was issued.

In China, the views expressed in *China's Destiny* were criticized in intellectual and even in official circles. The Generalissimo took cognizance of this criticism, but in a very strange way. He ordered all the leading members of the Government to write their criticisms of the book and send them to him, but he insisted that all such criticisms should be signed. In view of what is known of the workings of the Chinese governmental bureaucracy, it was hardly to be expected that these officials, over their own signatures, would have risked saying what they really thought of the book. The result was virtually unanimous approval of almost everything in the book. Thus, when the revised edition was issued in January, 1944, the text remained substantially unchanged, with the exception of a few factual corrections and a slight toning down of some of the strongest attacks against Western imperialism. This revised edition (in Chinese) was officially published by the General Headquarters of the Kuomintang in the United States and can be bought for one dollar.

Even after the publication of the revised edition, however, no official English-language version was forthcoming. Once again, this may have been due to the appearance of still another book by Lin Yutang, *The Vigil of a Nation*, which was the product of Lin's visit to China in 1943. For in this book, Lin gave very full treatment to the one subject in *China's Destiny* that had not been covered in *Between Tears and Laughter*, namely, the issue of the Chinese Communists. Without even taking the trouble to visit them, he wrote a scathing attack on conditions in the Communist-controlled areas that all firsthand observers of Chinese conditions dismissed as being based solely on official handouts from the Kuomintang authorities. Lin himself virtually admits as much by stating in his introduction that he took to China "two big 150-page notebooks and came out again without writing a single line in them. . . . My whole diary runs under a thousand words." Yet on the basis of blank notebooks and a brief diary, he wrote a book of some one hundred and twenty thousand words, replete with names, dates, facts, and figures in great detail.

Readers of *The Vigil of a Nation* found it hard to believe that this was the same man who in 1935 wrote *My Country and My People*, in which he delivered the following scathing attack on the attempts of the ruling clique in China to revive Confucianism in order to avoid democratic government by law: "What China needs is not more morals but more prisons for politicians. . . . [Official] privilege is the antithesis of equality and the officials are the natural enemies of democracy. . . . The sooner we stop talking about moral reforms of the people, the sooner shall we be able to give China a clean government."

Thus, in various forms, the ideas voiced in *China's Destiny* received world-wide publicity. But there appeared at the same time, over Chiang Kai-shek's signature, *Chinese Economic Theory*, a book which even more than *China's Destiny* gives a detailed exposition of the theoretical basis of the economic philosophy underlying the Kuomintang's program for China's future. While *China's Destiny* was read by millions in China, this small book was not released for general circulation, but was published by the Generalissimo's Adjutant's Office of the National Military Council for use as a textbook in the Kuomintang's Central Political Training Institute, where all high Party officials receive training. Except for its publication in the January 1946 issue of *Amerasia*, its existence is thus almost unknown in the United States. As in the case of *China's Destiny*, this book was "ghosted" for Chiang Kai-shek by Tao Hsi-sheng, with the assistance of Chen Pao-ying, who reportedly contributed most of the material on Western economics.

With the war over, one might have expected that both *China's Destiny* and *Chinese Economic Theory* would have been withdrawn from circulation, and that the new world situation would have inspired a readjustment of the author's approach to the future of China. But Chiang Kai-shek's speech on November 26, 1945, when he announced that "it is my intention to assume personally the general direction of China's economic reconstruction," plus the fact that both books are still prescribed reading in China, indicate that the present Chinese Government is still determined to shape

China's future development in accordance with the principles expounded in *China's Destiny* and *Chinese Economic Theory*.

The translations of both *China's Destiny* and *Chinese Economic Theory* appearing in this volume were done very carefully through the combined efforts of two Chinese scholars, each one checking the other's work. Great pains were taken to make the translations both accurate and readable. Differences between the original and revised editions of *China's Destiny* are indicated in the text within square brackets or in footnotes. Other material within square brackets was inserted by the annotator for purposes of clarification. The annotator has also added footnotes of two kinds, explanatory and critical. Both *China's Destiny* and *Chinese Economic Theory* are so full of omissions, distortions, and inaccuracies that ten times the number of footnotes used would be necessary for an exhaustive annotation, but attention was concentrated on the most important textual requirements. A general commentary on both books will be found at the end of this volume.

PHILIP JAFFE

CHINA'S DESTINY

By Chiang Kai-shek

CHAPTER ONE

GROWTH AND DEVELOPMENT OF THE CHINESE NATION

Five thousand years ago, the Chinese nation established itself on the continent of Asia. Other states established five thousand years ago are now only matters of historical record. China is not merely the only ancient state still in existence, but also, in company with other peace-loving and anti-aggressor states, is fighting an unprecedented war for justice and righteousness, and for the freedom and liberation of mankind. We are now advancing on the broad road to a brilliant victory and everlasting peace.

We know that a nation is formed naturally, while a state is built by the collective strength of the people.[1] During the process of natural formation, the Chinese nation was also established as a state through common resistance against foreign aggression and collective action for survival. Our nation is of one stock, and due to its fertility the population has greatly increased and the nation has become stronger and bigger. Consequently, the domain of the state has expanded. Nevertheless, the Chinese nation has never overstepped the limits required by its natural growth, and at no time has it used military force to expand. Whenever any foreign aggressor has forcibly broken through the defense lines of our state and occupied territory needed for our nation's existence, the Chinese nation, impelled by a sense of humiliation and the need for survival, has had no alternative but to rise and fight until that territory was restored to us.

1. Throughout the book, the author distinguished between "nation" and "state." "Nation" refers to the people or peoples within China, while "state" refers to the political and governmental structure of that nation.

According to its historic development, our Chinese nation
was formed by the blending of numerous clans.[2] This blending of various clans continued, dynasty after dynasty, but
the motive power was cultural rather than military, and it
was accomplished by assimilation rather than by conquest.
Three thousand years ago, many clans spread along the
valleys of the Yellow, Yangtze, Heilungkiang [Amur], and
Pearl rivers. [In the revised edition, the preceding three
sentences were expanded to read: "According to its historic
development, our Chinese nation was formed by the blending of numerous clans. These clans were originally branches
of the same race, spreading to the east of the Pamir plateau,
along the valleys of the Yellow, the Huai, the Yangtze, the
Heilungkiang, and the Pearl rivers. They maintained different cultures according to the differences in their geographical environment. And cultural differences gave rise
to differences among the clans. However, during the past
five thousand years, with increasing contacts and migrations,
they have been continuously blended into a nation. But
the motive power of that blending was cultural rather than
military, and the method of blending was by assimilation
rather than by conquest."]

After the period of the "Five Emperors,"[3] written records
were kept in greater detail so that the organization of the
different clans can be studied historically. Within the Four
Seas, the clans of the various localities were either descend-

2. The Chinese character here
translated as "clan" is sometimes
translated as "race," "tribe," "people," or even "nation." Its most literal meaning, however, is "clan,"
and in this particular instance this
most accurately conveys the author's
romanticized version of Chinese history—namely, that the Chinese, Mongols, Manchus, Tibetans, Mohammedans, etc., derive from a common
stock and are really members of the
same family. Although this thesis is
rejected by all modern historians,
both Chinese and foreign, it is important to study it carefully since it is the
basis of much of the author's social
philosophy.

3. The period of the "Five Emperors" is known in the Chinese classics
as the "Golden Age" when the government of the world was perfect. The
last of the "Five Emperors"—Shun—
was succeeded by Emperor Yu, who
according to orthodox Chinese tradition founded the first dynasty, the
Hsia, in 2205 B.C.

ants of a common ancestor or were interrelated through marriage. The *Book of Odes* [4] states: "The descendants of Wen Wang extend to hundreds of generations, but all come from the same family tree." This means that the main and branch stocks all belong to the same blood stream. The *Book* also states: "He is not an outsider but a cousin or an uncle." That is to say, among all the clans there were either blood relationships or connections by marriage. This is how the Chinese nation was formed in ancient times. Therefore, all Chinese citizens share the same lofty ethical concept that "within the Four Seas, all are brothers," and possess the same magnificent spirit of kindness and love. These are not just empty words.

During the Ch'in and Han dynasties,[5] Chinese military exploits figure prominently in the historical records. However, when these exploits are examined, it is found that in the north they were undertaken for the defense and survival of the nation, and in the south for the development of the people's livelihood. Clans from the grasslands of the desert zone in China's northwest often migrated into the agricultural areas in the Central Plains [the western part of Shantung, Honan, the southern part of Hopei and Shansi, and the eastern part of Shensi], and both large and small wars resulted from these migrations. The Government resisted the migratory clans with military force when they came as invaders, but accorded them civilized rule when they pledged obedience.[6] Thus, at that period, China's domain extended to the desert in the north, to Liaotung in the east, and to

4. A Chinese "classic" consisting of very old poems and songs, allegedly dating from the legendary period of Chinese history.

5. The Ch'in dynasty was founded by Ch'in Shih Hwang who reigned from 221–209 B.C. The name China comes from this dynasty. The Han dynasty (206 B.C.–A.D. 221) occupies a special place in the traditions of the Chinese, who call themselves the "Han" race, or "Men of Han."

6. The author neglects to mention the other side of the picture, namely, that the Chinese were constantly encroaching on the territories of the nomadic tribes in search of new agricultural land, and that this Chinese expansion outward was also the cause of "large and small wars."

the Belurtagh Mountains in the west [the mountains that form the western boundary of Sinkiang Province, known in Chinese as the Chungling Mountains]. At the same time, the Government developed the agricultural areas in the southeast, and the high plateau in the southwest was also linked up economically with the Central Plains. Therefore, at this period, China's territory in the south extended to the South Sea [more commonly known on Western maps as the South China Sea], in the east to Wu-Yueh [Kiangsu and Chekiang], and in the southwest to Cochin-China.[7] Due to economic interdependence and the spread of a common civilization, the numerous clans in various localities had already blended together and formed one great nation.

During the period of the Three Kingdoms [221–265], although the Central Plains were divided and in conflict, the governments of the Three Kingdoms each worked for the survival of the nation. They continued the policies of the two Han dynasties, either strengthening the frontiers or developing waste lands. The Western Tsin dynasty [265–317] suffered from Tartar attacks; the Hans migrated southward; and the clans of Hsiung Nu and Hsien Pei [western and eastern Tartars] occupied the Yellow River Valley. However, these clans gradually acquired the civilization of the Hans. As a result, the Tsin and the Wei [dynasties], though they established themselves along the Yellow River for longer or shorter periods, adopted Chinese dress, methods of government, and culture. The unification accomplished by the Sui [589–618] and T'ang [618–907] dynasties was the fruit of four hundred years of nation-blending during the Wei, Tsin, and the North and South dynasties. During this period, the nation was composed of innumerable main and branch

7. In the revised edition, Cochin-China is given as Yuehnan, or Indo-China, and Burma is mentioned as the western limit of China. In this connection, it may be noted that the map of present-day China appearing in the original edition of *China's Des-* *tiny* included Hong Kong, Outer Mongolia, Tannu Tuva, and Tibet. In the revised edition, this map was altered to include also North Burma including the Hukwang Valley, as well as the Liuchiu Islands.

stocks with rich and flourishing cultures. Thus, in the entire domain east of the Belurtagh Mountains, west of the Yellow Sea, south of the Gobi Desert, and north of the South Sea, the many varieties of religion, philosophy, literature, art, astronomy, astrology, law, institutions, and social customs were gathered together and synthesized.

During the Sung dynasty [960–1280], national defense was not adequate to protect the state or assure the survival of the nation. The Ch'i-tan[8] [Liao] and Nuchen [Chin] Tartars were clans of China's north and northeast which had not been completely assimilated. They took advantage of the Sung dynasty's low morale, political confusion, and military decline to conquer their neighbors and become a strong aggressive power. But though they occupied the Central Plains, they were eventually absorbed by Chinese culture. The rise of the Mongols to power followed a similar pattern. The realms trampled by the hooves of Genghis Khan's horses extended far beyond any domain essential for the survival of the Chinese nation. But after Kublai Khan proclaimed himself emperor, those regions beyond China's original domain were separated away from the state organization of China, and only the main and branch clans under Kublai Khan were assimilated into the Chinese nation. [The revised edition uses the word "blended" instead of "assimilated."] When the Manchus occupied China, they were assimilated in the same way as the Nuchen Tartars [Chin dynasty]. Thus, after the Revolution of 1911, the Manchus and the Chinese were really blended into one body, without the slightest trace of any difference between them.

From the foregoing, one can discern the steadfastness of the national consciousness of China, the stoutness of the nation's strength, and the enduring quality of its culture. This has enabled the Chinese nation to resist external aggression and

8. The Ch'i-tan Tartars are sometimes called "Khitans." They held possession of North China for a considerable period, and it was from early Russian contact with the Khitans that the Russian name *Kitai*, and hence the English name Cathay, for China was derived.

humiliation, and has made it unwilling to encroach upon or humiliate other nations. Because it would not yield to aggression and humiliation, the Chinese nation always rose together and drove out any alien clans[9] to recover its territory when the Central Plains were invaded. Because it would not encroach upon and humiliate other clans, the Chinese nation, in the process of eliminating the sufferings and misfortunes of internal conflict, was able by virtue of its great and enduring civilization to blend these neighboring clans into the nation. In short, our Chinese nation has resisted the armed might of alien clans, but has not resorted to armed might against others. Instead, it has accepted and absorbed their civilizations while at the same time imparting to them on a wide scale the civilization of China. This has been the outstanding characteristic of the survival and expansion of our Chinese nation.

In regard to the living space essential for the nation's existence, the territory of the Chinese state is determined by the requirements for national survival and by the limits of Chinese cultural bonds. Thus, in the territory of China a hundred years ago, comprising more than ten million square kilometers, there was not a single district that was not essential to the survival of the Chinese nation, and none that was not permeated by our culture. The breaking up of this territory meant the undermining of the nation's security as well as the decline of the nation's culture. Thus, the people as a whole must regard this as a national humiliation, and not until all lost territories have been recovered can we relax our efforts to wipe out this humiliation and save ourselves from destruction.

Within China's territory, the customs of each clan, and

9. If this phrase is intended to refer to the Mongols or Manchus, the use of the word "alien" is confusing, since the author constantly stresses the view that all these clans were actually part of the same "family" or stock. It is also difficult to reconcile the statement that the Chinese nation always expelled the invaders of the Central Plains, with the previous argument that these invaders were always "assimilated" by the Chinese and blended into the Chinese nation.

the way of life in each locality were different. Yet the customs of each clan were unified to form China's national culture, and the combination of the ways of life in each locality made possible the existence of the Chinese nation. This outstanding fact of China's history is based on her geography, her economic structure, the requirements of national defense, and a common historical destiny, and is not merely the result of political necessity.

With regard to her geographical configuration, China's mountain ranges and river basins form a self-contained unit. Taking a bird's-eye view from west to east, starting from the Pamir plateau on the "roof of Asia," we have in the north the Tien Shan and Altai mountain ranges leading to the Three Northeastern Provinces; in the center, the K'un-lun Mountains extending down to the plains of southeastern China; and in the south the Himalayas extending down to the "Mid-South Peninsula [i.e., the Malay Peninsula, that consists of Indo-China, Siam, Burma, and Malaya]. Within these three great mountain chains lie the Heilungkiang, Yellow, Huai, Yangtze, and Pearl river basins. The Chinese nation has lived and developed within these river basins, and there is no area that can be split up or separated from the rest, and therefore, no areas that can become an independent unit.

As for China's economic structure, each region within the geographical setting described above has its own particular soil and natural resources. The way of life in each region differs accordingly. It may be one of hunting or of a nomadic pastoral type; it may have reached the stage of farming and industry or be adapted to mining; or it may specialize in salt production or fishing. This division of labor among the different areas is largely determined by their physical conditions, while trading among them has developed as the result of the needs of each area for the products of others. Long before the invention and use of railways and steamships, there was a very close commercial relationship between one area and another. Such a common economic life was and is the basis of political unity and harmonious relations among all the people of the nation.

As regards national defense, if any region within this geographical system is occupied by an alien nation, then the whole nation and state lose the natural bulwark that protects them. There are no natural frontiers in the areas of the Yellow, Huai, Yangtze, and Han rivers where a strong defense line can be prepared. Therefore, Formosa, the Pescadores, the Four Northeastern Provinces [Manchuria], Inner and Outer Mongolia, Sinkiang, and Tibet are each a fortress [or strategic area] essential for the nation's defense and security. [The revised edition adds the Liuchiu Islands.] The separation of any one of these regions from the rest of the country means the disruption of our national defenses. Furthermore, from the point of view of natural resources needed for the support of the state, the coal, iron, and agricultural products of the northeast, the horse hides and wool of the northwest, the copper and iron of the southeast, and the tungsten and tin of the southwest, are all essential for the maintenance of our national security. [The revised edition reads: "the tungsten and lead of the southeast, and the copper and tin of the southwest."] The loss of these resources would mean the destruction of the foundations of the state.

The common historical destiny of the various clans is due to China's ancient virtues that enabled her to bind them in friendship toward her, and also to convert [revised edition: "harmonize"] their original characteristics. In return for the tribute offered by her neighbors, China responded with luxurious gifts and favors, and never harbored designs of economic exploitation. In the conflicts among her neighbors, China always adhered to the principle of "re-establishing interrupted dynasties and reviving dismembered states," and never adopted the policy of taking advantage of the precarious position of other countries to seize their territory.[10] Thus, the neighboring clans that occupied the Central Plains were assimilated. Those clans that lived in peace with China evolved from the status of tribute bearers to feudatories, and from feudatories to self-governing units; the status of each being determined by its economic needs and its cultural level. In the case of Mongolia, the process began with the Yen-Yung [Hsien-yun] [11] in the Chou dynasty and continued with the Hsiung Nu in the Ch'in-Han period. After this, it was continued with the Tu-chueh [Turkis] during the early T'ang dynasty, and with the Ch'i-tan [Liao] at the end of the T'ang and during the two Sung dynasties, and with the Mongols themselves during the Ming [1368–1644] and the Ch'ing [Manchu] dynasties [1644–1911]. As to Sinkiang, the Hsi-yung [12] came under the domination of the state of Ch'in during the period of the Spring and Autumn Annals [722–481 B.C.] and the process was continued during the Han dynasty and by the T'ang dynasty which fixed the Tien Shan as its western frontier. It was finally completed when Sinkiang was opened up and colonized during the Yuan [Mongol] dynasty [1280–

10. Whether ancient China was or was not an aggressor is only of academic interest today. But what is important is this further example of the author's distortion and romanticizing of history to sustain his thesis that ancient China was perfect in all respects. In this connection, it is interesting to quote a few sentences from Dr. Sun Yat-sen, to whom the author so frequently refers to sustain his own conclusions. In the *San Min Chu I*, Dr. Sun writes that before Asia was invaded by European imperialism, "the only power of Asia that deserved to be called imperialistic was China. The weaker and smaller nations were afraid of China and her political domination. . . . Our fore-fathers constantly employed political force to encroach upon weaker and smaller nations; but economic force in those days was not a serious thing, so we were not guilty of economic oppression of other peoples. . . . China used peaceful means to influence others and what was called the 'royal way' to bring the weaker and smaller states under her rule."

11. The Hsien-yun were a tribe that invaded China during the reign of Hsuan Wang of the Chou dynasty, about 827 B.C.

12. Hsi-yung is a comprehensive term for all the tribes living in the western part of China on the borders of Tibet.

1368] and the Ch'ing dynasty. Thus the assimilation of these two regions [Mongolia and Sinkiang] has been taking place for more than two thousand years.

Following the conversion of the Tufans in Tibet to Buddhism, the orientation of Tibet's development was toward China. Under the Sui and T'ang dynasties, Tibet looked to China for direction.[13] During the Yuan dynasty, Tibet was under the jurisdiction of the Hsuan Cheng Yuan [the government department responsible for Tibetan and Buddhist affairs], and during the Ch'ing dynasty, it was under the Li Fan Yuan [the government department responsible for Mongolian and Tibetan affairs]. Thus, Tibet's period of assimilation has lasted over thirteen hundred years.

The northeast started its inward orientation [i.e., toward China] even earlier. The affiliation of the Su-Shen [14] began in the Chou dynasty. The development of this area by the Han clan was most extensive in the two Han dynasties. Through the dynasties of Sui, T'ang, Sung, Yuan, and Ming, it was a territory in which the Han clan and the Tung-hu coexisted.[15] By the time of the Ch'ing dynasty, the development of agriculture, industry, and commerce in the region depended almost entirely on the efforts of the Han clan, while the Manchus were assimilated into the Chinese nation.

Formosa and the Pescadores were originally opened up by the Hans. They stand firmly in the southeast and have long been the bulwarks of China. They were invaded and occupied by the Dutch at the end of the Ming dynasty, but were eventually recovered by Cheng Cheng Kung [known to foreigners as Coxinga], whose deeds were epic. China's relations with the clans of the "Mid-South Penin-

13. The characters translated "looked to China for direction" mean literally "toward the inside." The exact degree of political dependence implied is not clear. Some translate it as "owed allegiance to" and others as "affiliated with China."

14. The old name for the region now known as Kirin, also including the district around Vladivostok.

15. A Mongolian tribe known as the Tung-hu in the Ch'in and Han dynasties, and as the Hsien Pei in the Chin dynasty.

sula" were even closer.[16] History continuously records the dispatch of armies "to revive dismembered dynasties," and of battles fought "to help the weak and support the fallen." All in all, China's history during the past five thousand years is the record of the common destiny of all these clans. This common record constitutes the history of how all these various clans were blended into the Chinese nation, and of the building of the Chinese state by the Chinese nation for common defense against foreign aggression and to assure national survival.

[The following paragraph was added in the revised edition.]

Throughout this lengthy historical process, these various clans, on the occasion of the contact and blending of their cultures, often traced their respective genealogies and discovered their common origin. For example, the Mongols are the descendants of the Hsiung Nu, and according to the *Shih Chi* and *Han Shu*, the rulers of Hsia were their distant begetters. The Nuchen of the Northeast and the Tufan of Tibet are the descendants of the Hsien Pei, and according to the *Tsin Shu* and the *Wei Shu*, Huang Ti [first of the "Five Emperors"] was the distant ancestor of both. Again, when we study the *Chou Shu*, the *History of Liao*, and the *Documentary History of Institutions*, it is revealed that he [Huang Ti] was the forefather of both the Manchus and Tibetans of today. As to the so-called Mohammedans in present-day China, they are for the most part actually members of the Han clan who embraced Islam. Therefore, the difference between the Hans and Mohammedans is only in religion and different habits of life. In short, our various clans actually belong to the same nation, as well as to the same racial stock. Therefore, there is an inner factor closely linking the historical destiny of common existence and common sorrow and joy of the whole Chinese

16. In the *San Min Chu I*, Sun Yat-sen writes that "Annam and Burma were both formerly Chinese territory," and that "Siam paid tribute to China."

nation. That there are five peoples designated in China [i.e., Chinese, Manchus, Mongols, Tibetans, Mohammedans] is not due to difference in race or blood, but to religion and geographical environment. In short, the differentiation among China's five peoples is due to regional and religious factors, and not to race or blood. This fact must be thoroughly understood by all our fellow countrymen.[17]

This long history is based on the inherent moral character of the Chinese, which, in turn, has developed China's exalted culture. We know that the ethical tenets of a Chinese citizen are loyalty, filial piety, benevolence, love, faithfulness, righteousness, peace, and harmony, and that the basic principles on which the Chinese state is founded are propriety, righteousness, modesty, and honor.[18] Under the influence of these eight virtues and four principles, the Chinese nation conducts itself by fully utilizing its own resources without

17. This paragraph was added to the revised edition, presumably in an effort to counteract the belief, deeply implanted in the minds of the Chinese people, that China is a nation of five peoples, as symbolized by the five-barred flag of the Republic, and to give further emphasis to the author's thesis of common blood ties uniting all the Chinese people. As pointed out previously, this theory completely distorts Chinese history. To cite only one example, it would follow from this theory that the overthrow of the Manchu dynasty in 1911 was not a nationalist revolution, but merely a civil war. The author himself appears to contradict his own theory in later chapters where he praises the "nationalist revolution" that overthrew the Manchus. All scholars recognize that China is made up of a number of peoples or nationalities. Moreover, this fact has been publicly recognized by Chiang Kai-shek's own party, the Kuomintang. The declaration of the First Congress of the Kuomintang in 1924, for example, specifically stated that "the right of self-determination of the various nations within China is recognized, and a free, united China, by the free association of these nations, will be organized after the victory of the anti-imperialist and anti-warlord revolution."

18. It is difficult to translate these Chinese words accurately. For example, the word "jen," here translated "benevolence" also means "kindness" or "perfect virtue;" the word "hsin," here translated "faithfulness," also includes the idea of sincerity and reliability; "li" or "propriety" is an essentially Chinese concept involving the idea of good manners, good discipline, obedience to law, etc.; "lien," here translated "modesty," is sometimes translated as "integrity" and conveys the idea of an ability to discriminate between right and wrong; "ch'ih" or "honor" means literally a sense of shame, and conveys the idea of an awakened conscience.

excess, and it benefits other people by extending its blessing without demanding concessions. When propriety is required, it yields to no one in practicing benevolence. When its own self-interest is involved, it acts without the slightest selfishness. It neither fears the strong nor takes advantage of the weak.

Through five thousand years of alternate order and confusion and the rise and fall of dynasties, our nation has acquired the virtue of modesty, a sense of honor, and the ability to endure insult and shoulder hardships. Because of its modesty, it is capable of contentment with its lot. Because of its sense of honor, it is capable of developing its own power. Because it is contented with its lot, it does not trespass upon other nations. Because it is capable of developing its own power, it does not tolerate the aggression of other nations. Because it can endure insults, the strength of the nation is accumulated inwardly and not exposed outwardly. Because it can shoulder hardships, the aspirations of the nation are enduring instead of spasmodic. Because of the development of these virtues, the various clans and branches of the Chinese nation are capable of sacrificing their personal interests for the benefit of the whole community. There has thus been produced a spirit that is firm and determined in self-defense, that is peace loving in its relations to the world—a spirit of benevolence that "saves the lost, restores the vanquished, relieves the weak and supports the fallen." This spirit puts into practice the great principle of loyalty and tolerance, and the principle that "in establishing oneself, one establishes others, and in enlightening oneself, one enlightens others." Consequently, during the past five thousand years, all the various nations of East Asia, whether they have been affiliated with or assimilated by China, or have joined together for mutual self-protection, or have remained independent, have each in accordance with the aspirations and desires of its people, and following its own national temperament and social customs, developed the best points in its own culture and thus contributed to the common progress of humanity.

During the last hundred years, China's national position and the morale of the people deteriorated to such an extent that an unprecedented situation developed. Territories required for the survival of the Chinese nation experienced the painful process of partition. The oppression and bondage of the unequal treaties further undermined the vitality of the Chinese state and the nation. A survey of our long history of five thousand years reveals the alternate rise and fall of states and the survival and extinction of nations. Yet the national decay during the last hundred years reached a point unequaled in our history. The state and the nation became weakened and encountered inner crises in the political, economic, social, ethical, and psychological spheres, until the basis of rebirth and recovery was almost destroyed.

If the Father of our Country [Sun Yat-sen][19] had not promoted the Three People's Principles[20] and led our National Revolution, China would have suffered the same fate as Korea, and would have been swallowed up by the Japanese invaders with their methods of "nibbling like a silkworm or swallowing like a whale." Fortunately, Sun Yat-sen, with his prophetic foresight, applied his great courage and wisdom to the task of establishing China's freedom and equality, and of arousing the whole nation. He fought for forty years, directing the common aspirations of all the Chinese people into the right channels. On his deathbed, he designated the abolition of the unequal treaties as the first objective of the Chinese Nationalist Revolution, and

19. Throughout the book, the author uses this title when referring to Dr. Sun Yat-sen. In order to make him a more recognizable figure in the minds of non-Chinese, this translation has for the most part rendered the phrase "the Father of our Country" as Sun Yat-sen.

20. The three principles of Nationalism, Democracy, and the People's Livelihood were expounded by Sun Yat-sen in a series of speeches delivered in Canton between January and August, 1924, and subsequently published under the title, San Min Chu I, or Three Principles of the People.

left to us, the comrades who survived him, and to the citizens of the entire country, the accomplishment of this great task. We have continued the fight till this day, and have finally succeeded in the first step. Thus the opportunity for the recovery of the nation and the hope of the rebirth of the state are now presented to the citizens of the entire country. I, Chiang Kai-shek, have been identified from the beginning with restarting the Republic of China on the road to independence and freedom. Surveying the present in the light of the past, and planning for the future on the basis of the lessons of history, I am going to describe the experience of our state and nation during the last hundred years and point out the direction to be followed from now on by our state and nation. I especially hope that all citizens of the country will realize that China's destiny rests on their shoulders, and that our destiny will be definitely decided by the war situation as it develops today. There is no room either for hesitation or for an attitude of blind acceptance and reliance on the help of others. I wish all my countrymen to examine thoroughly what I have written, and carry these precepts into practice.

CHAPTER TWO

THE ORIGINS OF NATIONAL HUMILIATION AND SOURCES OF THE REVOLUTION

1. Political, Social, and Cultural Decline in the Ch'ing [Manchu] Dynasty and Fundamental Errors of Its Domestic Policy

THE deterioration of China's national position and the low morale of the people during the last hundred years can be largely attributed to the unequal treaties. The implementation of the unequal treaties constitutes a complete record of China's national humiliation. To find the cause of this national humiliation, one must go back to the political decay, and especially the academic and social decline in the Manchu dynasty.

As the Manchus were originally a small clan, how could they conquer the Central Plains? It was because at the end of the Ming dynasty politics was corrupt, opinions were divided, political parties were at loggerheads, and banditry was rampant. In addition, the eunuchs [1] usurped power and the generals were disobedient, with the result that domestic disorder and foreign encroachments steadily increased. Thus the three-century regime of the Ming was overthrown by the concurrent blows of the roving bandits of Li Tzech'eng and the "Banner Soldiers" of the Manchus. [The Manchu troops were divided into groups, each designated by the color of its banner.] After the entry of the Manchus,

---

1. Eunuchs were frequently the most powerful section of the bureaucracy in imperial China. Regarded as the most trustworthy advisers for an emperor who maintained a harem, they were favored for positions of power and influence because of their physical inability to create family dynasties.

China's national consciousness received a serious blow. Sun Yat-sen said: "After Emperor Shun Chih [of Manchu] over-threw the Ming dynasty and became China's sovereign, the Ming's loyal officials and heroic citizens rose in various parts of the country and offered resistance until the be-ginning of the K'ang Hsi reign. Thus up to that time China was not yet conquered by the Manchus."

He also said: "During the K'ang Hsi and Yung Cheng reigns, anti-Manchu sentiment among the followers of the Ming was still strong. Therefore, during these reigns, many books were published, such as *Great Truth to Dispel Illusions*, stating that the Han people should not object to the Manchus becoming emperors. Their reasoning was that 'Shun was a foreigner from the east, Wen Wang was a foreigner from the west; thus the Manchus, though foreigners, could be em-perors of China.' During the reign of Emperor Ch'ien Lung, even mention of the words Han [Chinese] and Man [Man-chu] was not permitted. Any part dealing with the historical relation between the Sung and Yuan dynasties, and between the Ming and Ch'ing dynasties in any book was omitted or altered. All books concerning the Manchus, Hsiung Nu, and Tartars were forbidden. They were all destroyed, not permitted to be read or even kept in any home."

The rule of the Manchus was certainly oppressive. But its severity fell far short of the cruel rule of the Japanese in Chosen [Korea]. Chosen has been conquered for only thirty years, but its people are already poisoned by the slave-like education instituted by the Japanese. All the original history and culture of Korea have been completely destroyed. Not a trace of national consciousness has been permitted to be retained by its people. Therefore, the people of Chosen nowadays, on hearing the term Han-Kuo [the name for Korea], do not understand its meaning. [In the revised edi-tion, this sentence reads: "Therefore very few Korean people nowadays, on hearing the term Korea, would understand its meaning."] The speed and severity with which contem-

porary imperialists subdue conquered states and nations,
and the dire consequences of their rule ought to chill any-
body's heart.

Under the enslavement and brutal repression of the Manchus, China's original excellent academic tradition became
greatly corrupted. The [Confucian] school of Chu Hsi, introduced at the beginning of the Ming, developed certain
undesirable tendencies during the middle of the dynasty.
Those scholars taking literary examinations spent their time
studying words and sentences and composing "eight legged"
[stereotyped] essays. Even those engaged in academic studies
were merely concerned with composing philosophical discourses. Wang Yang-ming [Wang Shou-jen] started the
school of "oneness of knowledge and action" to correct such
tendencies. In his latter years, he advocated the "extension
of conscience"[2] to liberate the scholars from their tortuous
literary studies and confused thinking. This school, however,
also became impractical. When Chang Chiang-ling became
premier, he urged the "practice of practical learning" as a
remedy for the undesirable aspects of both the Chu Hsi
and the Wang Yang-ming schools. During the late Ming
and early Ch'ing dynasties, although Wang's school had
become Buddhistic, and the teachings of the Tunglin scholars
were vague and impractical, there were some students of
science, such as Hsu Kuang-ch'i, Li Chih-tsao, Mei Wen-
ting, and Sung Ying-hsing, who carried on research in the
fields of agriculture, astronomy, and manufacturing. All of
them endeavored to seek the truth through practical action
and to promote continuous progress. The great scholars like
Huang Li-chou, Ku Ting-lin, Wang Ch'uan-shan, Li Ehr-
ch'u, Yen Hsi-chai, and Fu Ch'ing-chu, were versed in both
philosophy and economics, and placed equal emphasis on
theory and practice.

2. This expression is difficult to translate into English. It signifies both knowledge of material things and com- plete understanding of intangible, spiritual values.

The development of nationalist and democratic ideas aroused the particular hatred of the Manchus. Following a number of academic inquisitions, the study of government and economics declined. During the reigns of Ch'ien Lung and Chia Ch'ing [1736–1820] a new school of research developed, which had its origin in the teachings of Ku Ting-lin and Huang Li-chou, who believed that research was worthless when divorced from the basic principles of government and economics. The students of the Ch'ien Lung and Chia Ch'ing period, however, abandoned the practical approach of Ku and Huang, and concentrated on the study of terms, words, and phrases. As a result, learning was separated from human life as well as from politics. Under such an eclectic and hodge-podge academic tradition, scholars generally misinterpreted the teachings of the "mean." They developed a habit of ambiguity and fence-sitting, and lived in what Tseng Kuo-fan described as "a world neither white nor black, neither itchy nor aching [i.e., a blank and senseless world]."

However, the broad and far-reaching scope of the state organization and the refined and detailed political institutions and legal enactments of the Ch'ing dynasty were worthy continuations of the achievements of the Han and T'ang dynasties, surpassing those of the Sung and Ming, and certainly leaving those of the Yuan dynasty far behind. This period of two hundred and sixty years was the period during which the modern countries of Europe and America cast off the Dark Ages, began to build their states, and endeavored to develop their power. If the Manchu dynasty had treated the Hans, the Manchus, the Mongols, the Mohammedans, and the Tibetans within the state without discrimination; if it had recognized the five clans as integral parts of a single whole and granted equality to all clans irrespective of religion, occupation, class, or sex; and if the dynasty had aided the frontier clans to develop their self-government and had guaranteed them a position of equality, it can be definitely said that China would have been able to advance together with the contemporary European and American countries. She would have become healthy, happy, rich and strong, and would not have been forced either to suffer the humiliations of the unequal treaties during the past hundred years, or to tolerate the Japanese invasion of the continent of Asia.

This, of course, is a question of policy in relation to a particular historical era, and we cannot be such perfectionists as to believe that the Manchus at that time should have been able to put such a policy into effect. But the Manchus were not only unable to recognize the desirability of such a policy; they followed exclusively a policy of slaughter and enslavement in governing the different clans. Thus during the two-hundred-and-sixty-year reign of the Manchus, our people in the whole nation never saw a single day of light. Although the Ch'ien Lung period was hailed as a period of good government, the Manchu ministers in power, such as Ho Shen, were selfish, autocratic, and greedy. From that period on, open and unrestrained bribery and extortion became common practice among the Manchu officials, while Han officials and scholars who offered themselves as slaves to the Manchu court confined themselves to empty gestures, seeking self-preservation by closing their eyes to realities. The truculent, unscrupulous elements took pride in gaining admittance to the ranks of the Manchu army, where their duties were to oppress their own fellow countrymen.

Social corruption and academic degeneration became more pronounced each day. The methods adopted by the Manchus for dealing with the clans within the country are even more heartbreaking and hair raising to describe. The vicious policy adopted by the Manchus was designed solely to divide the clans within the state and provoke friction and fratricide among them, so that the Manchus could enjoy the benefits of their imperial position without fear of united opposition. Thus, with regard to the Mongolians and Tibetans, the Manchus made use of the "Lama" religion to destroy their martial spirit, and even endeavored to annihilate these clans entirely. Against the Hans and Mohammedans, political and religious restrictions were rigidly enforced, and Manchu Banner Troops were used extensively to control these clans. However, the greatest weakness in this policy lay in the marked distinction drawn between the soldiers and the ordinary citizens. The Ch'ing court followed a policy of compelling the Han to pay taxes to support the Banner Troops, which in turn received military training in order to suppress the Han and other clans. They did not recognize that when soldiers are not also farmers, they become loafers and hoodlums. Although every male Manchu was a soldier, the final result was that all the Manchus became parasitic loafers. By the time of the T'ai-p'ing Rebellion,[3] the Banner Troops as well as the Green Battalions were degenerate and useless. It was then that the Hsiang [Hunan] Militia and the Hwai Militia [from northern Anhwei] earned fame as the beginning of local armed forces [i.e., farmer-soldiers].

These domestic policies of the Manchu Government, destructive to others as well as to itself, were pursued throughout the reigns of Tao Kuang and T'ung Chih, until the spirit with which the dynasty was founded became lost, together with its traditional institutions. The result was political disintegration and the deterioration of national defense. A general situation of chaos and collapse developed.

During this period, China, in the face of aggression by the great foreign powers, underwent ever-increasing national humiliation as a result of the conclusion of a series of unequal treaties that increasingly weakened the position of the state, while the imperial house itself found it difficult to escape total extinction.

Sun Yat-sen saw that the domestic policies of the Manchu Government would eventually destroy both the state and the nation. Therefore, beginning with the Hsing Chung Hui [Society for the Regeneration of China], and continuing with

3. For discussion of the T'ai-p'ing Rebellion, see footnote, p. 194.

the T'ung Meng Hui,[4] these policies were made the object
of revolutionary attack. As soon as the Hsin Hai (1911)
Revolution had succeeded, Sun Yat-sen enunciated the great
principle of "A Republic of Five Peoples" in order to eliminate the friction among the clans within the state and bring
them to a status of unity and equality.[5] From that time until
this day, the Nationalist Government has persistently upheld
the testament of Sun Yat-sen and the successive manifestoes
of the Kuomintang. These call for making a clean sweep of
the detestable domestic policies of the Manchus, and for establishing complete equality among all clans within the state.
They also call for rendering positive assistance to develop the
ability of self-government and to improve the status of the
border clans, granting them religious, cultural, and economic
opportunities for a balanced development, so that all of them
will love, cherish and support the whole state and the central
government through harmonious endeavor and mutual concern, to the end that our Chinese Republic may become
stronger, richer, and happier each day, and that the Three
People's Principles may shine gloriously throughout the world.
This is the underlying spirit of the Revolution of the Kuomintang of China and the one and only mission of its domestic
policy.

4. The predecessor of the Kuomintang, the T'ung Meng Hui (United
League of Revolutionaries) was a
revolutionary party organized by Dr.
Sun Yat-sen in 1905 by the amalgama-
tion of his own party, the Hsin Chung
Hui (Association for the Regeneration
of China) with the Hua Hsin Hui
(organization of Chinese students in
Japan) and the Kuan Fu Hui, a group
of intellectuals headed by the noted
scholar, Chang T'ai-yen. The chief
aim of the T'ung Meng Hui was the
overthrow of the Manchu dynasty.

5. This entire analysis of the Manchu dynasty is contradictory. The author was apparently trying to reconcile the two conflicting ideas that, on
the one hand, the Manchus were
alien, oppressive aggressors, and on
the other, that they were one of the
five clans sharing a common Chinese
bloodstream. Sun Yat-sen does not
speak of "eliminating friction among
the clans," but rather of assimilating
the peoples of China in a "free association of nations." That the Manchus
were finally absorbed by the Chinese
nation was due to the numerical superiority of the Chinese people, in addition to the greater strength of their
cultural and economic institutions.

2. *The Conclusion of the Unequal Treaties and the People's Reaction*

The unequal treaties between China and foreign countries began with the Sino-British Treaty of Nanking, signed in the twenty-second year of Tao Kuang [1842].[6] The Nanking Treaty was the result of the Opium War. Defeat in the Opium War was China's "First National Humiliation" and the Nanking Treaty was the result of this humiliation. China's international relations from the Opium War to the 1911 Revolution may be divided into three periods.

The first period dates from the Opium War to the war of [the year of] Chia Wu [Sino-Japanese War of 1894], with the Treaty of Tientsin [1858] marking a decisive turning point. During this period, foreign powers opened trading ports in China, and these became footholds for the establishment of all forms of special privileges. The first trading ports opened by them were Canton, Foochow, Amoy, Ningpo, and Shanghai, which constituted the so-called "five ports for trade." The special privileges secured by the foreigners were that the citizens of their countries could live and trade under the jurisdiction of their own consuls [extraterritoriality]. Foreigners were also permitted to carry on unrestricted import and export trade under a conventional tariff. Subsequently, countries such as England and France opened more commercial ports in the areas in which they planned to expand their influence and, taking advantage of the stupidity of the Man-

6. Throughout this section in which there is an extensive listing of treaties signed between the Manchu dynasty and the foreign powers, the dates are given by the year of the reigning emperor. To make the translation more readable, dates have been substituted. For example, "the fifth year of T'ung Chih" has been translated 1866; the "seventh year of Kuang Hsu" as 1881, etc. Since very few Chinese know the dates of past centuries in terms of the years of an emperor's reign, one can only conclude that this is an effort on the part of the author to inspire his readers to think in terms of ancient China, even though in this case it concerns the hated Manchu dynasty.

chu diplomatic officials, obtained additional privileges. Whenever one country obtained a new privilege from its treaty with China, all the other countries would, under the evil "most-favored nation" clause, enjoy the same benefits. The special privileges provided in a treaty were often amplified by the foreign interpretation of its terms, or a *fait accompli* was created to force China to acquiesce in still more far-reaching privileges. Take the concessions and settlements for example. There were no provisions in the treaties between China and foreign powers granting special privileges to the latter, but through the expansion of the right of consular jurisdiction, the "guests" gradually usurped the position of the "host."

In what way is the Treaty of Tientsin the pivotal point of this period? Subsequent to the conclusion of the Treaty of Nanking, Canton became the most prosperous port for foreign powers trading with China under the unequal treaties. The imperialist influence upon China's economic and cultural life was strongest in the two Kwang provinces [Kwangtung and Kwangsi], where the people's reaction was also the most violent. The residents of Canton were vigorously opposed to the opening of the city as a trading port and to the entry of foreign steamships. In 1850, nine years after the conclusion of the Treaty of Nanking, Hung Hsiu-ch'uan [of the T'ai-p'ing kingdom] led an insurrection in Chin T'ien, Kwangsi, and his forces spread to the Yangtze Valley and almost overthrew the Ch'ing Government. During the same period, the allied forces of England and France suddenly attacked Canton, invaded Tientsin, and entered Peiping. The Ch'ing Government, ignorant and confused, signed the Treaty of Tientsin under the coercion of the allied forces. Prior to this, the Ch'ing Government had consistently maintained a chauvinistic attitude toward foreign nations and adopted antiforeignism as its only foreign policy. But at this point, the Ch'ing Government, beset internally by popular revolutionary forces and externally by pressure from the foreign powers, chose to yield to the demands of the foreign nations. Hence the treaties concluded with the foreign powers contained many voluntary concessions.

The attitude of the Han scholars and ministers toward the foreign powers had also been chauvinistic. Most of them were still arrogant and ignorant, despising foreign matters as not worth a single glance. Some of them, however, understood and appreciated the mighty effect of Western rifles, cannons, and steamboats, and began to advocate imitation of the West and to promote "Ke-chih" [the study of physical sciences]. Tseng Kuo-fan, Tso Tsung-t'ang, and Li Hung-chang, who suppressed the T'ai-p'ing Rebellion, were the forerunners of this "New Deal" of the Manchu Government. What they advocated, however, was merely the building of factories for the manufacture of copies of Western firearms and communications equipment, and the establishment of schools to teach Western languages. They failed to recognize that a knowledge of foreign languages does not automatically produce a diplomatic expert, and their efforts to build steamboats, coastal defenses, and railroads, without a comprehensive national plan, merely indicated their amazement at the strength of the ships and the effectiveness of the guns of the West. The funds raised for the government's reforms were freely appropriated by the imperial family for extravagant personal expenditure. All officials also regarded the reform program as a source of remunerative positions which enabled them to indulge in corrupt practices to fill their own pockets. The Navy Yamen [Office of Naval Affairs] was in reality busily engaged in the service of the Summer Palace of the Empress Dowager. The Foreign Affairs Yamen was an office in name only. Actually, it became a center where powerful princes, dukes, and ministers divided their spoils. With the Sino-Japanese War of 1894, China's defeat was complete. Li Hung-chang was ordered to Japan to conclude the Treaty of Shimonoseki, which undermined China's sovereignty and the position of the state, and added one more national humiliation. The weaknesses and malpractices of the Manchu dynasty over a period of two hundred years were fully exposed to the world. And this display of weakness and corruption gave rise to the Japanese militarists' contemptuous view of China and their ambitions toward the continent of Asia.

A general survey of the unequal treaties of this period would place all the treaties made following the Opium War into one period, and those made following the Anglo-French joint expedition [1858] into another. The important treaties in the first period were the Sino-British Treaty of Nanking in 1842, the Opening of the Five Treaty Ports (the Tiger Gate Treaty) in 1843, the Sino-American Wang-hsia Treaty in 1844, the Sino-French Huangpu Treaty and the Sino-Swedish-Norwegian Treaty in 1847, and the Sino-Russian Commercial Treaty in 1851. The chief special privileges received by the powers from these treaties were as follows:

A. *Consular Jurisdiction* [Extraterritoriality]
  1. Cases involving only foreign subjects may not be interfered with by Chinese officials.
  2. Civil cases involving Chinese and foreigners shall first be mediated by foreign consuls. If not settled, they shall then be "tried jointly" by local Chinese authorities and foreign consuls.
  3. In criminal cases involving Chinese and foreigners, the Chinese shall be tried by local Chinese authorities according to Chinese law, while foreigners shall be tried by their own consuls according to the laws of their own country.

The establishment of foreign consular jurisdiction in China undermined the judiciary power of China as well as infringed upon the sovereignty of the state; moreover, trade and intercourse between Chinese and foreigners were no longer on an equal footing. Thus a fatal blow was struck against both the welfare of the state and the livelihood of the people.

B. *Conventional Tariff*
  1. With the exception of tea, lumber, metal, and spices, the duties on which shall be ten per cent ad valorem, all

imports from and exports to foreign countries shall be taxed at the rate of five per cent *ad valorem*.

2. On foreign merchant vessels of over one hundred and fifty tons entering a port, the duty shall be five *ch'ien* (1/20 *tael*) per ton, and one *ch'ien* (1/100 *tael*) per ton on those under one hundred and fifty tons. [One *tael* equals approximately seventy-five cents U.S.]

Following the conclusion of the conventional tariff agreement, China's economic and financial power fell completely into foreign hands. The economy declined and the lifeblood of the state was cut off.

Among the unequal treaties following the Anglo-French joint expedition, the most important were: the Treaties of Tientsin in 1858 between China on the one hand and England, France, America, and Russia on the other; the Renewed Treaty between China and Russia in 1861; the Tientsin Treaty between China and Germany in the following year; the Tientsin Treaty between China and Portugal in 1862; the Sino-Dutch and Sino-Danish Tientsin Treaties of 1863; the Sino-Spanish Treaty of 1864; the Sino-Belgian Peking Treaty of 1865; the Sino-Italian Peking Treaty of 1866; the Sino-Austrian Peking Treaty of 1869; the Sino-Peruvian Washington Treaty of 1874; the Sino-British Chefoo Treaty of 1876; the Sino-American Addendum Treaty of 1880; and the Sino-Brazil Tientsin Treaty of 1881. After the conclusion of these treaties, the foreign powers opened many commercial ports along the coast and on the rivers of China, and secured various special privileges. The most notable ones were as follows:

Consular Jurisdiction: Under these treaties, in addition to reaffirming the consular jurisdictional provisions secured previously, the foreign powers obtained the following two special privileges:

1. The privilege of attending trials: The phrase "joint trial" contained in all treaties concluded after the Nanking Treaty

was a mistranslation made by officials of the Ch'ing Government. When the Tientsin Treaties were signed, the powers, taking advantage of this mistranslation, secured the privilege of attending trials. Whenever a civil or criminal case between a Chinese and a foreigner arose, the foreign consul could send a representative to attend the trial.

2. The privilege of joint trial: In 1886, local authorities in Shanghai and the British and American consuls conferred and formulated "Regulations for Foreign Representation in Joint Trials." Thereafter, not only were civil cases involving Chinese and foreigners to be tried by a joint court, but also all cases involving only Chinese, if they occurred within a foreign concession. Subsequently, every country followed this precedent, and as a result there appeared the French Concession's "Joint Court" in Shanghai, Hankow's "Foreign Office," Harbin's "Head Office of Railroad and Foreign Affairs" and the Kulangsu "Joint Court" [in the International Settlement at Amoy].

After the consuls of the foreign powers in China obtained the special privilege of attending trials, and of joint trials, the foreigners not only avoided the jurisdiction of Chinese law but also interfered with Chinese justice. They were not only placed outside the jurisdiction of Chinese courts, but were also given the right to try Chinese citizens.

Concessions: During this period, foreign concessions were established in different localities. In addition to Shanghai's International Settlement, established in 1845, and the French Concession in Shanghai, established in 1849, there were the British and French Concessions in Hankow, Kiukiang, Chinkiang, and Amoy, and the British and French Concessions in Shameen, Canton, established in 1861; and the International Settlement in Chefoo, established in 1866. Consular jurisdiction was originally intended to be applied to persons and not to places or localities. But after the establishment of the concessions, consular jurisdiction was applied to all designated areas. This was tantamount to the establishment of many states within the territory of China.

The Privilege of Navigation and Anchorage of Foreign Warships: The right of foreign warships to cruise and anchor along China's coast and in her inland ports was not explicitly provided for in previous treaties, but through the misinterpretation of these treaties, such actions had become established practices. In the Tientsin Treaties, however, this privilege was specifically granted, with the result that China's coastal defenses became nonexistent, and there was not a single large city that was not dominated by the "gunboat policy" of imperialism.

The Privilege of Controlling Customs: Prior to the Treaties of Tientsin, the custom house at Shanghai was in fact administered by foreigners. The Tientsin Treaties expressly provided that China should engage Britishers to assist in tariff administration, and since that time the Chinese customs has had a British High Commissioner. In 1864, the "General Office for Foreign Affairs" of the Ch'ing Government promulgated "Regulations for the Employment of Foreign Subjects in Tariff Affairs," permitting the chief commissioner to engage foreigners, and since then the tariff office in each port has been headed by a foreigner. After the direct control of our customs by foreigners, not only were the tariff rates determined by the foreign powers, but tariff revenues were also subject to their appropriation; not only was the import of foreign commodities placed under their control, but exports of Chinese goods were subject to their inspection and restrictions.

Conventional Tariff: The Tientsin and other subsequent treaties revised the tariff system of China, the salient points being as follows:

1. Revision of the tariff rate to five per cent *ad valorem.*
2. Inland port duties fixed at half the regular tariff rate, or two and one-half per cent.
3. Reduction of duty on ships to four *ch'ien* per ton.
4. Revision of tariff convention every ten years.

The purpose of these provisions was to fix the duty on imports on the basis of actual value, so that the duties would be reduced when prices fell. The provision fixing inland port duties was to enable foreign goods to be transferred freely from port to port in China with no additional payment. In short, each time the tariff provisions in the unequal treaties were revised, foreign goods received more elaborate protection.

The Right of Coastal Trade and the Right of Navigation: All the ports opened by the treaties concluded subsequent to the Nanking Treaty were coastal ports; therefore the navigation of foreign steamships along the coastline of China was already an established practice before it was provided for in the treaties. After the conclusion of the Tientsin Treaties, explicit provisions to that effect were made. The Tientsin and subsequent treaties also opened more ports along the Yangtze to foreign trade; the powers thereby securing the right of inland navigation. As the powers had the rights of coastal trade and inland navigation, it was not only possible for foreign goods to be marketed in all parts of China, but the control of China's maritime trade also fell into the hands of foreigners. Not only were foreign goods transported by foreign ships to different localities, but domestic goods also depended upon foreign ships for transportation.

The period from the war of 1894 to the time of the Expedition of the Eight Allied Powers constituted the "second period" in China's international relations. The powers, taking advantage of the results of Japanese aggression against us, vied with each other to acquire Chinese territory as concessions or spheres of influence. They built military barracks and naval bases, and obtained railroad building and mining rights. The memory of the disastrous loss of Ryukyu [Liuchiu Islands], Hong Kong, Formosa, the Pescadores, Indo-China, Burma, and Korea was still fresh, while the final calamity of the partitioning of the whole country was impending. Then

a movement for avenging national humiliation and strengthening the state sprang up among the Chinese people. In this
period, both the scholar and the statesman were also gradually learning that China's decline was not only due to the
inferiority of her guns and steamships to those of the West,
but was mainly caused by her political degeneration, the
chief source of which was absolute monarchy. How could
this political system be revolutionized? Those that were aware
of this problem gave different answers. Dr. Sun, responding
to the times and the people, advocated a revolution and organized the Hsing Chung Hui [Society for the Regeneration
of China] in Honolulu. There he recruited comrades, adopted
the slogan of "Drive out the Tartars [Manchus], recover
China, establish a people's state, and equalize land rights."
[The revised edition very significantly omits the last two
points in Sun Yat-sen's program, i.e., those pertaining to the
establishment of a democracy and the equalization of land
rights.] With the Three People's Principles as the basic program, he proceeded actively with the Revolution. No other
parties or political factions achieved this level of understanding. For example, K'ang Yu-wei favored safeguarding the
sovereign position of the monarch, organized the "Protect
the Emperor Party," and advocated the establishment of a
constitution [in the revised edition, K'ang is credited with
advocating "reform" instead of "the establishment of a constitution"]. This reform movement precipitated the *coup d'état*
executed by the Empress Dowager in 1898 which resulted in
the Emperor's imprisonment and the abandonment of the
reforms. The failure of K'ang's reform movement as a result
of the *coup d'état* intensified the reaction of the Ch'ing Government. Rallying around the imperial court, scholars and
statesmen of the conservative clique refused to discuss foreign
affairs and opposed the new reforms. The stupid and stubborn
among them even went so far as to employ amulets to resist
the military weapons of the foreign powers, and sponsored

the so-called "Boxers" to mislead and confuse the people.[7]
As a result, China suffered national humiliation at the hands
of the Eight Allied Armies in 1900, and signed the Hsin-
Ch'ou Peace Treaty in 1901. [Hsin-Ch'ou is the Chinese
name for the year 1901.]

From a general survey of the unequal treaties concluded
during this period, it is clear that the Sino-Japanese Treaty
of Shimonoseki was the turning point in the relations between
Japan and China, marking a shift from equality to inequality.
The main features of this period were the treaties providing
for the leasing of territories and the agreements for railroad
loans concluded between the Ch'ing Government and foreign
powers, and the unilateral declarations made by the powers,
concerning their respective "spheres of influence." The salient
features may be listed as follows: spheres of influence, leased
territories, rights of railroad construction, rights to land adjacent to railroads, and mining rights.

Great Britain: Before 1894, the powers had already established the precedent of setting up spheres of influence in
China. After the ceding of Hong Kong, Great Britain inserted in the Sino-British Treaty of 1846 providing for the
return of Chousan Island, the stipulation that the Ch'ing
Government was "not to cede Chousan Island to any other
country." In the Yunnan-Burma Boundary and Commercial
Convention between China and Britain in 1894 it was also
stipulated that "the area of Meng-lien and Kianghung shall
not be ceded to other countries in whole or any part thereof."
After 1894 [in 1898], Weihaiwei and Kowloon became British
leased territories by virtue of the Sino-British Treaties, both
concluded in 1898. In 1899, Great Britain and Russia agreed
that the Yangtze Valley should be a British sphere for rail-

7. In an effort to divert a popular uprising against themselves, the Man-chu bureaucracy, led by the Empress Dowager, succeeded in corrupting and converting the rising mass revolt into an antiforeign movement. The insurgent organization, known to for-eigners as the "Boxers" because its Chinese name was "Fists for the Pro-tection of Public Peace," changed its slogan from "Down with the Man-chus! Protect the Chinese!" to "Down with the Foreigners! Long Live the Imperial Dynasty!"

road building. At the same time, a British firm, Fu & Co., also obtained mining rights in the two provinces of Shansi and Honan.

France: After occupying Indo-China, France obtained in 1897 the Ch'ing Government's guarantee that "Hainan Island shall not be ceded to any other country" and, in the next year, the pledge that "the three provinces of Kwangtung, Kwangsi, and Yunnan shall not be ceded to any other country." During this period France obtained the right to extend the Lungchow Railroad, to build the Yunnan-Indo-China Railroad, and to exploit the mineral resources of Kwangtung, Kwangsi, and Yunnan. In 1899, she concluded the Kwangchowwan Treaty with the Ch'ing Government, by which Kwangchowwan became a French leased territory.

Germany: Germany concluded the Chiao-Ao Treaty with the Ch'ing Government in 1898, by which she secured Kiaochow Harbor as a German leased territory, with permission to build the Tsingtao-Tientsin Railroad and to exploit the mineral resources within thirty *li* of the railroad. [Three *li* equals one mile.]

Czarist Russia: Czarist Russia concluded the Sino-Russian Tao-Sheng Bank and the Three Eastern Provinces [Manchuria] Railroad Agreements in 1896, designating the Three Eastern Provinces as her sphere of influence. Two years later, she concluded a treaty leasing Port Arthur and Dairen Harbor, and by a subsequent agreement she obtained special rights to railroads, mines, manufacturing, and commerce in the Port Arthur-Dairen area. In 1899, England and Russia agreed that the region north of the Great Wall should be a Russian sphere of influence for railroad building purposes.

Japan: After her occupation of the Pescadores and Formosa, Japan obtained a guarantee from the Ch'ing Government in 1898 that "Fukien Province and its coastal regions shall not be ceded to another country."

This division of various Chinese regions among the powers as their respective spheres of influence was a prelude to the complete partition of China. Although the calamity of partition did not materialize, the powers made extensive use of their special rights of railroad construction, mining, manufacturing, and commerce.

Concessions: The concessions subsequently granted during this period were: the German Concessions in Tientsin and Hankow in 1895; the Russian and French Concessions in Hankow and the Japanese Concession in Hangchow in 1896; the Japanese Concession in Soochow in 1897; the Japanese Concessions in Tientsin, Canton, and Hankow in 1898; and the Japanese Concessions in Amoy and Foochow in 1899.

Rights of Foreign Garrisons: During this period, Czarist Russia forcibly stationed the so-called "Chinese Eastern Railroad Guards" along the Chinese Eastern Railroad. Thereafter, the powers had the right to station troops in China.

The Employment of Foreign Postal Employees and Foreign Post Offices: In 1898, France forced the Ch'ing Government to employ foreigners in post offices, and the powers then opened their own post offices in China. Thereafter, China's communications fell under the control of the powers.

The Right to Establish Factories: In the Treaty of Shimonoseki, the Japanese inserted a provision granting Japanese subjects in China's treaty ports the right "freely to pursue various lines of manufacturing and freely to ship and import all kinds of machinery, provided only that a fixed import duty be paid." All articles manufactured in factories in the treaty ports were to be treated as imports, and duties and taxes were to be exempt or reduced accordingly. On the basis of "the most-favored nation clause," other countries secured the same privileges.

With the conclusion of the Hsin-Ch'ou Peace Treaty in 1901, China's international relations entered the third period. In the first period, the imperialist powers competed in China on a basis of equality; in the second period, this situation changed into one of imperialist rivalry, which produced the Anglo-Japanese Alliance and the Russo-French Alliance. At the time of the Expedition of the Eight Allied Armies, international policy toward China was hovering between the Open Door and Concerted Partition. The Open Door Policy was initiated by the United States and seconded by Great Britain. But the Japanese aggressors were not satisfied with their concessions on the Liaotung Peninsula, while Czarist Russia continued her efforts to monopolize the northeast. Hence the Russo-Japanese War was fought in 1904 to decide their respective spheres of influence in the northeast—another national humiliation for China. Thereafter, the Japanese aggressors laid the foundation of their "continental policy"— the beginning of the present calamities wrought by them in Asia and the world.

The unequal treaties of this period, such as the Hsin-Ch'ou Peace Treaty, the Sino-British Treaty of 1902, the Sino-American Commercial Treaty of 1903, the Sino-Japanese Supplementary Navigation Agreement, the Agreement between China and Japan concerning Manchuria in 1905, and the Sino-Swedish Treaty in 1908, all contained provisions for additional special privileges. The chief of these were as follows:

Legation Areas: The Hsin-Ch'ou Peace Treaty provided for the establishment of a special area for foreign legations in the then national capital, Peking, to be jointly administered and defended by the legations. This is the T'ung Chiao Min Hsiang Legation Area. Within this area foreign troops were stationed regularly and it was constantly patrolled by special police, thus becoming actually a "state within a state."

Right to Station Foreign Troops: In addition to the stationing of foreign troops in the legation area, the Hsin-Ch'ou Peace Treaty provided that foreign troops should be stationed along the railroad from Peking via Tientsin to Shanhaikwan, to protect the communication line from Peking to the sea. Our fortifications at Taku and between Peking and Haikow were demolished, and China was deprived of the right to establish coastal defenses.

Japan's Sphere of Influence: After the Russo-Japanese War, the Japanese aggressors occupied Port Arthur, Dairen, and the southern section of the Chinese Eastern Railway and its branches. The Ch'ing Government, in the so-called Basic Sino-Japanese Agreement on Matters Concerning the Three Eastern Provinces, recognized this *fait accompli* by making the southern part of Manchuria, i.e., the Liaotung Peninsula, a Japanese sphere of influence, while Port Arthur and Dairen became Japanese leased territories.

Concessions: Concessions added during this period were the Russian and Belgian Concessions in Tientsin and the Japanese Concession in Chungking in 1901, the Italian Concession in Tientsin and the International Settlement in Kulangsu [Amoy] in 1902, and the Austrian Concession in 1903.

The Right to Control Customs: In 1907, the Japanese obtained control of the Customs House in Dairen.

The Right of a Conventional Tariff: Changes were made with respect to the tariff system in the Hsin-Ch'ou Peace Treaty and the Mackay Treaty of 1902. The important points were as follows:

1. Import duties were fixed at five per cent *ad valorem*, supplemented by a specific duty.
2. Revenues from inland ports were placed under the control of the Customs House.
3. It was specified that after the abolition of *likin* [inland transit duties] import duties might be increased to twelve and one-half per cent and export duties to seven and one-half per cent.

These provisions were intended to reduce or remove inland duties on foreign imports. The Hsin-Ch'ou Treaty had forced a huge indemnity on China, and in order to pay it, China was compelled to increase her taxes. But since foreign imports enjoyed reduced tariff rates and exemption from the *likin* tax, the burden of the indemnity payment fell entirely on native goods. Thereafter, the inability of native goods to compete with foreign products in the Chinese market became increasingly apparent.

Right of Appropriation of Customs Revenues and Custody of the Surplus: Customs revenues were pledged for indemnity payments and were placed under the control of the Commissioner of Customs, who was a foreigner. The surplus, after the annual payment of indemnity installments, was deposited in foreign banks and was still subject to the Commissioner's control. Thus not only was the cream of the Chinese economy drawn off by the imperialist powers, but even the leftovers were expropriated.

Right to Clear the Channels of Inland Waterways, Employing Foreign Pilots, Erecting Lighthouses and Navigation Buoys, etc.: The Hsin-Ch'ou Treaty granted to foreign countries the right to dredge the North River [the entrance channel from Taku] and the Huangpu River [the entrance channel from Wusung]. It also granted them the privilege of employing foreign river pilots, and erecting buoys, navigating marks, lighthouses, and watch towers. Thereafter, the conditions and strategic importance of China's principal harbors and inland waterways became well known to the imperialists and subject to their control.

In this period, there was first the Hsin-Ch'ou Treaty which not only discredited the Ch'ing Government once and for all, but also resulted in the continuous decline of the national economy. Though China luckily maintained her formal existence as a result of the conflicts and rivalries among the powers, the Ch'ing Government's fear of the foreign powers was at its height, leading it to try to curry favor with the foreigners. Following this, there was the Russo-Japanese War in which Japan finally triumphed over Czarist Russia—a victory that left a deep impression on both the Government and the people of China. The Ch'ing Government, sensing the unalterable trend toward reform, was forced to promulgate a "New Deal." It abolished the literary examination, established [modern] schools, trained new armies, built ar-

senals, mints, and shipyards, and prepared for the promulga-
tion of a constitution and the calling of a parliament, in order
to conceal its political corruption and diplomatic humiliations, and thus mislead the people. The people recognized the
impending calamity in the foreign relations of the state, as
well as the ignorance and helplessness of the Ch'ing Government. They also saw that the so-called movement for constitutional reform had secured from the Government only a
series of decrees. It was then that the revolutionary program
advocated by Sun Yat-sen took root among the broad masses
of the people who had been secretly cherishing a nationalist
ideology. The prestige of the constitutional monarchists and
royalists was increasingly undermined, while an upsurge of
revolutionary anti-Manchu sentiment rose higher and higher.
The new schools established by the reforms of the Ch'ing
Government became hotbeds of revolutionary ideas, and the
new army became the springboard of the revolutionary movement. Popular belief in Sun Yat-sen's revolutionary program
became stronger. The active movement within the country
was led by secret societies and parties, while financial support
came mainly from overseas Chinese.

Such being the situation within the country and outside,
the revolutionary storm could not be averted. However, as
the revolutionary movement grew, the Ch'ing Government
became increasingly reactionary. It clung firmly to the policy
that "it is better to give to friends than to one's own slaves,"
which made the people realize that they were suffering from
the double oppression of imperialism and autocracy, and
that they must fight for a government of as well as by the
people. The revolutionary movement aimed at strengthening
the state, overthrowing the Manchus, and avenging the national humiliation. Through the rallying of volunteer armies,
the launching of insurrections, the shedding of blood, and the
sacrifice of lives on the part of the martyrs of the T'ung
Meng Hui, the objectives of the Revolution became clarified
and the will of the people more and more determined.

Thus the insurrection of October 10th, 1911, in Wuchang brought an immediate response from the whole country. The Ch'ing Emperor abdicated and the Republic was established. Although there were alternately external encroachments and internal troubles, and many obstacles were encountered, they all add up to one historical lesson; without determined effort on the part of the people, humiliation cannot be avenged and strength cannot be built up; without a people's revolution, the people's aspirations cannot be satisfied and their will cannot be unified for the task of avenging humiliations and building up the country's strength. Ninety-three years of history since the T'ai-p'ing insurrection has proved that the people's revolution and the Three People's Principles initiated by the Father of our Country are the only right road for rehabilitating our nation. From the Revolution of 1911 to the present war of resistance and national reconstruction, we have followed this road without hesitation or retreat, advancing with courage and speed, and we will never halt until the goal is attained.

3. Lessons from the Accomplishments and Failures of the 1911 Revolution

Although the public supported the people's revolution, their understanding of its fundamental meaning was not sufficiently deep. They knew that making copies of guns and steamships could not strengthen the state. They also knew that if absolute monarchy and feudal partition were allowed to continue, the state could not strengthen itself and become independent. But when the absolute monarchy had been overthrown and a Republic of Five Peoples had been proclaimed, they thought that the Nationalist Revolution was a success and that democratic government had become a reality. They only knew how to imitate the form of Western democracy, and were content so long as the Central Government had a president, a cabinet, and a parliament. They did not recognize that the main objective of the Nationalist Revolution was to escape from the bondage of the unequal treaties, and especially to overcome the habits of arrogance, extravagance, immorality, lawlessness, and the attitude of servile dependence upon foreign powers that had been fostered under the unequal treaties. They did not know the real meaning of democracy, nor did they realize that the principle of the people's livelihood is the basic aim of the Revolution. They had overthrown the absolute monarchy, but they could not eliminate the bad habits of idleness, greed, and aimlessness developed under autocracy, nor the tradition of unrealistic learning and discussion without regard for practical results. With such habits and traditions, the copying of Western firearms resulted in the substitution of sand for gunpowder,[8] and the operation of the parliamentary system was marked by bribery and the [illegal] revision of the provisional constitution. Even members that joined the revolutionary party were so governed by bad habits that they lacked steadfastness. Once they encountered defeat, their faith was shaken, they became despondent, lacked courage to face difficulties, and resorted to actions that bore no relation to their verbal protestations. Thus, although the Chinese Republic was founded in 1912, there was a period of thirteen years, until the reorganization of the Kuomintang, in which the Nationalist Revolution experienced innumerable difficulties and obstacles. In retrospect, the history of that period is certainly a matter for profound regret. The experience of those thirteen years may be divided into two periods.

The first period dates from the insurrection of 1911 to the death of Yuan Shih-k'ai in 1916. At the time of the 1911 Revolution, Sun Yat-sen's purpose was to overthrow the three-thousand-year monarchy, and establish a democratic state. He did not consider that democracy consisted merely of a president, a parliament, a provisional constitution, and

8. This is intended to indicate the graft practiced by Chinese officials who substituted sand for gunpowder and pocketed the difference in cost.

a cabinet. Because of this, he turned the presidency over to Yuan Shih-k'ai. He believed that the revolutionists should constitute a nongovernmental party, devoting their energy to education and industry, and to implanting the foundations of the Three People's Principles in the minds and life of the people. There were very few men in the Party that understood this idea. Attention was generally centered on the text of the provisional constitution, in the belief that if only a system of responsible government could be enforced, Yuan Shih-k'ai could be prevented from abusing his authority as president. They also thought that if a powerful political party could be organized to control the parliament, a responsible cabinet could be maintained to carry out the task of restricting the authority of the president. They also copied the form of British and American politics, believing that if two major parties existed side by side, the mold of democracy would have been set. However, though two major parties were organized, they did not help the parliament to increase its authority. Even though there was a majority party whose members engaged in legal activities in the parliament, they could not establish a responsible cabinet, nor could they prevent a president like Yuan Shih-k'ai from abusing his prerogatives.

What Yuan Shih-k'ai feared was not the parliament, but the influence of the revolutionary party in the Yangtze Valley and the southern provinces. Therefore, after the failure of the Second Revolution in the provinces of Kiangsi, Kwangtung, and Fukien, and in Nanking in the second year of the Republic [1913], the parliament was dissolved by the president it had elected, and the decree of dissolution was countersigned by none other than the prime minister of a cabinet responsible to the parliament. Immediately after the dissolution of the parliament, the cabinet collapsed. Thereafter, the so-called parliament, the so-called cabinet, and the provisional constitution itself, were all controlled by Yuan Shih-k'ai, and were maneuvered at his pleasure.

But Sun Yat-sen had long anticipated that Yuan Shih-k'ai would reject the provisional constitution and attempt to make himself Emperor. Thus, following the assassination of Sung Chiao-jen [a leading organizer of the Kuomintang], Sun Yat-sen immediately advocated the prosecution of Yuan and the launching of a punitive expedition. Unfortunately, there were again very few leading members of the Party that understood this idea. Being low in morale and lacking in determination, they merely waited for Yuan Shih-k'ai to complete his preparations for war, thus leaving their own fate in his hands. As a result, the Revolution met a disastrous defeat. In the third year of the Republic [1914], Sun Yat-sen organized the China Revolutionary Party on a basis of strict discipline for a determined effort to realize the aims of the Revolution. When Yuan Shih-k'ai declared himself Emperor Hung Hsien, all citizens of the country once again realized that our leader had not misled them with his revolutionary platform. In other words, historical facts once more proved that the Nationalist Revolution is the most effective means for the rehabilitation of the Chinese nation, and that it is also the only correct platform.

With the death of Yuan Shih-k'ai [in 1916], the country entered the second period. Dissension among warlords throughout the country led to internecine strife. The dream of the northern militarists to achieve unification through military conquest failed to materialize. The movement for a federation of self-governing provinces, serving as a mask for a feudalistic partition of the country, produced no results. A political set-up in which rival warlords and corrupt politicians vied for power became bankrupt. But even in this darkest and most miserable stage, the Nationalist Revolution saw a glimmer of hope.

The First World War took place in this period, and for four years the strength of the great powers—England, France, Germany, Italy, Russia, and Turkey—was concentrated on the European battleground, and their manpower, materials, and money were expended there. The United States granted loans and shipped supplies to Europe, and finally also sent its troops to participate in the great war. Great hopes were aroused in the minds of the Chinese people, who thought that China could now escape from imperialist oppression and become free and independent through self-help and self-endeavor. Moreover, China's new industries suddenly prospered, the textile industry in particular undergoing a profitable expansion. China's balance of trade, which had been unfavorable since the end of the Ch'ing dynasty, became favorable, with an excess of exports. This economic progress further enhanced the hope and self-confidence of the people. But the warlords and politicians had no idea of modern politics or economics, nor could they understand the people's aspirations or express the people's will. Instead they brought about an even greater national humiliation. This was, first, the so-called "Twenty-One Demands" presented by the Japanese imperialists, who took advantage of Yuan Shih-k'ai's overweening desire to become Emperor. Following this, the Japanese took advantage of the civil war policy of the Peiyang clique [northern militarists], granted political loans [to this clique] and later concluded the so-called "Sino-Japanese Military Agreement" whereby their army was sent into Chinese territory. The Japanese army also unlawfully attacked and seized Tsingtao and demanded the transfer to Japan of German rights in the railroads and mines of Shantung.

This national humiliation, so contrary to the aspirations of the people, gave rise to strong revolutionary sentiments. The May 4th [1919] Movement was the clearest evidence of that feeling. Under the pressure of this strong popular revolutionary sentiment, the government of the warlords and politicians could not hope to survive. Even the various paper plans for constitutional reform failed to arouse any interest among the people. The power of the Anhwei clique had declined, and the Chihli [Hopei] and Fengtien [Manchurian] cliques could muster no support among the people. The [presidential] election conducted by the Chihli clique was equivalent to the digging of their own graves. When events reached this stage, there was no way to fulfill the people's aspirations, voice their demands, and strengthen their self-confidence except by a Nationalist Revolution led by the Kuomintang of China. Thus the power to the Three People's Principles and the Nationalist Revolution, riding the thunderous tidal waves of world events, rallied the entire country unitedly beneath the banner of the blue sky and white sun [of the Kuomintang] with one purpose: to fight determinedly for the abolition of the unequal treaties, to lay a foundation for the rehabilitation of the nation, and to secure freedom and independence.

Of all the unequal treaties of this period the "Twenty-One Demands" of the Japanese aggressors were the most brutal and vicious. They demonstrated that the Japanese imperialists' policy toward China had advanced another step, from partition to monopolistic possession. The main points of these "Demands" were as follows:

The first group of articles concerned Shantung. Article 4 demanded that the special privileges accorded to Germany in Shantung be transferred to Japan by the government of the Peiyang [northern] clique. These included mining and other rights in Kiaochow Bay and along the Kiaochow-Tsinan Railroad. Shantung Province, with all territory and islands along the coast, was "not to be ceded or leased to any other country." The right to build a railroad connecting Yen-tai or Lung-kou with the Kiaochow-Tsinan Railroad, and the opening of all important cities in Shantung as trading ports were also specified. In short, Japan demanded that the whole province of Shantung be designated as her "sphere of influence."

The second group of articles concerned the southern part of the Three Eastern Provinces [Manchuria] and the eastern part of Inner Mongolia. Article 7 of Group II demanded the extension of the leases of Port Arthur, Dairen, and the South Manchurian and Antung-Fengtien [Mukden] Railroads to ninety-nine years; the right of Japanese subjects to own or lease land, reside, travel, engage in industry and commerce, and to extract minerals in "southern Manchuria" and "eastern Mongolia"; the employment of Japanese in these two areas as political, financial, and military advisers and instructors; the right to administer and operate the Kirin-Changchun Railway and to forbid other countries to build railroads or invest capital in these two areas. In summary, Japan demanded the designation of the southern part of the Three Eastern Provinces and the eastern part of Inner Mongolia as her "sphere of influence."

The third group of articles concerned the Hanyang-Tayeh-Pinghsiang Iron Company. These articles demanded that this company be made a "joint enterprise" of Japan and China, and that Japan be given the exclusive right to operate all mines adjacent to those owned by the company.

The fourth and fifth groups of articles concerned the whole of China. The first article of Group IV demanded the exclusive occupation by Japan of all harbors and islands along the entire coast of China. The seventh article of Group V demanded that China employ Japanese as political, financial, and military advisers, and also demanded that Japanese subjects be given the right to own lands in the interior of China; joint administration of China's police; the right to supply China's armaments and joint management of China's munition works; the right to build railroads between Wuchang, Kiukiang, and Nanchang, between Nanchang and Hangchow, and between Nanchang and Chaochow; the designation of the entire province of Fukien as a Japanese "sphere of influence"; and the right of Japanese subjects to conduct missionary work in China. In summary, Japan intended to monopolize all China as a feudatory or slave colony.

The "Twenty-One Demands" aroused the people of China

and shocked the world; yet, if we examine their implications, they were really no different from all the other unequal treaties between China and the foreign powers. [The revised edition omits the preceding sentence.] All political, judicial, military, police, customs, communications, mining, religious, and educational matters—all the factors of culture, national defense, and economy essential to the maintenance of China's statehood—had long been sold out through the successive treaties concluded with the powers. The "Twenty-One Demands" were simply intended to transfer the special privileges separately enjoyed by the powers to the exclusive control of the Japanese imperialists. Therefore, I have often said that the spirit of the "Twenty-One Demands" was in reality nothing more than the grand culmination of all the unequal treaties. [The revised edition omits the phrase "nothing more than" in the preceding sentence.]

Sun Yat-sen said: "It is easy to feel the pressure of political power, but it is generally not easy to feel the pressure of economic power." We may also say that the people in general did not readily grasp the effects of the treaties fatal to the state and enslaving to its people that were concluded piece-meal as a result of the continuous pressure brought to bear by the foreign powers on the Manchu and Peking Governments. But an inclusive and clear-cut set of articles, like the "Twenty-One Demands" could be easily understood. Because of their frank and clear-cut character, they aroused the indignation and the united opposition of the entire country. Yet it should be understood that the piecemeal concessions previously made by the Manchu and Peking Governments to foreign countries, whose fatal and enslaving effects upon the state and its citizens had not been so clearly recognized, were, just because of this popular apathy, more dangerous than the "Twenty-One Demands." [For the phrase "more dangerous than the 'Twenty-One Demands,'" the revised edition substitutes, "a severe blow to the independence and survival of the nation."]

For this reason, the Revolution of the Three People's Principles, while conducting a life and death struggle against the monopolistic aggression of the Japanese invaders, has also maintained equal vigilance with respect to the unequal treaties and demanded their complete abolition.

CHAPTER THREE

THE DEEPENING EFFECTS OF THE UNEQUAL TREATIES

1. Their Effects on Government and Law

Our Nationalist Revolution had its origin in the state's distress and the suffering of the people. If the Revolution fails, the state's distress and the people's suffering will deepen. During the Revolution of 1911, China was unable to transform destruction into reconstruction. During the First World War, she was unable to throw off the bondage of the unequal treaties and attain freedom and international equality. The Peking Government was unable fully to grasp the opportunity and wage an active struggle for the reconstruction of international relations in the Pacific when the chance was first offered by the Washington Conference of 1921. Although the "Nine Power Treaty" established the principles of the "Open Door" and "Territorial Integrity," the specific abolition of privileges specified in the unequal treaties, such as the recovery of concessions, the abolition of extraterritorial rights, and the withdrawal of foreign garrisons, were either vetoed or postponed. In particular, the signing of a treaty between China and Japan for the settlement of pending problems in Shantung met with successive difficulties that were not fundamentally solved. Moreover, the principles of the "Open Door" and "Territorial Integrity" only deepened the indolent psychology of the Chinese people and increased their dependence upon foreign countries, since they now felt confident that China would not be partitioned.

After the Treaty of Tientsin [1858], the despotism of the Manchu dynasty and the aggression of imperialism no longer opposed each other but were in league with one another. After the Revolution of 1911, the relations between the corrupt warlords and the imperialists advanced another step. Yuan Shih-k'ai's monarchy and Japan's "Twenty-One Demands" were interrelated. Okuma Shisenoba's interview [published in the press under the title "Supporting China's Monarchy"] obviously stimulated Yuan Shih-k'ai's ambitions. This is a concrete example that is familiar to us all.

The imperialists, in addition to employing all sorts of coercion and bribery to win over the warlords in order to obtain special privileges, intervened directly against China, particularly in regard to border questions. Outer Mongolia was dominated by Czarist Russia, and in 1911 it declared its independence [of China] and the control of all internal and external affairs in Outer Mongolia fell into Russian hands. After the Russian Revolution, the Mongols abandoned their independence and were planning to renew their allegiance to China. At that time, the Japanese, taking advantage of the so-called "Sino-Japanese Military Agreement," incited the Mongolian bandits and White Russians to carry out espionage activities in Outer Mongolia. The Tibetan problem was similarly subject to foreign influence. The British likewise took advantage of the conflicts between the Tibetans and the Szechwanese and Yunnanese. Their manipulation and control of the Dalai Lama was exactly the same as the Russian use of the Panchen Lama. [The last two sentences in this paragraph were omitted in the revised edition.]

In the first year of the Republic [1912], I publicly stated in the magazine, *The Voice of the Army:* "To conquer and pacify Mongolia and Tibet, one cannot look only at the ease or difficulty of the immediate circumstances, the advantages or disadvantages of the situation, and adhere to a fixed military strategy. We must carefully examine the present circumstances of Britain and Russia and their relations to Mongolia and Tibet and then make our decision accordingly. When Britain and Russia insist on intervention, our country, though not having the strength to declare war, should oppose them strongly on a basis of principles, and should demand the restoration of our sovereignty. Why does our government not act in this way, instead of repeatedly tolerating this oppression, and willingly retreating and withdrawing? There is no greater loss of our rights, no greater humiliation to our country than this."

These remarks clearly indicate the situation in China's border regions at that time. But were not conditions within the country the same? After the political *coup d'état* of 1898, the Empress Dowager Tsu Hsi lived in fear of interference by the envoys of the foreign powers resident in China with regard to the question of whether or not to dethrone the Emperor Kuang Hsu. At the time when Yuan Shih-k'ai declared himself Emperor, Japan incited him behind the scenes, though publicly Japan gave him warnings and reprimands. How dangerous and maliciously ruthless were the intrigues and methods of the imperialists. Although Tsu Hsi's stupidity and confusion and Yuan Shih-k'ai's treachery were denounced by the Chinese people at that time, foreign intervention [in China] set a bad precedent in international relations. The Peking Legation Quarter, the railway zones in the Northeastern Provinces, and the concessions in Tientsin and Shanghai were, under the pretext of protecting foreign residents and foreign trade, the real bases for interference in our internal affairs. One of the most illuminating illustrations of foreign intervention in our internal affairs was the Kuo Sung-ling affair in 1924, when the Japanese imperialists dispatched troops to the South Manchurian Railway zone and prevented the passage of Kuo's army. This incident permitted a further extension of the Japanese warlords' control over the northeast [Manchuria].

The secret activities of the imperialists were actually the chief cause of the civil wars among the warlords following the establishment of the Republic. Extraterritorial rights made possible the protection of their spies and secret service agents. Special areas like the concessions, leased territories, and railway zones, and the special rights enjoyed by the powers on the railroads and waterways, afforded facilities for the powers to store and sell munitions to local warlords, thus prolonging the internal disorders. We still remember that the Peking Legation Quarter and the international cars on the Peking-Mukden Railroad, as well as the Tientsin Concession, were the main places where the militarists and politicians plotted their political *coups d'état* during the regime of the Peking Government. The successes and defeats of the militarists and politicians; their ascension to power and their downfall, were all based upon these [foreign-inspired and supported intrigues]. The Manchurian and Mongolian princes and officials of Dairen, and the defeated warlords and bureaucrats of Tientsin and Shanghai all bowed their heads shamelessly and became puppets of the foreigners, serving as instruments for imperialism. Most heartbreaking of all was that in what was actually China's territory, Chinese laws could not be enforced, and China's armies could not trespass. From this, the evils of the unequal treaties can be clearly seen. They not only rendered China no longer a state, but also made the Chinese people no longer a nation. They completely destroyed our nationhood, and our sense of honor and shame was lost. [The preceding three sentences on the unequal treaties were omitted in the revised edition.] So long as the unequal treaties were still in existence, how could Chinese politics develop along the right lines? How could China's economy be built up? When one thinks or talks about this, can one fail to be bitter and enraged? [This sentence was deleted from the revised edition.]

The unequal treaties even went a step further in destroying China's national defenses. During the early years of the reign of Kuang Hsu, Li Hung-chang planned coastal defenses, trained a navy, and erected fortifications in important harbors. In the War of 1894, the North Sea naval squadron was defeated. The Treaty of 1901 explicitly required China

to raze "the Taku Fort and any forts obstructing communications between the capital and the sea." Thus, the defense
of the capital was destroyed, and China's right to national
defense was completely abolished.

The Tientsin Treaties between China and Great Britain,
the United States, France, and Japan had already provided
that foreign warships could enter any harbor in China, and
also permitted them to anchor in any treaty port. As a result
of the "most-favored nation" clause, other countries also
enjoyed these special privileges. Thus any foreign warships
could sail and anchor in Chinese waters and inland rivers;
China became an "open house" and the imperialists could
do as they pleased. The ports where they concentrated were
either the economically developed cities or the political and
cultural areas. Whenever any issue was to be negotiated, the
foreign navies could take off the gun covers, threaten the
Chinese officials and merchants, and coerce the Chinese
Government or local authorities into recognizing their demands. Under the "Gunboat Policy" China could only acquiesce in whatever they demanded.

The stationing of foreign troops in Chinese territory was
of two categories. In some cases it was based on treaty provisions; in others it was not provided for by treaties. The
stationing of troops in leased territories, and the foreign garrisons in the Legation Quarter and along the Peking-Mukden
Railway, were based on the terms of the 1901 Treaty. The
stationing of all other foreign troops in China was not explicitly provided for in any treaties. As for the Russian garrison on the Chinese Eastern Railway and the Japanese
garrison on the South Manchurian Railway, not only was
there no treaty provision for such garrisons, but the "railway
zones" was a term evolved by a misinterpretation of the
treaties. Garrisons in the concessions were also not provided
for by treaty, but developed from actual practice.

The foreign consular police and the concession police were
also not based on treaty provisions. On the excuse that en-

forcement of consular jurisdiction required a police force, the consuls of the various countries organized police forces, and the police department of the "Joint Court" in the Shanghai Concession was expanded to form the "patrol station" of the "Department of Public Works."

This equipping of troops and police meant that the "diplomatic areas" and "concessions" were definitely states within a state. Many states and political authorities were established within Chinese territory, and furthermore, the activities of foreign troops and police were not confined to these special areas. The number and duties of these troops were far in excess of what was required to carry out the Consular Court decisions. The Japanese garrisons and police in the northeast [Manchuria] were especially undisciplined. Incidents such as the Cheng-chia-tun incident of 1916, the Chang-ch'un and Foochow incidents of 1919, and the Miao-chieh and Huei-ch'un incidents of 1920 all occurred because Japanese troops and police stationed in China ran amuck and wantonly shot and killed Chinese citizens and attacked Chinese soldiers. In addition, there were innumerable incidents in which concession police and foreign troops intimidated Chinese soldiers and shot and killed Chinese citizens. For example, the Lao-hsi-kai incident of 1915, the May 30th [1925] incident in the Shanghai International Settlement, the tragic affairs [June 1925] in the Hankow Concessions and in Shakee [Sha-chi], Canton will be forever remembered by our people as causes of shame and humiliation. [In the revised edition, "causes of shame and humiliation" was changed to "facts."]

In Chinese territory, the troops and police of the imperialists could wantonly fire on Chinese soldiers, police, merchants, and citizens, while Chinese soldiers and police could not fight back. If Chinese soldiers and police made any move, the imperialists would immediately threaten them with war. Their armies would be mobilized; their navies would get up steam; and a series of strongly worded diplomatic notes amounting to ultimatums would follow. The Chinese Government and the people were conditioned to fear foreigners; treacherous officials took advantage of the opportunities offered to exploit the people; rich families transferred their wealth to the concessions and entrusted it to the protection of foreign troops and police. It became the established custom for Chinese banks, treasuries, greedy officials, and big merchants to use the concessions as a refuge for themselves and their fortunes. Thus a few foreign soldiers and police, who originally were only a symbol of imperialism, became a mighty power that throttled both the social and political life of China. As a result, when Chinese soldiers and officials were threatened by imperialists, they not only lacked courage to fight back, but did not even think of fighting back. This was the sad and tragic state into which the nation had fallen! The soldiers, whose morale had been undermined by the unequal treaties, completely lost their sense of responsibility to the state.

Confronted with China's demand for the recovery of all legal rights, the foreign powers always used the inadequacy of Chinese laws and prison regulations as an excuse to oppose it. But, during the past hundred years, Chinese judicial rights were not exercised in the foreign concessions, and as a result the concessions became havens for criminals, the prestige and dignity of Chinese laws were destroyed, and the law-abiding habits of the Chinese people impaired. Moreover, the courts and prisons within the concessions, as far as regard for human life, law and fair trials were concerned, compared most unfavorably with Chinese courts and prisons. Specifically, the inhuman torture of Chinese by the concession police was without human decency and is unbearable even to describe. [In the revised edition, this sentence was changed to "The unfair and unlawful treatment of the Chinese by the concession police is unbearable even to describe."] After a Chinese had been arrested, there was no way for him to receive a public trial, and in a [secret] trial, he could hardly receive a fair sentence. The wealthy were released on large bail, and allowed to move about freely, while the poor remained under sentence and endured cruel treatment, with no opportunity to prove their innocence. Such cruel methods were seldom seen even before the reforms in China's judicial and penitentiary systems. Chinese officials had no authority to investigate a legal case involving foreigners, nor to inquire into the injuries and tortures suffered by Chinese citizens in the police stations of the concessions. Nor was there any means of bringing such Chinese citizens under the protection and jurisdiction of Chinese law. It is clear from this that the effect of the unequal treaties upon the administration of Chinese law not only impaired the virtue and infringed on the human rights of the Chinese people, but also broke the world law of justice and humanity. As a result, the recovery of legal jurisdiction and the attainment of tariff autonomy became the two basic points in the movement for the abolition of the unequal treaties. These two points represented the unanimous demand of the Chinese people, and were also the most important objectives of the Chinese Nationalist Revolution.

2. Their Effects on Economics

The effect of the unequal treaties on China's economy also originated in the foreign concessions and areas where foreign troops were stationed. The agreement on customs and extraterritorial rights constituted the two instruments of foreign economic aggression. Furthermore, the right of the foreign powers to sail in inland waters, to trade along the coast, to establish factories in treaty ports, to build railroads, open mines and issue currency through their own banks, all tended to increase the effects of their economic aggression and caused the Chinese economy to suffer inestimable losses.

Sun Yat-sen pointed this out to us, saying: "Oppression by economic power is more severe than oppression by political power. Oppression by political power is visible, but when one

comes under oppression by economic power, ordinarily one
is not easily aware of it." The Father of our Country was the
first to emphasize the losses incurred from having our maritime customs under foreign control, and our customs revenues
determined by agreements with foreign powers. Following
the Treaty of 1901, which required China to pay an indemnity
to the foreign powers, receipts from the Chinese Maritime
Customs were mortgaged; control of the customs fell into the
hands of foreigners, and the surplus funds after the payment
of debts—the so-called "Customs Surplus"—were also under
foreign control. Then too, the tariff, jointly regulated by the
powers, provided for very low rates on foreign imports and
prevented Chinese industries from receiving tariff protection
to safeguard their existence and expansion. As a result, our
markets were flooded with foreign commodities and domestic
products could not be distributed. In consequence, the traditional handicraft industries declined and the newly established machine industries were unable to prosper. China's
unfavorable balance of trade increased with the years, and
her economy became weak and impoverished.

Sun Yat-sen also pointed out that the issuing of currency
notes by foreign banks in China caused China to suffer a
heavy loss. The people of our country, affected by the poison
of foreign economic oppression, trusted these foreign cur-
rencies, thus enabling the foreign banks to use their own notes
for the purchase of Chinese commodities. Deposits in foreign
banks constituted an additional heavy loss for China. Chinese
deposited their money in the foreign banks in the concessions,
and these banks invested this capital in China, thus deriving
both interest and profits. These revenues, together with land
rents and the profits derived from speculative enterprises in
the concessions and from foreign-controlled industry and
commerce in China, all depended upon the special privileges
accorded by the unequal treaties. These combined losses to
China caused our social structure to decay and threatened
our people's chance of survival. The number of unemployed

and bandits increased steadily, and national distress mounted.

In the course of Chinese history, the key area of China's economy has shifted three times. During the Ch'in and Han dynasties, the greatest economic development occurred in the Yellow River Valley. From the period of the Three Kingdoms to the Sui and Tang dynasties, economic activity in the Yellow River Valley declined, and was superseded by the economic development of the Yangtze River Valley. From the Sung to the Ch'ing dynasties, the state gradually came to depend upon the wealth and tribute of the southwest. After the Yuan dynasty fell, land communications between the continents of Asia and Europe were broken, and the cities of western China gradually declined in importance. The sea-borne commerce of Spain, Portugal, Holland, and England extended to the China coast, and the southeastern cities consequently flourished. Thus, the economic pattern of China for the past one thousand years can, in general, be described by the saying: "Use the wealth of the southeast to support the armies of the northwest." However, the basis of our country's economy was agriculture. And because agriculture was evenly distributed throughout the country, except in the border regions, there was a similarly even distribution of population. The policy of successive governments with regard to the development of communications was always based on the principle of paying equal attention to all parts of the country. And although the trend of economic development was from the rivers toward the coast, the economic structure of the country does not appear to have been one-sided.

But after the conclusion of the unequal treaties, the foreign concessions became the centers of newly developed industrial and commercial enterprises, and year after year our country's economic life was increasingly concentrated in these areas. Railroads and steamship lines originated from the treaty ports and extended into the interior. Traditional handicraft industries became bankrupt, and agriculture began to degenerate. In the impoverished agricultural villages, irrigation ditches went unrepaired, dikes deteriorated, famine spread, and hamlets became wildernesses. This was all due to the effects of the unequal treaties, which truly caused "the old and the weak to die in gutters, and the strong to wander in all directions [i.e., become bandits]."

Within the concessions, the only ones that prospered were the compradors [Chinese merchants and officials that became brokers for foreign capital], who distributed foreign goods and dealt in raw materials. Therefore, although the markets were prosperous, the buildings rich and impressive, and the population steadily increasing, no productive enterprises developed in these ports because they could not absorb the wandering and homeless people from the agricultural villages. Many of these people then became bandits or wandering brigands, and when civil war and banditry drove capital out of the interior, it tended to be concentrated in the concessions. This capital was invested in speculative activities which, not being based on productive enterprise, soon collapsed and created panics in banks, stock exchanges, trust companies, and currency markets.

Economic reconstruction is the essential first step toward national defense reconstruction, and must have its foundation in the national economy. Under the unequal treaties, there was no way to promote economic reconstruction for national defense, and the abnormal development of the national economy could not be adapted to the defense needs of the state. Our industrial and commercial enterprises were concentrated in the main coastal centers such as Dairen, Tientsin, Tsingtao, Shanghai, Amoy, and Canton, which were all under the control of the imperialists' "Gunboat Policy" and particularly subject to blockade by the Japanese. The main communication routes were based on these easily blockaded cities and penetrated from them to all parts of the interior. But the interior itself lacked modern means of communication and it was necessary to use foreign railroad routes and steamship lines to travel from one interior locality to another. As a result, the national economy of China was divided into several areas, each centered around one or more foreign concessions of leased territories, which served as their economic outlets and thus controlled them. Under such economic conditions, if China had endeavored to wage war against the imperialists, they could have blockaded our few ports and this would have been sufficient to strangle the country's economic life and cut the arteries of our communications. It is obvious that this situation left no room for even a discussion of national defense. Thus, under the effects of the unequal treaties, China's economy reached a point at which the state could not protect itself, and the people could barely exist.

3. Their Effects on Society

The effects of the unequal treaties upon Chinese society must be studied in relation both to the social structure and to social traditions and popular morale. Let us first discuss the effects of the treaties on the social structure.

China's [original] social structure, from the standpoint of blood relationships, proceeded from the individual to the family and then to the clan. From the standpoint of regional divisions, it proceeded from the family clan to the *pao chia*,[1] and then to the village community. These two sets of relationships were clearly distinguished, and the ancient sages and scholars devoted most of their efforts to formulating the precepts governing each of them. From the admonitions and regulations governing the individual's conduct in the family there developed the rules of family propriety and clan regulations. In the *pao chia*, there were *pao* contracts [for mutual protection]; in the villages and communities, there were village agreements and community regulations. The spirit of self-government was sufficient to ensure individual and family behavior without depending on legal intervention. The spirit of mutual co-operation was sufficient to ensure planning for

1. For an account of the *pao chia* system, see footnote on p. 134.

the public benefit without the need for government supervision. With regard to education, there were village and
community schools. As for relief, there were free lands and
free storage of grain in community warehouses. With regard
to protection against robbery and the apprehension of criminals, there was the *pao chia* system of collective responsibility.
As to dikes and irrigation works, roads and rivers, there was
none that was not built or dredged through the joint effort
of villages and communities.

Mencius stated: "Be friends when you are coming in and
going out; co-operate when you are on patrol duty; give
assistance when there is sickness." He also said: "Stress the
observance of ranks and positions [social status], amplifying
it with the doctrines of filial piety and brotherly love." Li
Yun stated: "The aged have their fulfillment; youths have
their usefulness; widowers, widows, orphans, and childless
ones are supported."

Such ideals were traditional in Chinese society and showed
their practical results. But during the past hundred years, as
a result of the oppression of the unequal treaties, the welfare
of the agricultural villages declined, while life in the cities
became extravagant. As a result, the traditional structure of
the family, the village, and the community was disrupted.
The virtue of mutual help was replaced by competition and
jealousy. Public planning was neglected and no one took an
interest in public affairs. Chinese society not only lost the
incentive to encourage the good and eliminate the bad, but
the country also lost the foundation for a strict and uniform
policy of administration and economic development.

During the past five thousand years, our country's sages
and scholars devoted their lives to teaching and advocating
the ideals of social conduct. They realized that changes in
social traditions and morale determine whether there is order
or chaos in the state, and whether the nation survives or is
destroyed. They therefore devoted themselves to training men
of loyalty, generosity, sincerity and honesty, and to cultivating

the traditions of friendliness, harmony, simplicity, and thrift. Consequently, though our history was marked by alternate periods of order and chaos, and of prosperity and decline, our social traditions and public morale retained their honesty and sincerity, diligence and modesty, virtue and righteousness, thrift and honor. These were the fundamental reasons why our nation was able to survive for so long.

But, under the oppression of the unequal treaties during the past hundred years, these social traditions and popular morale were gradually destroyed. If we examine the social habits [of that period], we find that the average citizen became disorderly and lacking in logic, as revealed by his recklessness and dissipation, his stupidity and confusion. No one was sincere and practical, and work was not done swiftly and promptly. The psychology of untrustworthiness, falsehood, and indolence was everywhere apparent. The people followed a blind routine; they were hesitant, careless, lacking in confidence and determination. They benefited themselves at the expense of others; promoted their private interests and neglected public affairs; and failed to understand the nature of the state or of the nation. They possessed no virtue or righteousness, no sense of thrift or of shame. The decline of the nation's virtue could not have been more extreme.

One of our ancient sages said: "Do not refrain from good deeds because they are little, nor proceed with evil ones because they are small." Every citizen should examine his thoughts and actions in his daily life; abandon self-interest and concern himself with the public good; work for the benefit of others, and at all times place the interest of the state and the nation above all else; cultivate simplicity and not extravagance, honesty and not deceit. Only by so doing can we fulfill our ideal of seeking happiness for society and the state. We should bear in mind the fact that the sages and heroes of history were honored and respected by the people only because each of them performed meritorious service to society and the state. Their thoughts and actions became social standards of right and wrong, good and evil. Therefore we should emulate the sages, worship the heroes, and follow the precepts of our forefathers in order to strengthen our own virtue and integrity.

For the past hundred years under the oppression of the unequal treaties, the people fell into decadent habits and evil practices in their daily life. Each person took his own selfish interests as the basis for determining right or wrong; his selfish desires as a basis for determining good or evil. As a result, depraved and frivolous persons attained power in the villages, and scheming citizens pursued their lawless way in the towns and cities, sacrificing public welfare and other people's happiness for their own selfish ends. Furthermore, literary theories and political writings were used to conceal, or even to justify the evils of this way of life. These writings glorified selfish desires and the quest for profit in order to incite social struggle. The tradition of emulating the sages, worshiping the heroes, and following the precepts of our forefathers not only tended to perish but was despised by the people. They even praised foreign figures and scorned the history of their own country. Confidence in the state declined, and the self-confidence of the people lost its center of gravity. As a consequence, the nation became like a pan of loose sand, and the state fell into disintegration and disunity; the people failing to realize that when the nation and the state are in danger of dismemberment, there is nothing that the individual can depend upon for his own existence.

The ancient sages said: "Propriety, righteousness, modesty, and honor are the four pillars of a state. If the four pillars are not strong, the state will perish." When we think and speak of the future, must we not tremble? Must we not be ashamed and disturbed?

4. Their Effects on Ethics

The evil effects of the concessions and consular jurisdiction upon China's ethics were limitless. The Nanking Treaty was signed at the conclusion of the "Opium War." That war was caused when Governor Lin Tse-hsu of Hu-Kwang [Hunan, Hupeh, Kwangtung, Kwangsi] prohibited the transport of opium to Canton. The import of opium at that time, valued at from twenty to thirty million *taels* annually, was, as Huang Chueh-tzu said, "using China's money to fill a bottomless foreign pit and taking in exchange a poison for mankind which gradually turns China into a sick nation." As Lin Tse-hsu declared: "If opium is not completely prohibited, the country will gradually become poor, and the people will gradually grow weaker. After several decades, there not only will be no source of government revenue, but also no effective army."

After China's defeat in the Opium War, the maritime customs had no means of stopping the entry of opium and other poisonous commodities, and the concessions and consular jurisdiction protected their transportation and storage. The smoking of opium was strictly forbidden by the laws of the country, but these laws could not be extended to the concessions and smoking could still be openly practiced there. Furthermore, following the Russo-Japanese War, the Japanese imperialists who coveted our territory applied the "poison policy" as one of their practical methods [of penetration]. Such vicious methods, because of the protection rendered them by the unequal treaties, could not be prevented by the Chinese Government beforehand, nor their effects restricted. Japan's plan of poisoning us became more and more open, and the degree of poisoning increased in severity. The damage from opium was less than that from the "red pills," and the damage from "red pills" was less than that from the "white powder" [various forms of heroin and other narcotics]. In many towns and villages in the northeast [Manchuria] and in Hopei and Shantung, the entire population was found to be using "white powder." The Japanese sold the poison along the coast and the Yangtze Valley, and even penetrated far into Szechwan and Hupei. They also compelled Koreans to violate the law in Peiping and Tientsin, and Formosans to do likewise in Fukien—all of them making the peddling of poison drugs their exclusive profession, with a view to poisoning our people until our country could be dismembered and our race eliminated.

The concessions were not only the source of drugs, but were also havens for prostitutes, gamblers, thieves, and bandits. When economic conditions in the interior were poor, the people migrated to the cities. But it was difficult to find employment and they were therefore forced to sell their sons and daughters, and fell into the evil habits of prostitution and kidnaping. Thus, during the past hundred years, beautiful and prosperous cities became hells of misery and chaos. As for gambling, its damage was not limited to the rich, but also spread to the poor. The rich lost their fortunes and went bankrupt, and the poor lost their livelihood and met disaster. Once tainted with the habit of gambling, the social order became completely lawless. The people's minds were paralyzed and their morality destroyed. Moreover, the practice of gambling was not limited to the gambling dens, but extended from lotteries to speculative activities in the market— activities that did not follow the laws of production and exchange, but depended solely on luck to obtain unmerited profits. The concessions became the concentration points for surplus capital, but there were no well-established industries to employ this capital. Consequently, many people, both rich and poor, engaged in gambling, spent money lavishly in houses of prostitution, and became paralyzed with drugs. After having gone bankrupt and broken up their families, they degenerated into thieves and bandits, using the concessions as their hideouts and engaging in all sorts of criminal activities. China's five-thousand-year-old tradition of diligence, thrift, and simplicity, of cotton clothes and a simple diet, of women weaving and men farming, were completely undermined by the opium, gambling, prostitutes, and thugs of the concessions.

China's ancient philosophy of ethics is based on a careful and thorough study of the interrelations of human society. Although social organization is in a state of constant evolution, yet the principles of the relations between father and son, husband and wife, elder brother and younger brother, friend and friend, between higher and lower ranks, the honorable and the humble, men and women, old and young, down to the duty of neighbors to protect each other and care for the sick, have remained the unchangeable ethical rules of social life. During the past hundred years, with the spread of the wanton customs of the concessions, the people not only neglected these ethical principles, but discarded and scorned them. As a consequence, between father and son, husband and wife, brothers, friends, high and low, old and young, neighbors and communities, there was no thought of reciprocal love and reciprocal friendliness, and above all, the virtue of co-operation and sense of unity were lost. Everything was planned for material interest, with a total lack of self-discipline. Duty was shirked in the struggle for profits. The high and the low deceived each other, and the people cheated one another right and left. The old and the weak received no consideration or relief, and the sick received no help. The people treated their own blood relations as strangers, and regarded their fellow countrymen as enemies. And they failed to recognize the error of such unethical and abnormal behavior. They transformed China, a propriety-loving and virtue-respecting country, into a country without modesty or shame. Such was the evil effect of the unequal treaties. If this can be tolerated, then what cannot be tolerated?

The steady deterioration of the people's virtue affected their physical condition, causing them to grow weaker day by day. The physical strength of the countless numbers of unemployed in the cities was, of course, completely exhausted, and as the merchants and ordinary people became accustomed to a life of luxury and dissipation, their health also deteriorated. The most serious danger was the threat to the health of the youth in the schools. Physical training could not include the entire student body, and ethical training had long been neglected by the principals and teachers. A life of luxury and dissipation outside the schools lured the youth and caused them to become physically weak and mentally decadent, while contagious diseases and syphilis from the cities further undermined their health. How could these physically and mentally weakened youths, after leaving school, promote scholarship, or reform the people's way of life so that they could assume the responsibilities of the state and develop social enterprises? It was indeed impossible to predict when this degeneration of the state and decline of the nation would end.

5. *Their Effects on Psychology*

The effects of the unequal treaties on the psychology of the Chinese people were as serious and harmful as their effects on politics, economics, and national defense. Some people argue that the missionary and educational work carried on by foreigners in different parts of China constitutes cultural aggression. Others, recognizing that many of the schools established by foreigners in China have been well run and beneficial to society and the people, deny that China has experienced cultural aggression. In my opinion, both these arguments show a lack of clear understanding of the focal point in the problem of Chinese thought and culture during the last hundred years.

From the record of history we can see that the character of the Chinese nation is marked by self-respect but not conceit; humility but not subservience. The statement "to be upstanding but not boastful, to be humble but not efface oneself" is a correct explanation of our nation's virtuous character. The attitude of our nation toward foreign religion and teachings, therefore, should be determined on the basis of our own character.

With regard to religion, China's own philosophy of life, developed by Confucius, amplified and propagated by Mencius, and further explained by the Han scholars, automatically became a lofty system, superior to any other philosophy in the world.[2] Yet the Chinese nation also accepted foreign religions and was able to select the most profound philosophical principles of those religions and develop them together with China's own ancient philosophy of life. Thus, after the Tsin and Wei dynasties, Buddhism from India and Central Asia was introduced into China. During the Sung and Yuan dynasties, Mohammedanism was introduced into China. At the end of the Ming and the beginning of the Ch'ing dynasties, Christianity was introduced into China. And all of these have benefited Chinese thought and learning. Because of this attitude toward religion, there were never any religious wars in Chinese history, such as those that took place in medieval Europe. During the past hundred years, Christianity in China exercised a beneficial effect in introducing scientific knowledge and reforming social traditions. The T'ai-p'ing revolution was based upon the teachings of Christianity. And even in the Nationalist Revolution, the principles of Christianity played an important part.

However, during the last hundred years, the Christian churches, because of their reliance on the unequal treaties, enjoyed special privileges and paid no attention to the spirit of the Chinese nation. As a result, some people came to regard

2. Confucianism is the philosophy expounded by Confucius, who lived from 551–479 B.C. Confucius is the Latinized version of the title, K'ung Fu-tzu, or "the Master K'ung," K'ung being his family surname. Confucius was the leading sage of ancient China—a philosopher and statesman at a time when the emerging feudal society was fighting the entrenched slave society. As spokesman for the new feudal order, Confucius played a progressive role in China's history. The application of the Confucian philosophy to later stages of Chinese social development, however, inevitably served a reactionary purpose, since this philosophy provided the ideological basis for preserving a feudal society. The present Kuomintang hierarchy has developed an extensive propaganda literature sustaining their right to positions of power on the basis of Confucian ideology. They have even attempted to emasculate and pervert the teachings of Sun Yat-sen to support their adaptation of Confucianism to present-day China.

foreign missionary work as cultural aggression, and even went
so far as to regard it as an enemy. Thus, the unequal treaties
caused untold harm to the religious teachings of the Christian
church. It is for this reason that I say that the unequal treaties
only damaged the Christian church and brought it not a
single benefit.

As for China's ancient learning, the wisdom and ability
of the Chinese nation have made great contributions to human
progress. For example, the dredging of the Yellow, Huai,
Yangtze, and Han rivers dates back to the time of Ta Yu
[Emperor Yu, legendary founder of the Hsia dynasty, 2205
B.C.]. The magnificent construction of the Great Wall was
completed in the Ch'in dynasty. The Grand Canal was completed in the Sui dynasty. Other achievements include such
things as the compass, gunpowder, arms, printing, and other
mechanical inventions, and particularly accomplishments in
law, mathematics, music, and medicine. One need only examine our past history to discover that the glories and the
scope of our ancient Chinese learning cannot be equaled in
the history of any of the strong Western nations of today.
In spite of this, however, the Chinese nation was still able to
absorb and adopt foreign culture and learning for its further
advancement. And because China could absorb other forms
of civilization, her own civilization became even broader and
greater. However, China's culture and learning have their
own ancient standards. China was able to absorb other forms
of civilization and learning precisely because she had her own
standards and her own system by which to judge these other
forms of civilization. Thus, when foreign civilizations were
transplanted to China, they became a part of China's national
economy and of the people's livelihood, and thus could remain
indefinitely as part of China's civilization.

For the last hundred years, Western science has greatly
benefited Chinese civilization. This cannot be denied. After
the Opium War, in the belief that the Western powers were
rich and strong because of their guns and ships, the Chinese

people began to study the technique of making guns and ships. After the War of 1894, the Chinese people also began to study foreign social and political institutions. Famous works of Western social science were translated into Chinese. Discussion of Western social and political theories began to appear in magazines and newspapers. For several decades after this, as a result of discussion, popular study, comparison, and observation, China's applied science, natural science, and social science all made progress. In some fields, we even made important new contributions to human knowledge. The power and prestige of science was fully recognized in Chinese thought and learning.

On the other hand, during the past hundred years, China's civilization showed signs of great deterioration. This was because, under the oppression of the unequal treaties, the Chinese people reversed their attitude toward Western civilization from one of opposition to one of submission, and their attitude toward their own civilization changed from one of pride to one of self-abasement. Carried to extremes, this attitude of submission [to Western theories] became one of ardent conversion and they openly proclaimed themselves loyal disciples of this or that foreign theory. Similarly, the attitude of self-abasement was carried to such an extreme that they despised and mocked the heritage of their own civilization. We should bear in mind that from the Opium War down to the Revolution of 1911, the unanimous demand of the people was to avenge the national humiliation and make the country strong, and all efforts were concentrated on enriching the country and strengthening the army. In other words, it was our unwillingness to become slaves that first caused us to study Western civilization. It follows that we should also study Western civilization for the purpose of winning our independence and making China strong. Unfortunately, after the Revolution of 1911, the will to avenge our national humiliation and make the country strong perished with the failure of the Revolution, and the effects of the unequal

treaties were further deepened after this failure. Unconsciously, the people developed the habit of ignoring their own traditions and cultivating foreign ways; of respecting foreign
theories and despising their native teachings; of depending
upon others and blindly following them. Thus, although the
Chinese people originally studied Western civilization because
of their unwillingness to become slaves, the result was that
they unconsciously became the slaves of foreign theories because of their studies of Western civilization.

After the May 4th [1919] Movement, the ideas of Liberalism [Democracy] and Communism spread throughout the
country. But those that advocated these ideas had no real
knowledge of the enduring qualities of Chinese culture; they
were simply looking for something new. Moreover, they
merely endeavored to copy the superficial aspects of Western
civilization without attempting to adopt its basic principles
for the benefit of the Chinese economy and the people's
livelihood. As a result, the educated classes and scholars generally lost their self-respect and self-confidence. Wherever the
influence of these ideas prevailed, the people regarded everything foreign as right and everything Chinese as wrong. [In
the revised edition, the foregoing passage was altered to read:
"After May 4th, two types of thought—individualistic Liberalism and class-war Communism—were suddenly introduced among the educated classes and spread throughout the
whole country. . . . As a result, the educated classes and
scholars generally adopted the superficial husks of Western
culture and lost their own respect and self-confidence—lost
their confidence in Chinese culture. Wherever the influence
of these ideas prevailed, the people regarded everything foreign as good and everything Chinese as bad."][3] They wor-

3. The May 4th Movement of 1919
was a great movement of students and
intellectuals that marked the beginning of China's modern revolutionary
history. It was both anti-imperialist
and antifeudal, and represented the
reaction of Chinese intellectuals to the
turbulent new forces unleashed by the
First World War. In specific protest
against the terms of the Versailles
Treaty as they affected China, and
against the terms of Japan's infamous
"Twenty-One Demands," huge student demonstrations were held in

shiped this or that foreign country in a similar manner. Different cliques existed among them only because there was more than one country and more than one foreign theory in the world. Each clique imitated one particular country and worshiped one particular theory, forming a group around its particular one, and declaring that all who belonged to that clique were right and all who did not were wrong. Since the theories of the various countries were constantly changing, each of these cliques had to change its theories repeatedly in accordance with these foreign changes. Their ideas circulated widely and disturbed the people. But from an objective point of view, their ideas and proposals did not coincide with our nation's psychology and character, and from the subjective point of view, they lacked a solid foundation, since they were based on foreign theories and were constantly having to change. Thus, all the movements led by them lasted only a short time.

If we examine the theories and political proposals put forward since the Revolution, we find that all of them were copies of foreign theories. In 1913, the arguments for a parliamentary system, a cabinet system, and a presidential system in reality reflected the differences between the British, the French, and the American political systems. In 1920, the opposing theories of a centralized as against a federal state reflected the differences between the French and the American systems of local government. The theoretical basis of the

Peking on May 4, 1919 to denounce the pro-Japanese Peking Government. This revolutionary tide spread rapidly throughout China, spearheading a rapid growth of a strong labor movement and culminating in the reorganization of the Kuomintang in 1924 and the establishment of a united front between the Kuomintang and the Chinese Communist Party. This united front laid the foundation for the Nationalist Revolution of 1925–27. The famous Northern Expedition of the Revolutionary Armies from December, 1926, to March, 1927, triumphed over all warlord opposition, but the Revolution sustained a serious setback when the right-wing elements in the Kuomintang under Chiang Kai-shek's leadership, soon followed by the faction led by Wang Ching-wei, broke the united front and launched a campaign of severe repression against the Communists, peasants, and workers.

monarchy of Yuan Shih-k'ai was provided by an American editorial, and the constitution of Tsao K'un was an exact copy of the Weimar Constitution of Germany.

As for the struggle between Liberalism and Communism, it was merely a reflection of the opposition of Anglo-American theories to those of Soviet Russia. Not only were such political theories unsuited to the national economy and the people's livelihood, and opposed to the spirit of China's own civilization, but also the people that promoted them forgot that they were Chinese and that they should study and apply foreign theories for the benefit of China. As a result, their copying [of Western theories] only caused the decay and ruin of Chinese civilization, and made it easy for the imperialists to carry on cultural aggression. China's theoreticians and political leaders, either directly or indirectly, intentionally or unintentionally, adopted the theories and interests of the imperialists as their own, and forgot their own origin and the purpose of their study. They even maintained this attitude in social propaganda and education, thus causing the people to accept without question the unequal treaties and the aggression and exploitation of the imperialists. This is the greatest single danger of cultural aggression, and the greatest threat to the nation's spirit. We citizens must wake up in time and correct this attitude. Only thus can we save our country and make China strong and independent, with a position of equality among the other nations of the world.[4]

4. This sharp criticism of those Chinese leaders that accepted foreign political theories ignores the fact that Sun Yat-sen himself based his political theories primarily on Lincoln's concept of "government of the people, by the people, and for the people," coupled with theories derived from the Soviet Union. It is also interesting to note that Chiang Kai-shek himself visited the Soviet Union for six months in 1923, sent his eldest son to study there, and publicly declared that "China's Revolution must be led by the Third International." When Chiang became anti-Communist, he went to Tokyo to interview the notorious Toyama, and stated that China and Japan must unite. Still later, following Hitler's rise to power, he sent another son to study in Germany, and employed German Reichswehr officers as military advisers. And even today he is employing a large number of Western political, economic, and military advisers. These actions hardly harmonize with his professed contempt for foreign theories.

6. *National Self-Examination and Self-Criticism*

[This entire section was added in the revised edition]

The previous chapter outlined the reasons for the imposition of the unequal treaties, and this chapter has explained the severity of the damage done by those treaties, with a view to proving by historical facts the truth that "people insulted you only because you had insulted yourself," and that "the country was subjected only because it had subjected itself." It was written in the hope that our citizens would subject themselves to self-examination and self-criticism. We must recognize that nations which become strong through their own efforts can surely obtain a position of equality and independence among the other nations of the world. Our numerous national humiliations of the past all resulted from the fact that we debased ourselves and scorned our own cultural heritage. Therefore, every national humiliation and every clause in the unequal treaties should serve as a basis for self-examination and self-criticism. The reason that I stress this repeatedly is because I wish all citizens to recognize our past sufferings and difficulties, and to understand the heavy responsibilities that await us in the future, so that we may free ourselves from past evils and struggle earnestly to become modern citizens, fitted for the new destiny that is assured by the abolition of the unequal treaties.

If our citizens fail to practice severe self-examination and self-criticism, and continue to cherish a narrowly nationalistic viewpoint, nurse grievances, and retain the reactionary attitudes of conceit and self-satisfaction, then they cannot live up to the spirit of nation-building and cannot be regarded as true supporters of the Three People's Principles. Therefore, at this time when the unequal treaties have been abolished, our citizens must be especially careful to maintain their self-respect, to ignore past wrongs and forget old grievances, and to work together with all friendly powers in sharing the responsibility of reforming the world and safeguarding the peace.

Our Allies have now voluntarily relinquished the special rights that they enjoyed under the unequal treaties, and have concluded new treaties with us which respect our freedom and independence. This fact proves not only that the nationalist spirit of China, as revealed in the last fifty years of revolutionary struggle and the five and a half years of the War of Resistance, has won the sincere recognition of our Allies, but also that the war which our Allies are fighting against the Axis powers is a war for righteousness, justice, and the freedom and equality of the peoples of the world. Thus this [abolition of the unequal treaties] is not only an epochal event in the history of China, but it also constitutes the most glorious achievement of our Allies in their joint effort for the creation of a new world. At this present decisive point in the war against aggression, and at this time of the beginning of equal and free relations between our country and the Allies, our citizens must further demonstrate the traditional virtues of our nation, strengthen China's good-neighborliness and friendship toward all friendly powers, and exert themselves in working for international co-operation. This is the responsibility and duty of our citizens.

I explained this point in detail in my broadcast to the army and the people on January 12th of this year [1943], which I reprint herewith for purposes of reference:

"To the Armies and the People of China:

"On the Double Ten anniversary last year [Oct. 10, 1942], the United States and Great Britain voluntarily announced their relinquishment of the special rights they had long enjoyed in China under unequal treaties. Yesterday in Washington and in Chungking our Government signed new treaties of equality and reciprocity with these two nations.

"Fellow countrymen, we recall that it was just a century ago that our country began to conclude unequal treaties with the foreign powers, in the later years of the Manchu dynasty. By fifty years of revolutionary struggle and five years and a half of sacrifice in the War of Resistance, our Chinese nation was finally able to transform this heartbreaking anniversary into an occasion of national rejoicing. This is not only the most important milestone in the history of China's struggle for survival; today, our Allies, Great Britain and the United States, have built a new lighthouse to guide man's progress toward freedom and equality for all the peoples of the world. Most important of all, our Allies have proved that the aim of this war is to fight for humanity and righteousness. This indeed is a most glorious and righteous action on the part of the governments and peoples of Great Britain and the United States. We are particularly gratified and satisfied with the United States Government, which is in complete agreement with the aspirations of our Government, and which makes no reservations and no demands on us. This action on the part of our Allies not only strengthens the fighting power of all of our Allies, but deals a severe blow to the spirit of the aggressor countries.

"But all our armies and people must recognize that the status of independence and freedom must be won 'by our effort.' I have often said to our countrymen: 'We must be self-reliant before we can be independent; we must be strong before we can be free.' The Chinese Republic must be self-reliant and strong before it can become an independent and free country. All the armies and the people of China must become self-reliant and strong before they can become independent and free citizens. Therefore, the abolition of the unequal treaties and the achievement of a position of independence and freedom can only increase the responsibility of our country, and can only strengthen the sense of duty of our people. Because one thing has been achieved, we must not harbor any sense of arrogance, laxity, or self-satisfaction. If all the armies and the people of our country do not assume the duties and responsibilities necessary to build the Chinese

Republic into a completely free and independent state that can fulfill its duty to the peoples of the world, then the position of independence and freedom that we have gained will be lost again. Even when the present war ends, we will not automatically escape from the sufferings and restrictions of the past. If we do not continue the struggle, there is no knowing how many centuries it would take for us to regain a position of independence and freedom, and the tragic destiny of our children's children would be to live out their lives as slaves.

"Henceforth, China's destiny rests upon the shoulders of the citizens of this generation. In order to safeguard the broad lands bequeathed to us by our ancestors, and ensure the survival and well-being of our posterity, every one of us must start today to serve the state loyally and to unite together so that we can effectively assume the responsibility of becoming strong and self-reliant.

"Today, we can already see the first signs of victory in the world war against aggression. The defeat of Japan, Germany, Italy, and the other aggressor powers is near at hand, and the determining point of victory in China's War of Resistance will be decided during this year. There are some who assume that China's destiny will be decided at international conferences following the end of the war. Others assume that once we have been victorious in the War of Resistance, China will be able to enjoy the fruits of righteousness, peace, and prosperity together with the other countries of the world, without further effort. These [erroneous] views arise from the psychology of self-satisfaction, laxity, and dependence upon others. All our fellow countrymen must realize that this psychology is wrong. China's destiny must be determined today when we are striving to become strong; we must not sit and wait until the peace conference after the war. We must decide today whether China shall survive or perish; whether she shall be the master in her own house or the slave of other powers. Our armies and our people must never again become the prey of procrastination, lethargy, and indecision. Henceforth we must work still harder and endure still greater privations than we have suffered in the past five years of war in order to catch up with other nations. At such a time, there is no room for laziness or shirking.

"Fellow countrymen: Until today we could rightly claim that the unequal treaties were the main cause for our failure to build a nation. For the past hundred years, the oppression of the unequal treaties caused political disunity, economic paralysis, and social chaos in China. The people developed a sense of inferiority; their ethical standards degenerated; and they were unable to feel a sense of shame. All this was caused, directly or indirectly, by the influence of the unequal treaties. In particular, the foreign concessions and the areas where foreign troops were stationed became centers of degeneration and corruption. But now that the unequal treaties have been abolished, the unhealthy phenomena that developed from them will lose their protection and they will no longer foster an atmosphere of degeneration and corruption. However, the bad habits and corruption that have developed during the past hundred years may still remain latent in our social structure. We may be unaware of the role that they play in obstructing progress, injuring the Nationalist Revolution, and threatening the nation's survival—all of which are menaced by selfishness, greed, and feudalistic ideas. Therefore, all our countrymen must with one mind encourage self-criticism and weed out these evils, so that we can unite in support of the Three People's Principles and devote ourselves to the gigantic task of winning the war and rebuilding the nation.

"The success of the Nationalist Revolution, which is the aim of all our efforts, is at last in sight. Henceforward, China's destiny depends upon the efforts which my countrymen unitedly devote to the attainment of this aim. We must sincerely accept the teachings of the Father of our Country, Dr. Sun Yat-sen, and have faith in the Three People's Principles, comply with the strategy of the Nationalist Revolution, and obey the orders of the Nationalist Government. We must all, each according to his status, devote our intelligence and loyalty to meeting the requirements of wartime existence by abiding by the plans for price control, obeying the general mobilization decrees, esteeming thrift, increasing production, and thus strengthening the war effort, while at the same time devoting ourselves to the rebuilding of psychology, ethics, society, politics, and economics, so that we may as rapidly as possible carry through the total plan for national reconstruction, which combines culture, economics, and national defense into a single entity and lays the basis for the permanent survival of our state and nation.

"Fellow countrymen: This turning point in China's destiny is the opportunity for each of our citizens to swear to work for his country. It is our good fortune to witness this day the end of our humiliation and the beginning of a new stage in our struggle for independence and freedom. Therefore, at this crossroads of survival or extinction, I urge you to use caution and vigilance, and especially to cultivate self-respect and self-esteem. Since our country has attained a position of equality, the citizens of all friendly powers will enjoy the protection of our laws. All those that treat us on a basis of equality and obey our laws should be treated with friendship and courtesy, regardless of whether they come to China as tourists, merchants, or missionaries. Only by so doing can we preserve the original reputation of our country as a nation that is known for propriety and righteousness. I sincerely hope that my countrymen will carefully observe the lessons of the past and perform their present tasks well. In particular, we must recognize that we cannot sit back and wait for independence [to be given us], but must all, regardless of rank, pay more attention to propriety and righteousness, cultivate a sense of humility and frugality, work together wholeheartedly, and redouble our efforts to secure a genuine victory, equality, and freedom. Only in this way can we march forward on a basis of equality with our Allies, sharing with them the responsibility of rebuilding the world, securing the peace, and liberating mankind. To my countrymen throughout the nation I extend a welcome on this memorial day of independence and freedom, and express my boundless confidence and enthusiasm for the task of fulfilling the new destiny of the Chinese nation. I can only repay with this sincere pledge the patriotic spirit of my fellow countrymen, who have followed me, Chiang Kai-shek, from beginning to end, in life and death, sharing all adversities regardless of the sacrifices and sufferings involved. With the same sincerity, I pay tribute to the souls of the soldiers and civilians that died for their country. Finally, I respectfully salute the common victory of our fellow countrymen!

"Long live the equality and freedom of the Chinese Republic!

"Long live the Nationalist Revolution!

"Long live the Three People's Principles!"

CHAPTER FOUR

FROM THE NORTHERN EXPEDITION TO THE WAR OF RESISTANCE

1. Reorganization of the Kuomintang and the Steps for Carrying out the Three People's Principles

AFTER organizing the China Revolutionary Party in 1914, the Father of our Country, observing the repeated failures of the Revolution, recognized that unless the organization of the Party was strengthened it would be impossible to meet the demands of the Nationalist Revolution. In October, 1919, therefore, he changed the China Revolutionary Party into the Kuomintang of China. [The Kuomintang, or People's National Party, has been the only legal political party in China since 1927, and completely controls both the Central Government and the Central Armies.] In January, 1923, the Kuomintang issued a public statement of aims; in November, 1923, a Declaration of Reorganization was published; and in January, 1924, a National Congress was held in Canton at which it was announced that the reorganization of the Party had been successfully completed.[1]

1. A notable omission in this description of the reorganization of the Kuomintang in 1924 is the absence of any reference to the share of the Chinese Communist Party in this reorganization. Following the overthrow of the Manchu dynasty, the Kuomintang became corrupt and was unable to play a dynamic role in the face of rapidly changing conditions, or to attract the support of the Chinese peasants and workers. Recognizing this fact, Sun Yat-sen began to reorganize the Kuomintang soon after the First World War. At first, he appealed to the United States for support. He even wrote his *Industrial Plan* in the English language to underscore his appeal. The United States, however, turned a deaf ear to Dr. Sun. Only the Soviet Union expressed sympathy for his program. As a consequence, he proceeded to reorganize the Kuomintang on the basis of his "Three Great Policies": alliance with the U.S.S.R. in foreign

The Three People's Principles are the basic principles of the Nationalist Revolution. In his opening speech at the National Congress, Sun Yat-sen stated: "The Three People's Principles that we advocate are forever unchangeable; everyone should put them into practice. These principles were determined before the organization of the T'ung Meng Hui, and the reason for forming the T'ung Meng Hui was to carry out these principles. The subsequent overthrow of the Ch'ing dynasty and the founding of the Republic were also for the purpose of putting these principles in practice." Consequently, during the reorganization of the Kuomintang, Sun Yat-sen endeavored to outline the methods for implementing these principles. He said: "No matter what you do, success depends upon having good methods. How can you achieve a good method? You get it from learning and knowledge. You must first have learning, then you will have knowledge; when you have knowledge, you will have a method. When you have a good method for revolutionary work, you will attain immediate success as soon as you go into action."

During the reorganization of the Kuomintang, Sun Yatsen emphasized that although we were to search for methods and put them into practice, we should understand that these methods must be adaptable to changing situations. In 1921, he gave us clear instructions: "In all matters, to put something into effect after complete understanding has been achieved, is very easy. But if one does not understand fully and wishes to put something into effect, the course one takes is bound to result in many errors. This is a difficult problem. Why can we not avoid making errors? Because it is very difficult to know everything. If we wait until we know, and

---

affairs; a united front with the Chinese Communists in internal affairs; and cooperation with the Chinese workers and peasants. Sun Yat-sen asked and received aid from both the Chinese Communists and the Communist Party of the Soviet Union. In his writings, Sun repeatedly stated that it was this united front between the revitalized Kuomintang and the Chinese Communist Party that gave the Chinese revolutionary movement the necessary spark and vigor. It certainly led it to its subsequent victories.

then act, hundreds and thousands of years will elapse before
we can take action. Therefore, sometimes we human beings
must act even without complete understanding."

At the time of the reorganization of the Kuomintang, there
had already been a thorough discussion of the methods of
revolution, and there was a clear understanding of the revolutionary movement before action was begun. Sun Yat-sen
stated: "If we are determined in our desire to make the nation
rich and strong, a method can be found. If this method is
clearly thought out, and if we do not shrink from difficulties
but consistently go forward, we shall succeed."

From this we see that revolutionary action must follow a
revolutionary method, and that the revolutionary movement
may alter or improve its method. Therefore, one can say:
The Three People's Principles are unchangeable, but the
method for putting these principles into effect is not unalterable.

Previously, the members of the Revolutionary Party and
the people as a whole did not clearly understand the theories
of the Father of our Country, nor had complete confidence
in them; therefore, the Father of our Country took upon
himself the entire burden of reorganizing the Revolutionary
Party. Reviewing the situation at that time, he said: "The
fact that, although our revolution had several military successes and yet the revolution itself was not completed, was
because the Party itself lacked a solid foundation. All Party
members did not observe Party rules, but acted independ-
ently. They did not even display the ancient virtue of unquestioning obedience to their leaders, much less possessing
the new ideal of winning freedom. . . . At that time, I had
no alternative but to take up the burden single-handed and
reorganize the China Revolutionary Party." He also said:
"There is one thing that everyone must note. Previously, the
reason that our Party was unable to achieve a solid foundation was not because of the strength of our enemies, but
because we fought among ourselves, and created unnecessary

misunderstandings. Consequently, the strength of the Party was dissipated and the Revolution was often defeated."

Thus, when Sun Yat-sen reorganized the Kuomintang, he wanted all of us to understand the importance of solid organization and strict discipline for carrying out our task in accordance with the aims and methods of the Nationalist Revolution.

The aim of the Nationalist Revolution was clearly stated in the Declaration of the First National Congress [of the Kuomintang]. Regarding politics, the Declaration stated: "There is not a single warlord that is not connected with the imperialists. The so-called Government of the Republic is controlled by the warlords, and the warlords use the Government to gain favors from the foreign powers in order to strengthen their own position. The foreign powers, in turn, exploit them and have loaned them large sums for military expenses, thereby prolonging China's civil wars in order to gain profits and privileges, with each power occupying a special sphere of influence. Viewed in this light, we see that China's civil wars were caused by the foreign powers. The foreign powers have conflicting interests in China, so they make use of the warlords who kill our citizens to settle their differences for them." Regarding economics, the Declaration stated: "Civil wars hinder the development of Chinese enterprises, and cause the market to be flooded with foreign goods. Because of this, Chinese products cannot compete with foreign goods even within the boundaries of China. The resulting damage is not confined to the exploitation of our people's political life, but also involves immeasurable losses to our economic life."

Therefore, the target of the Nationalist Revolution is imperialism and the warlords. Its task is to abolish the unequal treaties and overthrow the warlords, and thus remove from China every trace of the present co-operation between the militarists and imperialism. The methods and progress of the Nationalist Revolution are from military government to a government of political tutelage, and thence to constitutional government. Since the T'ung Meng Hui, this policy has never changed.

The First National Congress made the following statement concerning our tasks during the period of military government: "After the reorganization of our Party, the foundation of our Party's organization must rest on strict discipline and spirit. The Party shall employ various suitable methods to educate and train our members so that they can become effective in teaching the principles of the Party, mobilizing the people, and promoting political organization. Simultaneously, we should use all the power at our command to conduct general propaganda work among the people and induce them to join the revolutionary movement to obtain power and conquer the enemies of the people." Concerning our tasks during the period of political tutelage, the First National Congress stated: "When political power has been secured and the Government has been formed, we must make our Party the center of control of political power in order to suppress counterrevolutionary movements within the country, to defeat imperialist plots to crush our people's victory, and to eliminate all obstacles to the implementation of the Kuomintang's principles."

It is the responsibility of members of the Kuomintang to see that the Three People's Principles are fully understood by the people and deeply implanted in their minds. In his instructions to us, Sun Yat-sen said: "The foundation of a nation is built on the people's ideas." He also said: "When there is one purpose, and it is the purpose of the entire people, and when the people all work to achieve this purpose, it is easy to succeed. This is the reason for the saying, 'the united will of all can build a wall.' The case of the revolutionaries who wished to overthrow the Ch'ing dynasty and finally succeeded in founding the Republic is evidence that where there is a will there is accomplishment. . . . The anti-Manchu action of the Hans in 1911 was an action supported by all the people. That is called mass force. This sort of mass force is very powerful."

To mobilize mass purpose and centralize mass force, we must first cause the people to have a true understanding of the Three People's Principles and the Nationalist Revolution. Only on the basis of real understanding can the people's thinking be reformed, their purpose unified, and their strength mobilized. Therefore, Sun Yat-sen said: "The reason for our previous inability to act was lack of knowledge. . . . The ancients said that to know is easy, but to act is hard; my theory is that to know is hard, but to act is easy. That all Chinese affairs were corrupt in the past was due to wrong thinking. The thinking of the Chinese people needs to be thoroughly reformed. Apply my theory and any task can be accomplished."

Carrying out his theory that to know is hard and to act is easy, Sun Yat-sen during this period wrote: *Plans for National Reconstruction* and *Fundamentals of National Reconstruction,* and also lectured on the Three People's Principles as the permanent guide for the Nationalist Revolution. If our members will only accept the teachings of Sun Yat-sen, develop a real sense of responsibility, and learn to work together with one mind, then the great task of building a state based on the Three People's Principles and the Five Power Constitution can surely be accomplished.

With the principles stated, the objectives clarified, the stages fixed, and the methods specifically outlined, Sun Yat-sen hoped that we would make up our minds permanently and carry out our aims in actual practice. On this point he said: "This time we shall definitely succeed in the Revolution. But it is essential that we all have this determination and that we make up our minds permanently to carry on this work." He wished us to determine to make China the richest and strongest state in the world within ten years. And he wished us to persist in our efforts, saying: "If we really understand the principles of revolution, we shall have persistence.

A revolution has its ultimate goal, and we must not quit in the middle if we desire to attain that goal."

On this basis was formed the Kuomintang of China, which has certain special characteristics that differ from the political parties of other countries.[2] The starting point of the Three People's Principles is the idea of the "common good" and the basic impetus of the Nationalist Revolution is "sincerity." The greatness of the Three People's Principles lies in the fact that they combine many different ideas. As to "sincerity" the members of the Kuomintang must act in conformity with the strategy of the Nationalist Revolution and abide by the discipline of the Party. In general, the Kuomintang requires that the actions of Party members do not violate Party discipline or conflict with the Three People's Principles, but it does not impose severe restrictions on the liberty of individual thought. Therefore, within the Kuomintang, there are Nationalists, Liberals, Communists, and Anarchists. Even though persons of differing political views may formerly have been political enemies, once they declare their belief in the Three People's Principles and join the Kuomintang, no questions will be raised as to their past. As long as they are members of the Party, working together with one purpose and assisting and co-operating with each other, they will be trusted as honest comrades. The Kuomintang has this principle of the "common good" because it is organized to ensure the survival of the entire nation, and to carry through a revolution for the benefit of all the people. Therefore, every Chinese citizen has the privilege of joining the Kuomintang, and should fulfill his duty to join the Party. Because the Kuomintang is the leader of the revolutionary building of the state, the Party makes not the slightest distinction between

2. The summary of the declaration of the First National Congress of the Kuomintang given above is notable for its omissions. No mention is made of the principle of racial and national equality within the Republic, nor of the program of land to the toilers, nor of the provision for the distribution of powers between the Central and Provincial Governments, providing for provincial self-government within a unified state, nor of many other provisions more meaningful than those chosen for quotation.

the citizens of the country and the members of the Party, and does not discriminate between them. Moreover, it has the responsibility of training and leading them to devote their efforts to the Nationalist Revolution, to putting into practice the Three People's Principles, to national reconstruction, and to restoring the people's welfare. Therefore the Kuomintang does not favor any particular occupation or class, and does not neglect any particular occupation or class. More specifically, the Kuomintang does not discriminate among the people on the basis of sex, occupation, religion, or class; it protects each and every citizen within the state, and does not ignore a single individual of ability. The Kuomintang welcomes every one in the country that supports the Revolution, and urges all citizens to join the Party so that they may struggle together for the revolutionary building of the state, in order to fulfill the task of the Nationalist Revolution. In short, the Three People's Principles are based upon the principles of equality and sincerity. Therefore, the Kuomintang, which carries out the Three People's Principles, is organized in accordance with the ancient virtues of our nation, and is based upon the spirit of reason, responsibility, and duty. It is entirely different from the other parties of the past which resorted to Machiavellian intrigue and cruelty to consolidate their power.

Thus the Kuomintang, in the fifty-eight years since it was founded by the Father of our Country, has become like T'ai Shan [sacred mountain in Shantung] and the North Star, majestic and unchanging. Its strength is ever increasing, and it has become the permanent and unique revolutionary political party of China, differing completely from the numerous other parties that perished as times changed. This status has not been attained by chance, but by the impersonal, unselfish, generous, and tolerant spirit of the Kuomintang.[3]

3. It is difficult to reconcile this description of the tolerant and benevolent Kuomintang with the well-known and substantiated history of the Kuomintang's secret police, concentration camps, system of "thought control," record of political terrorism and assassination, and other measures

2. The Success of the Northern Expedition and Lessons of the Revolution

After the reorganization of the Kuomintang in 1924, all revolutionary movements in the country came under the Party's banner. That was just after the First World War, when economic crises occurred in rapid succession and revolutionary movements developed in other countries. The Revolutionary Government of Soviet Russia abandoned the policy of militant Communism and adopted a New Economic Policy, thus laying the foundations for the building of the Soviet state in the midst of watchful encirclement by the world powers. Turkey, after its successful revolution, established a free and independent national government which further stimulated and aroused the peoples of Asia. Thus our Chinese Nationalist Revolution occurred in the midst of world-wide instability. Its aim was to strengthen the people's morale, unify the will of the nation, clarify the objectives of the Revolution, build up the revolutionary movement, and defeat the secret intrigues of the imperialists and feudal warlords, who sought to sabotage the Revolution. Although the headquarters of the Revolution at that time was confined to the Canton area, the revolutionary spirit spread throughout the country.

During this period, Sun Yat-sen trained the cadres of the Nationalist Revolution in Huangpu, Canton, and, after the fall of Ts'ao K'un [the despised warlord President of China from October 1923 to October 1924], he went north despite his illness and, in response to the popular demand, called upon all mass organizations to convene a People's Congress. At the time of his trip north, he told the people that "the destiny of the state depends on the determination of the

for suppressing all those of whatever political belief that dared to criticize or challenge the monopoly of power by a small ruling clique within the Kuomintang bureaucracy. The Chinese Communists have by no means been the sole recipients of this form of treatment.

people." The object of the People's Congress was to have all the people unite to abolish the unequal treaties and solve China's internal problems. It was also hoped that the militarists would respond to the demands of the people and combine their various armies into a national army, which would become a powerful popular weapon.

The Peking Government had no desire to accept the proposal for convening a People's Assembly. It was deeply imbued with the psychology of submission to foreigners; it dreaded intervention by the foreign powers; and it was therefore fearful of the movement to abolish the unequal treaties. Sun Yat-sen, even when surrounded by the counterrevolutionary atmosphere of Peking, was determined to carry on the struggle regardless of consequences. He was unable to succeed, and he died on March 12, 1925, with a heavy heart. But in his final will, drawn up on his deathbed, he placed the responsibility for calling a People's Congress and for abolishing the unequal treaties upon all members of the Kuomintang, and upon all citizens of the country, in the hope that these two objectives might be attained in the shortest possible time.

At that time, the Nationalist Revolutionary Army was attacking Ch'en Chung-ming's rebellious army along the East River in Kwangtung, and in this moment of deep sorrow, it suppressed Ch'en, unified Kwangtung, and laid the foundation for the military stage of the Revolution.[4] In July 1926, the Nationalist Revolutionary Army, in accordance with the last will of Sun Yat-sen, took the oath and marched

---

4. The author here omits an important historical incident that helps to explain many subsequent events. On March 20, 1926, occurred the so-called "Incident of the Gunboat *Chungshan*." The climax of this incident was a coup executed by Chiang Kai-shek at Canton, aimed at weakening the military leadership of all Communists and progressives. Although Chiang backed down formally, and released from arrest some fifty military and political leaders, the coup established him as the military commander of the Northern Expedition. Following the coup, right-wing politicians poured into Canton from their hideouts in Shanghai and Hong Kong.

northward. The aim of this Northern Expedition was stated in the Declaration of the Nationalist Revolutionary Army: "The aim of the revolutionary war is to create an independent and free state, and to support the state and the interests of the people by applying the Three People's Principles. Therefore, we must unite all revolutionary movements under the Three People's Principles and must crush the warlords and the imperialists upon whom they depend for their existence."

Wherever the Revolutionary Army went, nationalist movements sprang up with the vigor of storms and cloudbursts. Nationalist sentiment at that time was stimulated and strengthened by the disorders following the May 30th incident, and the tragic incidents of Hankow and Shakee.

When the British Government recognized that the strength of Chinese nationalism could not be suppressed, it made the following proposal in a memorandum to the Nine Power Treaty signatories: "As soon as China has established a government with power to negotiate treaties, discussions should immediately be conducted concerning the revision of treaties. Before the establishment of such a government, all nations should adopt a policy in accord with the spirit of the Nine Power Treaty and applicable to the prevailing conditions, and one that will respect the wishes of the Chinese nation."

The United States Government, in Secretary of State Kellogg's formal note, showed its respect for the unity and independence of China: "The United States wishes to discuss with a representative of the Chinese Government, China's customs and tariff autonomy, and the abolition of consular jurisdiction."

At the beginning of the reoccupation of Nanking by the Nationalist Revolutionary Army, the unfortunate Nanking Incident occurred, and the five powers—Britain, America, Japan, France, and Italy—made serious demands. Of these powers, only the Japanese warlords stubbornly refused to recognize the strength of China's Nationalist Revolution, with the result that even by the beginning of the War of

Resistance on July 7, 1937, the Nanking Incident had not been fully settled. Within these nine months [July, 1926–March, 1927], the power of the northern warlords in the Yangtze Valley was destroyed by our Nationalist Revolutionary Army, and in this short period we were able to establish the preliminary foundation for eliminating both internal conflicts and foreign aggression.

At this time, we must recall the opening speech delivered by Sun Yat-sen to the First National Congress of the Kuomintang. In that speech he said: "There is one thing we must note. In the past, we were unable to achieve unity, not because of the strength of our enemies but because we fought among ourselves. . . . Therefore the unity of the Party was very weak, and as a result the Revolution failed."

This means that if there is no conflict within, no danger can penetrate from without—a fact which applies both to the state and to the Party. When the aim and the strength of the Nationalist Revolution was centralized and unified, the power of the warlords was crushed and China's relations with the foreign powers progressed favorably. Unfortunately, at this critical moment, when the success or failure of the Revolution was at stake, internal splits occurred in the ranks of the Nationalist Revolutionary Army and we almost failed to meet the heavy responsibilities and to grasp the great opportunities bequeathed to us by Sun Yat-sen. That was the darkest and most painful chapter in our history.[5]

5. This was indeed a dark and painful chapter in Chinese revolutionary history, and one of the darkest pages in that chapter was the betrayal of the workers of Shanghai, who had been organized to seize the city and welcome the conquering heroes of the Northern Expedition. Unknown to them, Chiang Kai-shek had previously reached an agreement with Tu Yueh-sheng, powerful Shanghai banker, opium czar, and secret society leader, by which the support of the powerful Ch'ing Pang (Green Circle) secret society would be given to Chiang. When Chiang's forces entered Shanghai in April, 1927, the Ch'ing Pang gangs rose according to plan, and acting in co-operation with the Blue Shirts of Tai Li, massacred thousands of labor leaders and militant workers, broke up the mass labor organizations, and enabled Chiang to take over the city. Tu Yueh-sheng and other prominent Shanghai as well as international bankers then helped to finance Chiang Kai-shek's efforts to establish a right-wing Nationalist

What almost destroyed the foundation of the Kuomintang, and nearly extinguished the life of the Nationalist Revolution was the promotion of factionalism within the Kuomintang by Wang Ching-wei and the Communist Party during 1926 and 1927. In view of these developments, the Kuomintang was forced to re-examine its policy of tolerating Communists as members of the Party. I am reluctant to recall this past history, but up to now I still do not know the inside story of the plot between Wang and the Communists. Did Wang make use of the Communist Party, or did the Communist Party make use of Wang, or did they make use of each other? This is still a question.[6] It is certain, however, that there was a plot between Wang and the Communists, particularly in view of the joint statement of Wang Ching-wei and Ch'en Tu-hsiu. [Ch'en was expelled from the Chinese Communist Party in 1927, and became leader of the Trotsky movement.] If we look upon Wang Ching-wei as a shameless traitor to his country, we might conclude that the Communists were used by him. But the real fact of the matter was that the members of the Chinese Communist Party within the Kuomintang violated their pledge to join the Kuomintang as individuals. Furthermore, they adhered to their theory that the Nationalist Revolution was a democratic revolution of the capitalist class, and that they must take advantage of the development of this Revolution to change it into a social revolution of the proletariat. They also maintained that the Kuomintang was

Government in the hope that they could thus protect their business interests against the social and economic reforms advocated by the left-wing sections of the Kuomintang. To further the policy of destroying the power of the Communists and labor unions, so-called "moderate" labor unions were established in Shanghai under Tu Yueh-sheng's control, and by 1931 the independent Chinese labor movement was completely crushed.

6. This may still be a question to the author, but certain facts are known: that Wang Ching-wei followed Chiang Kai-shek in breaking the united front in 1927 by only three months, and that subsequently, Wang became foreign minister and premier in Chiang's government as well as the closest collaborator of Chiang Kai-shek in the appeasement of Japan and in waging civil war against the Communists prior to 1937. Wang's appeasement of Japan continued until it reached its climax in 1940 when he became the No. 1 quisling of China.

not a political party, but only a political alliance of different classes, hoping in this way to take advantage of the development of the Nationalist Revolution to strengthen the Communist Party.

During this period, the leaders of the Communist Party, such as Ch'en Tu-hsiu, voiced these theories in *New Youth*, *Guidepost*, and other publications. They also fomented conflict between the right and left factions within the Kuomintang and encouraged class struggle and social revolution. In accordance with their slogan of the class struggle, they regarded the peasants and workers as the exclusive instruments of the Communist Party and encouraged production stoppages. It is unnecessary to mention the other economic and social losses caused by them. They even regarded students and intellectuals as counter-revolutionaries, while praising as progressive elements those who practiced dissipation and debauchery. They encouraged our youth to despise and abandon the ancient virtues of our nation, and even denounced the virtues of propriety, righteousness, thrift, and humility as reactionary, and treated filial piety, brotherly love, loyalty, and obedience with scorn. The situation resembled a raging flood that nearly got out of control. Again, during the period from 1931 to 1936, there was continuous war and disaster in southern Kiangsi, eastern Honan, western Anhwei, southern Honan, western Hupeh, Szechwan, and Shensi.[7]

All this suffering resulted from the so-called "Split between Nanking and Hankow," caused by the traitor Wang Ching-wei. As a result, there was dissension in the ranks of the Nationalist Revolutionary Army, and the Northern Expedition encountered difficulties and obstructions. This is the

7. A completely erroneous description of the events of this period and, at best, a highly euphemistic reference to Chiang Kai-shek's five major campaigns against the Communists (with German, Italian, and American support) that led finally to Chiang's being kidnaped at Sian in December, 1936, not by the Communists, but by his own followers who were deeply disturbed by the destructive civil war in the face of increasing Japanese aggression. Indeed, it was the Communists that were instrumental in securing Chiang's release from his captors.

most impressive lesson to be learned from the development of the Nationalist Revolution, and it is also the saddest and most tragic page in our history. In summary, the only national policies that can succeed are those that are based on the principles of complete sincerity and justice. In other words, when one person exploits another, or when one connives with others for seditious purposes, or when one is exploited by others, or selfishly makes use of others to achieve personal success, he can never escape the established rule that "only the sincere will succeed" and that "the insincere will acquire nothing." It is still more true that the Revolution, which is the enterprise of the state and the nation, cannot succeed by mere personal opportunism.

Why is it necessary to make such statements at this time? Because the lessons that we have learned from the Revolution have been so bitter, the damage done to the state has been so great, and the sacrifices made by the people so tragic. If there had been no civil wars during the years 1931–36, the condition of the present War of Resistance would be entirely different, and the Pacific situation as well as the world outlook would be greatly changed. The enemy would not have dared to attack us, because he would have been quickly driven beyond our borders. Therefore, these lessons [of the Revolution] are pertinent, valuable, and worthy of study, and will not lose their significance with the passing of time. I want all patriots within the country to take warning from the past for the sake of the future, so that our future revolutionary struggle may be benefited.

In order to put the Three People's Principles into effect, to further the progress of the Nationalist Revolution, to safeguard the morale of the Chinese nation, and to protect our ancient cultural heritage, the Kuomintang, in the spring of 1927, decided to carry out a thorough purge of the Party. Although at that time the Nationalist Government was beset by hardships and disunity, it still continued the Northern Expedition and established the capital at Nanking. However, as the foundation of the Revolution had been undermined, the Northern Expedition was unavoidably interrupted, and it was not until March of the next year that the army could continue its progress. The Japanese imperialists, faced with the threat of Chinese unity, immediately dispatched troops to Tsinan to obstruct our progress northward. Our Nationalist Revolutionary Army, however, continued their determined advance and in early July [1928] occupied the ancient capital of Peking, thus attaining the objective of the Northern Expedition. Toward the end of the year, the Northeastern Provinces acknowledged the leadership of the National Government and thus the first stage in the unification of the country ended successfully.

In the Tsinan Incident of May 3, 1928, the Nationalist Government and the Revolutionary Army were thoroughly humiliated by Japan and severely criticized by the people. At that time, I warned the officers and men of the army as follows: "In order to avenge our country's humiliation, you must free China from imperialist oppression and must attain the objectives of independence and liberty. Today you can only endure insults and prepare yourselves for vengeance. It will take ten years to train the population in the firm belief of our forefathers that the lost territories can and must be recovered and the national humiliation avenged. If you can do this, it will not be difficult to attain a state of liberty, equality, and harmony throughout the land." These words constituted an order to all members of the Nationalist Revolutionary Army, from commanders to privates, to avenge our national humiliation. For the past fifteen years, our commanders and soldiers have never forgotten this.

The success of the Northern Expedition may be described as a sad and painful, but nevertheless noble and heroic, page in history, written by the Chinese nation which rose up against one hundred years of imperialist aggression. It marked the first step in building up the people's morale, achieving political unity, and strengthening the army. When

we recall the violent and malicious methods used by the
imperialists and the counter-revolutionary forces to destroy
the Nationalist Government—particularly their use of all
kinds of false rumors and slanders—we realize that they
stopped at nothing. But the people's confidence in the ability
of the National Government to solve all difficulties and build
a new and independent China, and their enthusiastic support
of its policies, gave us boundless and unforgettable encouragement. Therefore, the Nationalist Government determinedly
pursued the aims bequeathed us by the Father of our Country
—to call a National Assembly and to abolish the unequal
treaties. Undeterred by obstacles and setbacks, we have
worked to carry out this mission in order to console the spirit
of the Father of our Country as well as those of our heroes
of the past.

3. Internal Difficulties and External Perils Following the Transfer of the National Capital to Nanking

The first measure of success in the work of the Northern
Expedition was achieved under very difficult and dangerous
circumstances, as well as conditions of great instability. After
this, the Nationalist Government assumed that it would be
able to proceed from destruction to reconstruction, and was
especially hopeful that it could use the strength of national
unity to lay the foundation for the liberation of the nation.
When the Nationalist Revolutionary Army recovered Peiping
and Tientsin, I, Chiang Kai-shek, took an oath to carry out
eight undertakings, and solemnly announced this before the
tomb of the Father of our Country. The last two of these
undertakings were my most treasured hopes.

One of them concerned post-war construction. I said:
"After destruction, reconstruction is urgently needed. *The
Plans for National Reconstruction*, and *Fundamentals of National
Reconstruction* [of Sun Yat-sen] have already clearly outlined
the stages and methods, and if all our comrades will sincerely

and earnestly carry them out, there will be no difficulty in building a state based on the Three People's Principles and completing the task of the Nationalist Revolution. Now that the stage of military government is completed, the strength of revolutionary reconstruction must be demonstrated through practical political plans. Otherwise, the accomplishments of our comrades on the battlefields will not easily be preserved because the people will be disillusioned."

The other undertaking concerned the post-war movement for national independence, of which I said: "Because of the stubbornness of the warlords and politicians, our *Tsung-li's* [Leader's, i.e., Sun Yat-sen's] policy of national salvation by peaceful means could not be carried out, and our Party in its determination to eliminate all obstacles was compelled to resort to force. But when we turned to war, this caused great suffering to our fellow citizens in the war-torn areas, and necessitated heavy sacrifices by our commanders and soldiers at the front. I have always felt that definite efforts must be made to eliminate civil war after the success of the Revolution. The military power of a state should be employed only to defend the interests of the nation, and civil war is thus the most humiliating of all kinds of war. In the present Northern Expedition, over a million troops were mobilized, fighting back and forth in areas covering thousands of miles. But the damage was done to Chinese territory, and the dead and wounded were all our fellow citizens. Hereafter, the whole country must recognize that civil war is humiliating, and concentrate its entire energy on the defense of the state. We should learn the art of war solely for purposes of self-defense, and we should be prepared by our bitter experience to carry out the will of our Leader with respect to national independence and freedom."

Thereafter, the Nationalist Government, under difficult and dangerous circumstances, proceeded steadily along the course already adopted. That China has been able to fight the enemy in such a protracted struggle is due to the strength originating from this spirit of revolutionary reconstruction.

According to the steps outlined in *The Plans for National Reconstruction*, the period of political tutelage follows the military stage, and its chief task is to introduce local self-government. The criterion for the practice of self-government is based on the *Regulations for Starting to Practice Local Self-Government*, drawn up by Sun Yat-sen. As for the beginning of the period of constitutional government, it depends upon the results of practicing local self-government. The steps in this program are clear and logical, and provide no grounds for controversy.

But for ten years after the removal of the capital to Nanking, circumstances hindered progress in the basic task of political tutelage, from both the practical and theoretical points of view. On the practical side, the greatest political blow suffered by the Nationalist Government was the opposition to the unification of the state. On the theoretical side, the question of how to carry out the work of political tutelage became a controversial issue and the question of how long this period of political tutelage should be continued was also hotly debated. Such dissension not only provided the feudalists and counter-revolutionists with pretexts [for opposing the Government], but also gave comrades within the Party the appearance of wavering, with the result that arguments became more numerous and there was no unity of action. We all know that political tutelage is the path that must be followed to attain democracy, without which the people's rights cannot be protected, and that otherwise the constitution to be framed in the future can only become a worthless piece of paper. After the Revolution of 1911, our citizens did not realize the need for revolutionary reconstruction, and they devoted their efforts to studying the articles of the constitution and the forms of various political systems, thus opening the way for the plots of the warlords to seize control of the state, and giving the imperialists the opportunity to extend their exploitation.

Plans for Industrialization [written by Sun Yat-sen] is the classic guide to China's material rehabilitation. However, during the ten years after the Nationalist Government moved the capital to Nanking, economic rehabilitation in practice did not develop according to schedule, due to interference by the imperialists and obstruction from counter-revolutionary influences. From the theoretical standpoint, the economists at that time were equally divided between the theories of Liberalism and Communism. The Communists directed their efforts toward a so-called "land revolution" and a "peasants' revolution," and wherever their armies arrived, thousands of miles became barren and our peaceful villages were destroyed. They had no desire to preserve or protect the industry and commerce of the nation, and preached only the theory of hatred and strife in order to obstruct the increase in production. As a result, capital fled to the concessions, thereby encouraging imperialist aggression and intensifying its effects. Those who favored the theories of liberalism approached the problems that faced China as a result of the prolonged oppression of the unequal treaties, without recognizing that·the trend in world economics after the First World War had been from free competition toward monopoly and centralization.[8] They regarded themselves as new and modern when they were actually applying the economic theories of the first industrial revolution to a China that was faced with the second industrial revolution in Europe and America. As a result, the Principle of the People's Livelihood and *Plans for Industrialization* became obscured.

At that time, the Nationalist Government frankly admitted that its plans for reconstruction had not achieved the expected

---

8. The author fails to recognize that there is a world of difference between monopoly and centralization in a highly developed industrial country, and the same process in a very backward country where the ruling class consists almost entirely of landlords and bureaucrats. In the one, the step is a logical, historical development; in the other, it is retrogressive and tends to stifle the only forces that could replace a feudal with a modern economy.

results. It might be said that the revolutionary work of reconstruction had not been started, and that there was no
way to get it started. It must be realized that after the Tsinan
Incident of May 3rd [1928], the aggressive character of
Japan's "continental policy" became increasingly apparent,
and we were constantly threatened with Japanese military
aggression. China was never able to carry on reconstruction
as planned, nor had she the opportunity to realize the Three
People's Principles and complete the Revolution in a leisurely
manner. The Nationalist Government had to engage in social
and economic reconstruction while at the same time conceal-
ing its preparations for military resistance against aggression.

During this ten-year period, the Nationalist Government,
working under conditions of restraint and silence, and fear
of imminent attack, nevertheless achieved a steady improvement in the country's economy. Imports of luxury goods
gradually decreased, while imports of machinery and mechanical equipment increased, indicating the progress made
in China's agriculture, industry, and mining. The most notable results, however, were achieved in the field of communications and finance. Over a period of forty-eight years preceding the sixteenth year of the Republic [1927], eighty-three
hundred kilometers of railroads were built, and during the
ten years after 1928, seventy-three hundred additional kilometers were built, while over one hundred thousand kilometers of highways were completed. The construction of tele-
graphic communications was also successful; the most outstanding achievement being the construction of a nation-wide
network of thirty-three thousand kilometers of telephone
wires. In the field of finance, the *likin* tax was abolished, tax
rates were lowered, the maritime customs regulations were
revised, and domestic and foreign debts were adjusted. The
tael was replaced by the *yuan* [Chinese dollar], and the unification of the currency system and the adoption of a new
monetary policy were particularly instrumental in laying the
foundation for national unity and independence. That today

we can fight this War of Resistance and still remain unde-
feated, militarily and economically, is due to these reforms.

The manuscript of Sun Yat-sen's *Ten Year Plan for National
Defense* was destroyed during the revolt of Ch'en Chungming,
and only the table of contents remains. But his views on military matters may be ascertained from his speech concerning
the establishment of the Huangpu [Whampoa] Academy;
his economic views are set forth in his *Plans for Industrialization;* and his views on social psychology may be seen in his
speech on *The Spiritual Education of the Soldiers.* The Nationalist Government, after the removal of the capital to Nanking,
tried earnestly to attain its objective of peaceful unification
and national security. It also recognized that domestic dissension and foreign oppression were interrelated, and that
unification and independence were also interrelated. Therefore, it did not falter in the face of criticism and attacks by
those that used the crisis in foreign relations as a pretext for
spreading internal dissension. And it was eventually able to
achieve sufficient military preparation to enable the nation
to launch the all-out War of Resistance.

After the success of the Northern Expedition, the relations
between the Nationalist Government and the imperialists[9]
reached a climax. The failure of the Nationalist Revolution
would mean success for the imperialists;[9] if the Nationalist
Revolution succeeded, the power of the imperialists[9] would be
forever eliminated within China. During this stage, the internal difficulties and external perils confronting the Nationalist Government were almost beyond control. Moreover,
the various aggressor powers within China intrigued against
each other, and either by direct coercion or secret plotting
stirred up trouble and confusion everywhere. The disasters
caused by them were worse than at any time during the
preceding hundred years. [These two sentences, beginning
with "Moreover," are omitted in the second edition, and

9. In the revised edition, the word "Japanese" was inserted before the word "imperialists," in both these sentences.

replaced with the statement: "The destiny of China now entered on a period of greater peril than it had experienced during the past hundred years."] Had the Nationalist Government been careless in its handling of the situation, or had it wavered in its course, the outrageous behavior of the feudal forces following the Revolution of 1911 would inevitably have been repeated.

We all know that the united demand of our four hundred and fifty million compatriots for the past hundred years has been to avenge our national humiliation and build up our national strength. Moreover, history has proved that the most effective way to achieve this purpose is by a Nationalist Revolution. Yet, at that time, there were some that slandered the Nationalist Revolution, accused it of being transitional, reformist, and ineffective, and opposed and obstructed it. We know too that the united demand of our four hundred and fifty million countrymen during the last thirty years has been for unification, and that the Nationalist Revolution is the most peaceful and most logical way to attain this goal. Nevertheless, there were some that used the pretense of "democracy" to cloak their feudalistic ideas and their divisive activities; employed the slogan of "freedom" to conceal their reactionary and rebellious actions; and made use of such insulting terms as "tyranny" and "dictatorship" in their efforts to discredit the great task of national unification. Traitors such as Wang Ching-wei even borrowed the names of the Kuomintang and the Nationalist Government, and the names of the Three People's Principles and the Nationalist Revolutionary Army, in an effort to destroy the Kuomintang and the Three People's Principles and undermine the Nationalist Revolution. Such were the treacherous actions of those that betrayed the state and revolted against the Party during the past fifteen years. Every available theory and slogan were employed by these scoundrels to foment disunity in the nation and the state. As a result of their propaganda, the united will of the people was split, with some becoming radical and others becoming decadent. Those that were radical became bandits, while those that were decadent became passive and discouraged, with disastrous results for our culture and social traditions. The difficulties and obstacles encountered in politics, economics, and national defense were equally serious. Yet the Nationalist Government, during the ten years after the removal of the capital to Nanking, was able by vigorous effort to curb the activities that threatened to divide our state, our nation, and our culture, as well as our thought.

Take education for example. The Government's educational policy was defined as follows in 1929: "The objective of education derives from the Three People's Principles, and aims at enriching the people's life, aiding social progress, improving the people's livelihood, and prolonging the life of the nation, in order to attain national independence, widespread democratic rights, and rising living standards for the people, so that peace may prevail."

In 1932, the resolution on education adopted by the Third Plenum of the Central Committee, elected by the Fourth Congress of the Kuomintang, stated that the policy on education is "to arouse the nation's spirit, cultivate nationalist thinking, and revive the people's self-confidence in order to attain the objective of independence, liberty, and equality for the Chinese nation."

Thereafter, our educational program both in the schools and in society laid its chief emphasis on cultivating nationalist thinking and stimulating a nationalist spirit; making certain that learning and culture were suited to the economy of the state and the livelihood of the people; and eliminating the prevalent habits of disunity, disloyalty, vanity, and instability that had resulted from the effects of the unequal treaties. That our people have been able to show such great determination and self-sacrifice for the state during the War of Resistance is due to their education in the Three People's Principles during the last ten years.

The damage done to the revolution by internal strife had a profound effect upon China's foreign relations. When the Nationalist Government established the capital in Nanking in 1927, the Ministry of Foreign Affairs issued a public statement declaring that there was no ground for the continuance of the unequal treaties made by the Peking Government with the foreign powers, and that the Nationalist Government would negotiate new treaties with the various nations. It also stated specifically that tariff autonomy would become effective on September 1, 1927, and that the state's temporary regulations for tariff rates would be put into effect soon. However, the military progress of the Northern Expedition was obstructed by both domestic and foreign difficulties, and the Japanese took advantage of this to declare their opposition to the new tariff regulations. Their example was followed by other countries, and our revolutionary diplomacy was thus brought to a standstill.

After the completion of the Northern Expedition in 1928, the Nationalist Government again announced its intention to negotiate new treaties. All countries having treaty relations with China began to discuss new agreements, with the question of tariff autonomy constituting the central problem. The first treaty completed was that between China and the United States, regulating the trade relations between the two countries. Subsequently, other countries also negotiated and signed tariff agreements with China. Only the Japanese imperialists delayed taking action, and it was not until 1930 that the Sino-Japanese Tariff Agreement was signed, with part of the old provisions still retained.

Negotiations for the abolition of consular jurisdiction [extraterritoriality] began in 1929, but unfortunately, civil war broke out and all the foreign powers adopted a policy of watchful waiting. In December, 1929, and again in December, 1930, the Nationalist Government set a date for the return of China's jurisdictional rights, but due to the civil war nothing was accomplished. In May, 1931, the "Regulations for Controlling Foreign Nationals in China" were published, to become effective as of January 1, 1932, but this date was subsequently postponed as a result of the "September 18th" incident [Japanese invasion of Manchuria, September 18, 1931].

The Japanese imperialists, in addition to passively delaying negotiations, actively sought opportune moments to provoke our country in order to bring pressure against us. During the ten years following the removal of the capital to Nanking, the Western powers, although they did not fully understand our nationalist movement, nevertheless recognized that there was hope for the political unification of China; the prestige of the Nationalist Government was heightened; and they made appropriate concessions. But the more successful China became in achieving political unity, the more actively the Japanese imperialists pursued their secret schemes for a military offensive against China. Following the May 3, 1928, incident [of Tsinan], there were the "Wan-pao Shan" incident and the "Nakamura" incident [1931] which led to the "September 18th" incident. After the "September 18th" incident, there were the battles of "January 28th" [Shanghai, 1932], "Yu Kuan" [Shanhaikwan area], "Jehol," and "the Great Wall"; and the "Ishimoto," "Chengtu," and "Pakhoi" incidents, leading up to the incident of the "Marco Polo Bridge" [July, 1937] and the beginning of the total War of Resistance.

From the "September 18th" incident to the beginning of the War of Resistance, the main issue in China's foreign affairs was the problem of Japan, and the main issue in domestic affairs was also what measures to take in order to resist Japan. We all know that modern warfare is scientific warfare, and that China's scientific inventions and industrial skill were in their infancy and inferior to Japan's. Modern wars are also wars involving the entire population, but China's feudal and counter-revolutionary forces were still engrossed in civil strife. Under these circumstances, the Nationalist Government could only adopt the following policy: "Not until there is no hope of peace shall we abandon efforts to preserve peace, and not until sacrifice has reached its ultimate limit shall we scorn sacrifice."

Politically, the Nationalist Government endeavored to be lenient and to make concessions to all factions in the hope of stopping all internal strife in order to unite against the foreign enemy. Socially, it launched the New Life Movement to arouse the people's spirit of self-confidence and self-respect. Militarily, it enforced the *pao chia* system and trained able-bodied young men with a view to making every citizen a soldier.[10] It also expanded war industries and accumulated munitions and other military supplies. Since China had for so long been reduced to the status of a subcolony [Sun Yat-sen's term to describe China's status as even worse than that of a colony subject to the rule of only one country] and subjected to such intensive exploitation by the imperialists, it is

10. Under the *pao chia* system, the population is registered and organized into units for conscripting soldiers and labor, for taxation, and for the suppression of "banditry." Ten households make up one *chia*, and ten *chia* constitute one *pao*. Ten *pao*, or a thousand households, constitute a *hsiang* (rural township) or a *chen* (urban town). First instituted in the Sung dynasty (960–1279) primarily as a means of military conscription, the *pao chia* system was reintroduced in the Ch'ing (Manchu) dynasty as a method of suppression by which groups of households were held collectively responsible for any individual member's opposition to the alien government. In 1936, the system was re-established by the Kuomintang Government as the basis for county self-government, and is represented by Kuomintang spokesmen as the true foundation of democratic government.

Its actual purpose, however, is the same as in former times: to check subversive activity by means of the theory of collective responsibility, and to facilitate military and labor conscription. A modification of this system was adopted by the Japanese after their invasion of Manchuria in 1931, when they converted hundreds of Manchurian villages into "concentration villages" and ruthlessly punished the entire village for any opposition to Japanese rule that might have been displayed by one or more villagers. The re-establishment of the *pao chia* system by the Kuomintang, coupled with its ruthless destruction of labor unions, and its continued armed campaigns and secret police suppression of all opposition groups, makes the use of the word "lenient" in the first sentence of this paragraph a bitter mockery.

hardly necessary to point out how difficult it was for her to prepare for a war against imperialism. Furthermore, during those six years, there were not many that showed real consideration for the needs of the Nationalist Government. Our central organization was naturally different from the governments at the end of the Sung and Ming dynasties, but the severity of the struggles among various factions within the country and the laxity of morale were far worse. Those that were decadent and passive wanted to live quietly under the Japanese and therefore advocated a policy of nonresistance. The militant radicals, on the other hand, urged a policy of immediate war by which they hoped to strengthen their own position within the country. The first group forgot that the policy of appeasement followed at the end of the Sung dynasty had led the nation to the verge of total destruction. The second group failed to realize that the policy of immediate war pursued at the end of the Ming dynasty had resulted in heavy losses for border troops, whose defeat finally led to the tragic subjugation of the state. The Nationalist Government at that time [1931–37] was unwilling to explain its position to these various factions, because by so doing it would reveal to the imperialists its plans for resistance. What it relied upon was its deep confidence that despite nearly three hundred years of tyrannical rule by the Manchu dynasty, the people had preserved their sense of national consciousness; that after a century of imperialist aggression, they would be eager to avenge our national humiliation; and that in their desire for unity and independence, they would, in the final crisis, vigorously support the Nationalist Revolution and the Nationalist Government. The Government was also confident that those counter-revolutionaries that scorned our ancient virtues and attacked the Nationalist Revolution would ultimately be rejected by the people, while the correctness and realistic character of the Nationalist Revolution would eventually be demonstrated by the final results.

4. Internal Effects of the War of Resistance

On July 7, 1937, the Japanese enemy, under the pretense of maneuvers, forcibly occupied the Marco Polo Bridge and seized the Wanping District in order to cut communications between north and south, thus hoping to gain complete control of Peiping. We recognized that the development of this incident would determine not only the question of China's survival or destruction, but also the fate of all mankind. We also knew that since Japan had long planned to subjugate us, peace could not easily be obtained, and that China had reached the final, unavoidable crisis. We further realized that in this final crisis, there could be no question of compromise, for such a compromise would lead only to surrender and complete extinction. We could only fight to the end, and only if we were determined to sacrifice everything could we hope to win final victory. We were, of course, a weak nation but we could not refuse to fight to preserve our nation, nor could we refuse to assume the responsibility passed down to us by our forefathers. We therefore decided upon a policy of total resistance, and once the War of Resistance was launched, we were determined to see it through.

In Chinese history there are many precedents for national wars. But the present War of Resistance, in its immense scope, in the sacrifice entailed, in the difficulty of the task, and the greatness of its importance, is without precedent. The nature of this War of Resistance differs from the national wars in any other period of history. We must recognize that the present War of Resistance is not only an essential part of the National Revolution, but that victory in the War of Resistance will ensure the success of the Nationalist Revolution, the liberation of the nation, and the building of the state. Therefore, at the beginning of the war, the Kuomintang and the Nationalist Government immediately adopted the dual policy of resistance and national reconstruction.[11] This policy was described in the Program of Resistance and National Reconstruction which was approved by the Provisional National Congress of the Kuomintang and adopted by the People's Political Council, and which should be strictly adhered to by all citizens.

There are four main points in this program: In the field of international relations, we must unite with all anti-aggressor nations in support of the principles of independence and self-government, and fight shoulder to shoulder against imperialist aggression in order that all the peoples of the world may live together in peace. In the field of domestic politics, we must establish local self-government as the basis for constitutional government and, prior to the establishment of constitutional government, we must organize a body through which the people can participate in politics in order to enlist the support of the entire country for our national program. With regard to the national economy, we must initiate a system of planned economy that will combine national defense with the people's livelihood and thus transform China into a strong and unified fighting body. In the cultural and intellectual field, we must cultivate our own ancient virtues, expand our scientific knowledge, and revive our traditional customs, in order that the wisdom of the people may be increased. In other words, this program represents, in essence, the Three People's Principles and the strategy of the Nationalist Revolution. Thus, during the past five years, although both foreign and domestic conditions have constantly changed, the policies set forth in the program have remained unaltered. If only all our citizens would unite and co-operate in carrying

11. The literal meaning of the two characters that are most frequently translated "national reconstruction," is "state building," which some translators take to mean that what the author had in mind was primarily the state or governmental apparatus. Nevertheless, to American readers, the phrase "national reconstruction" is a more understandable concept than "state building" and that phrase is therefore used throughout this translation.

out this program, our victory in the War of Resistance and our success in national reconstruction would be assured.

After July 7, 1937, public sentiment was aroused, and public opinion was unified as a result of the Government's unfaltering policy. Wherever its influence prevailed, the supporters of a nonresistance policy either disappeared or became traitors and were rejected by the people, and those that had previously urged immediate war had no further opportunity to promote their radical ideas. Popular morale was strengthened and national unity increased as the War of Resistance continued, with the result that great progress was made in the unification of military command. The enforcement of orders from the Central Government and local authorities began to improve, and there was rapid progress in the planning of production and state control of industries, thereby establishing the basis for implementing the principle of the people's livelihood. At the same time, internal dissension diminished as a result of the growing recognition that "the state is supreme; the nation is supreme."

As a result, various organizations and parties pledged their support to the Government and their willingness to co-operate in meeting the national crisis. Even the Chinese Communist Party, in a public statement, made four solemn promises: "To fight for the realization of the Three People's Principles; to discontinue the policy of violent insurrection, Communist propaganda, and the forcible confiscation of land; to dissolve the Soviet Government in order to promote the political unification of the country; and to discard the name and insignia of the Red Army and reorganize it as part of the Nationalist Revolutionary Army, under the jurisdiction of the National Military Council, to await orders to move into action and assume duty in the front line of the War of Resistance."[12]

12. The author here refers to the Chinese Communist Manifesto issued on September 22, 1937, but does not mention that these four pledges were preceded by three other points, calling for the immediate establishment of a democratic form of government, the convoking of a National Convention

At that time I, Chiang Kai-shek, made known in a public statement that "the object of the Nationalist Revolution was to strive for China's freedom and equality." Our Leader [Sun Yat-sen] had clearly explained that the Three People's Principles are the doctrine of national salvation, and I had hoped that every citizen would join in a common effort to save the country from subjugation. Unfortunately, during the ten years following the successful completion of the Northern Expedition, the people as a whole did not sincerely believe in the Three People's Principles, and did not fully realize the danger that confronted the nation. As a result, the process of revolutionary reconstruction encountered many obstacles; the vitality of the nation was weakened; the people were compelled to endure many sacrifices; foreign aggression was intensified; and the position of the state was imperiled. During that period, however, the Central Government adhered to its policy of resistance based upon unification; of tolerating insults and shouldering heavy responsibilities, without for-

---

to draft and promulgate a constitution, and social and economic reforms to improve the people's welfare. In his formal statement acknowledging the Communist Manifesto (September 23, 1937), Chiang Kai-shek also made no reference to these three points, but merely expressed the hope that the Communists would carry out their pledges. These two statements formed the basis of the so-called United Front agreement between the Kuomintang and the Communists, but since this agreement was never embodied in a single document officially accepted by both sides, interpretations of the rights and obligations of both parties inevitably differed and a wide area of controversy developed. The Chinese Communists claimed that in return for their willingness to become a special administrative district under Central Government authority, to incorporate their troops in the Central Armies, to modify their land policy, etc., the Central Government had agreed to the introduction of political reforms in China. The Kuomintang leaders, on the other hand, refused to admit that the United Front Agreement involved anything more than a recognition by the Communists of the Central Government's authority, and did nothing to establish a representative government that would give all Chinese political parties a voice in determining Government policy. Under these circumstances, the Communists suspected with reason that the Kuomintang's demand that they surrender their armed forces to Central Government control was really intended to eliminate them as a political force— a view in which they were confirmed by the treatment meted out to the minority parties in Kuomintang China which possessed no armies.

getting for a single day the need for unity and co-operation in meeting the crisis confronting the state.

People that had formerly doubted the Three People's Principles began to place the interest of the nation uppermost, discarded their previous differences of opinion, and worked together to achieve unity. This indicated that all citizens had come to realize that if we live we all live, and if we die we all die, and that the life or death of the nation as a whole is more important than the fate of any individual or group. The declaration made by the Chinese Communist Party at that time testified to the growing strength of national consciousness. It also proved that only the Three People's Principles can increase our national consciousness, and that the Kuomintang is the only revolutionary party representing the demands of the entire nation and the interests of all classes. Any theory that is in opposition to the Three People's Principles will soon be rejected by the nation. Therefore, the highest guiding principle in the War of Resistance is the Three People's Principles, and the highest directing organization is the Kuomintang. If there was no Three People's Principles, there would be no War of Resistance; if there was no Kuomintang, there would be no Revolution. No political party and no political activity can aid the War of Resistance or promote the revival of the nation if they differ from the Three People's Principles and from the Kuomintang. This obvious fact ought to be fully recognized by all the people, and particularly by the intellectuals.

5. *The International Setting of the War of Resistance—An Account of the Military Strategy and Diplomatic Battles Before and During the War of Resistance*

The effects of our War of Resistance upon the world may be divided into two phases. The first phase concerns the relation of China's War of Resistance to the World War and to

international peace, while the second concerns the understanding of China's War of Resistance by the foreign powers.

As to the relation of our War of Resistance to the World
War and international peace, I want to point out first that
our Nationalist Government knows that world peace is in-
divisible. Thus, before the outbreak of the World War, China
refused to shirk her responsibilities toward international peace,
and after the outbreak of the World War, China determined
to do her full part in sharing the burden of the war. During
the past five and a half years, we have shattered Japan's
grandiose dream of dividing the world and caused her to
lose the power of initiative. Hereafter, China must continue
her vigorous efforts and, together with her friendly Allies,
destroy completely the power of Japan and her Axis partners
to disturb the world.

After the September 18th [1931] incident the Japanese imperialists, in pursuit of their "continental policy," proposed
the so-called "Three Principles" and tried to force their
acceptance by the Nationalist Government. These so-called
"Three Principles" were "Friendship between China and
Japan," "Economic Co-operation," and "Joint Defense
against Communism." "Friendship between China and Japan" in reality meant the political absorption of China by
Japanese imperialism. "Economic Co-operation" meant the
economic monopoly of China by Japanese imperialism. And
"Joint Defense against Communism" was a Japanese plot to
use our four Northeastern Provinces as a base from which to
continue their encroachments on Chinese territory, to black-
mail the Chinese Government, and to synchronize their military activities with those of the Axis countries in Europe for
a joint attack against Soviet Russia from the East and West.

Our Nationalist Government recognized that these were
the aims of Japan's "Continental policy," and adopted a
stern attitude in refusing to accept these "Three Principles."
China then signed the nonaggression treaty with Soviet
Russia in August, 1937, to frustrate Japan's secret plan.

Japan immediately abandoned the methods of diplomacy, in the belief that by using "local incidents" as a pretext for quick action, she could cut the Peiping-Hankow Railway, occupy Peiping and Tientsin, and establish the area northeast of the Yungting River as a Japanese base from which to attack and occupy Siberia. Our Nationalist Government not only refused to yield to Japanese pressure, but decided to send troops north to strengthen our garrisons in Peiping and Tientsin, and to fight the War of Resistance. After the outbreak of the war in Wusung and Shanghai on August 13th [1937], Japan's plans for rapid aggression on the mainland were completely frustrated by our policy of protracted resistance. Thereafter, China fought the war single-handed for two years before the outbreak of the European War; four years later the Pacific War began. China's policy has been consistent from beginning to end, and has never wavered. If one examines Japanese policy, however, one can see that there has been no such consistency, and that, furthermore, Japan must eventually abandon the "continental policy" that she has pursued since the days of Emperor Meiji. Therefore, we can state that between the incident of July 7th [1937] and the incident of August 12th [1937], when China's War of Resistance was launched, we had already defeated Japan's traditional policy both politically and militarily, and had laid the foundation for our own victory.

¦ China's total war and her determination to fight to the end have been clearly made known to the world. The Japanese imperialists, however, are as stubborn as ever, and are unwilling to abandon their long-prepared plans. The Konoye Cabinet repeatedly announced its "nonexpansionist" program. Its first move was to try to take advantage of the opportunity when our capital was in danger to secure a quick peace, with Germany acting as a mediator. When our Nationalist Government refused to enter into peace talks, and reiterated its determination to continue the War of Resistance, Japan's next move was to stop military aggression after the battle of Wu-Han [Wuchang and Hankow], and to employ both a peace offensive and a political offensive against China in the hope of ending the war, while still cherishing her desire to advance northward [against the Soviet Union]. The incidents of Changkufeng [1938] and Nomonhan [1939] were evidence of this desire.[13] However, the Japanese were forced to change their policy toward China from one of gradual encroachment to one of complete annexation, and were compelled to devote their entire strength to settling the "China incident." Japan's "nonexpansionist" program had to be altered to that of a "long-term war" in September 1938. And the "Three Principles" of "Friendship between Japan and China," "Economic Co-operation" and "Joint Defense against Communism," had to be openly announced by Premier Konoye. Following the Konoye declaration, the Nationalist Government thoroughly exposed the Japanese scheme, and the Konoye Cabinet thereupon fell.

In January, 1939, the Japanese Government was reorganized under the premiership of Baron Hiranuma. Germany demanded that, on the basis of mutual agreement and joint defense against Communism, Japan conclude a tripartite alliance [with Germany and Italy] aimed at launching a world war. But Japan, tied down by China's War of Resistance and having already lost the initiative, was forced to seek a postponement. In the autumn of that year, Hitler suddenly shifted his strategy and signed a nonaggression pact with the Soviet Union, and the European War then broke out. The Hiranuma Cabinet had no alternative but to resign in August, amidst widespread confusion and apprehension. The two succeeding cabinets of Abe and Yonai could only adopt a policy of "staying out of the European war" in order to save the situation temporarily. During this period, in February, 1939, the Japanese had extended their military activities to Canton and occupied the harbor of Hainan Island, thereby

13. Border incidents in which Japanese troops attacked Soviet forces and were defeated.

giving the first indication of their plan of military expansion southward. The war situation in the Pacific then changed sharply. Japan's policy of expansion northward had been altered to expansion southward, but expansion southward was hindered by China's War of Resistance, which caused Japan to hesitate and delay her attack on Great Britain and the United States for almost three years. This fundamental change in Japan's policy was the result of the complete success of our national policy. That this was the crucial factor in the failure of Japan's "continental policy" has been generally recognized by all students of world affairs. [The revised edition adds the following passage: "The day after the Japanese seized the island of Hainan, I warned the two friendly nations of Great Britain and the United States that this was the Mukden incident of the Pacific, and that all Pacific powers ought to adopt a common policy. But at that time these friendly nations regarded my warning as an exaggeration to attract attention, and took no notice. They sat still and watched Japan prepare a base for her southward expansion, and allowed her to complete her preparations for war. The reason why Japan was still not able to advance rapidly, and take advantage of the opportunity presented by the lack of preparation on the part of Britain, the United States, Holland, and France, was because her southward advance was hindered by Chinese resistance, from which she could not free herself."]

During May and June, 1940, Denmark, Norway, Holland, Belgium, and France were successively conquered by the German Army. Japan was amazed. The demand for the conclusion of a tripartite military alliance was again raised by the militarists. Konoye took this opportunity to form a cabinet, and he soon signed the Tripartite Pact. Its first strategy was to remain on the defensive in the north and undertake an offensive in the south, and as a consequence, the Soviet-Japanese Neutrality Pact was concluded in April, 1941. These two documents [the Tripartite Pact and the

Soviet-Japanese Treaty] raised Yosuke Matsuoka to the status of Japan's "super statesman." Not long afterward [June 22, 1941], the Soviet-German war suddenly broke out; Matsuoka resigned; and Konoye's second cabinet had to be reorganized. But the recklessness of the [Japanese] militarists could no longer be controlled. Konoye's third cabinet, which was formed after the attempted assassination of Hiranuma, was forced to sign its own death warrant by resigning in October of that year. Then Tojo, as war minister, formed a cabinet committed to the strategy of "southern expansion first, northern expansion afterward," and on December 8, 1941 [December 7th, in the U. S. A.], under cover of the American-Japanese negotiations, Japan suddenly attacked British and American Pacific possessions and points of strategic importance.

An examination of the history of this period shows that not only did the people of the world fail to understand the reasons for the changes in Japanese policy and strategy, and the results that these changes inevitably produced, but that even the Japanese militarists themselves failed to understand their real significance. Although the Japanese militarists considered themselves extremely clever, they were really stupid and stubborn. In their war of aggression against our country, they thought they had the initiative in their hands, and that they had China completely under their control, and therefore they did as they pleased without the least scruple. What they did not know was that, from the beginning of the war, their policy and military strategy were entirely under our control. As a result, their tactics in combat were basically controlled by us, and they were everywhere placed in a defensive position, advancing in the direction that our strategy dictated, and proceeding along the road to inevitable collapse. Japan was bogged down at the beginning, and finally became so hopelessly trapped in our net that she could not extricate herself.

From this we should realize that, as far as the question of

the survival or destruction of the state is concerned, the correctness or incorrectness of the policy decided upon by the Government is more important in its invisible influence than in its visible results in victory or defeat. Therefore our citizens must pay special attention to, and not for a moment neglect, the duty of obeying the state's policy and working to carry out that policy. If there is the least carelessness in carrying out the correct state policy, or if we permit it to be destroyed by those who are superficial, dishonest, or radical, then the future of the state and the nation will be one of a myriad calamities from which we will be unable to recover.

After the outbreak of the Pacific War, our War of Resistance and the World War against aggression were merged into a single giant force. The revolutionary spirit, based on right-eousness, justice, and the freedom and liberation of mankind, continuously strengthened this great force. The Joint Declaration against Aggression, signed in Washington on January 1, 1942 by the peace-loving countries of the world, was in reality the crystallization of the revolutionary spirit of mankind in its fight against tyranny. Our Nationalist Government, in accord with our already established policy, signed this declaration with the other anti-aggressor countries, and our country was recognized as one of the four Great Powers.

At that time, American and British preparations in the Pacific were inadequate, and Japanese aggression was victorious on all sides. But in the midst of this succession of triumphs, our army dealt a crushing defeat to the Japanese in the battle of Changsha, and thereby crippled them in the Chinese theater of war. In this battle, Japanese morale received a severe blow and Japan was compelled to recognize the strength of our army. The result was that on her western front she did not dare attack India after the occupation of the Malay Peninsula and Burma; on her southern front she abandoned her plan to invade the Australian mainland after the conquest of the Netherlands East Indies and the Philippines; and on her northern front she could not carry out her long-cherished plan to invade the Soviet Union after the attack on the Aleutians.

Japan's hesitation and indecision as to her future course gave Britain and the United States an opportunity to prepare their battle lines in Western Asia and the South Pacific and to strengthen the defense of North America, while Soviet Russia was able to concentrate on the war with Germany. Since November, 1942, the victories of the United Nations in all theaters of war have placed Japan in a hopeless position, surrounded on four sides, and even the Axis powers have shown their distrust of Japan because she failed to adhere to the Tripartite Pact and thereby missed a timely opportunity. It is universally recognized, however, that Japan's inability to advance on the eastern, southern, western, and northern fronts to carry out her "Great East Asia War Strategy" was due to one major obstructing force—China's War of Resistance. Thus, the status of our War of Resistance in relation to the World War, and particularly to the Pacific War, can be described without exaggeration in the words of the old saying: "An anchorage in midstream; a dike to stem the raging flood."

Because China's War of Resistance has played such an important role in world affairs, the foreign powers' understanding of our state and our nation has deepened as the war has continued. At the beginning of our war, the Great Powers assumed that it would surely be over in a short time. British and American attention was centered on the problem of how to protect their interests in China from destruction by Japan, and how to maintain their position in East Asia after the end of Chinese resistance. Germany and Italy wanted Japan to extricate herself from the Chinese war and join with them in prosecuting the World War. But when China demonstrated her determination to fight to the end, Germany and Italy had to abandon their hopes, and Britain, America, and Russia were compelled to recognize the strength of the Chinese nation. In particular, they were forced to recognize not only that China's War of Resistance represented the demand of the Chinese people for national independence and a stabilizing force in Asia, but also that it constituted a strong link in the chain of collective security that could alone ensure world peace. After the outbreak of the European War, when the Axis Powers and Japan revealed their monstrous plan to divide the world, Britain, America, and Russia began to realize that China's War of Resistance was restraining the world's most vicious aggressor, and that China had thus assumed one of the heaviest responsibilities of all the Allied nations. In other words, China's War of Resistance not only marked the beginning of opposition to aggression, but also constituted the Asiatic base for the World War against the aggressors. This has been proved by past events.

CHAPTER FIVE

CONTENTS OF THE NEW EQUAL TREATIES AND THE ESSENTIALS OF THE FUTURE WORK OF NATIONAL RECONSTRUCTION

1. The Abandonment of the Unequal Treaties and the Meaning of the New Equal Treaties

As STATED above, the Great Powers' appreciation of China deepened with the development of the War of Resistance. But to advance from this to the attainment of our major objective—the abolition of the unequal treaties—required vigorous diplomatic efforts on the part of the Nationalist Government. During the past five years, the foreign diplomacy of the Nationalist Government has been based on the spirit of nationalism and the objectives of the War of Resistance. This basic aim has never been altered, either by changes in the international situation or by internal criticism, and it has finally achieved the objective of abolishing the unequal treaties.

Let us first discuss the spirit of Chinese nationalism. China has long been a weak country because of the bondage of the unequal treaties, and she was therefore compelled to obtain international assistance in order to resist a powerful enemy. Since the beginning of the war, however, the Nationalist Government has based its policy on the ancient proverb: "one must do one's utmost," and has emphasized the principle of "salvation through self-endeavor." In five and a half years of war, the international situation has changed frequently, but the foreign policy of the Nationalist Government has remained consistent and we have never become pessimistic because of discouraging developments, or been dismayed by precarious situations. We have neither gone out of our way to make enemies, nor displayed a readiness to compromise. We have never lost an opportunity to seek help from friendly countries, but at the same time we have never lost the spirit of self-reliance.

Let us next consider the objectives of the War of Resistance. China is fighting not only for the independence of the state and the survival of the nation, but also for world peace and righteousness. At the beginning of the war, these two great objectives were definitely proclaimed. The Nationalist Government firmly believed in the indivisibility of world peace, and therefore, in the midst of disunity and discord among the Great Powers, it foresaw the inevitable formation of an international front against aggression. The Nationalist Government also believed that the righteousness of the world could not be destroyed, and therefore, during the difficulties and reverses of the Allied nations, it foresaw the inevitable defeat of the aggressor nations. [It recognized that] the independence of the Chinese state and the survival of the Chinese nation will be assured simultaneously with the restoration of justice and peace to the world and the victory of the principles of human freedom and liberty, which in turn will depend on the independence of China. Such being the objectives of the War of Resistance, the Nationalist Government pursued a foreign policy of not shirking its own responsibility or depending exclusively on foreign help, and at the same time emphasized not only the principle of "self-help" but also the principle that "to help oneself is to help others." From this it is clear that the reason why China could weather many difficulties and in the end attain a position of independence and equality among the Allied nations was not a matter of chance or luck, but was the result of great suffering and sacrifice on the part of the state and the nation.

After the incident of September 18, 1931, the Great Powers

ceased negotiations with China concerning the abolition of extraterritorial rights. In May, 1941, in an exchange of notes between China and the United States regarding the revision of the unequal treaties, the United States agreed to abolish extraterritorial rights and related special privileges, but the date for negotiations was postponed until "after the restoration of peaceful conditions." In July of the same year, China and Great Britain exchanged similar notes, and Britain agreed to abolish extraterritorial rights, return her concessions and revise her treaties in accordance with the principles of equality and mutual assistance, but the discussions were also to be postponed until "peace in the Orient has been restored." On October 10, 1942, the American and British Governments simultaneously informed our Nationalist Government of the abolition of extraterritorial rights and related special privileges in China, and announced their readiness to begin the negotiation of new treaties based upon the principles of equality and mutual benefit. On January 11, 1943, the new equal treaties between China and the United States, and China and Great Britain were signed. At that time, I told the entire country:

"Last year [1942] marked the one hundredth anniversary of the first unequal treaties with the Great Powers, concluded in the latter part of the Ch'ing dynasty. After fifty years of revolutionary struggle and five and a half years of sacrifice in the War of Resistance, our Chinese nation has transformed this painful anniversary into a glorious occasion, marking the abolition of the unequal treaties. This is not only an important milestone in the history of the revival of the Chinese nation, but is also a brilliant lighthouse erected by Britain and America to guide men's progress on the road to freedom and equality for all mankind. It is especially significant that our Allies have thus demonstrated that the present war is being fought for justice and humanity. This action on their part not only strengthens the fighting power of our Allies, but strikes a heavy blow at the morale of the aggressor nations."

[Because in the revised edition, the full text of Chiang's speech was added (see Chap. III, Section 6), this summary quotation was deleted, and the following passage substituted: "All of you should note that the significance of these two treaties lies not only in the fact that they represent greatly improved relations between China and America, and China and England, but also that they will serve as a model for all future treaties that may be concluded between our country and other free and independent nations of the world."]

These new treaties will also be a model for equal and mutually beneficial treaties between China and other free and independent nations. Furthermore, after the conclusion of the present war, China will negotiate additional treaties of friendship, commerce, navigation and consular jurisdiction, in accordance with the letter and spirit of these two treaties. Therefore, it may be said that, beginning today, the letter and the spirit of the unequal treaties of the past hundred years have been permanently abolished. [In the revised edition, the following was added to this sentence: "and the unhappy and discordant feeling between our country and others was also completely abolished, with no trace of distrust or suspicion remaining."]

The special privileges relinquished by these two treaties may be summarized as follows:

1. *Consular Jurisdiction [Extraterritoriality]*: Consular jurisdiction heretofore enjoyed by nationals or organizations of the United States and Great Britain was relinquished, and such organizations or nationals residing in Chinese territory were made subject to the jurisdiction of the Chinese Government in accordance with the principles and established practices of international law.

2. *The Legation Quarters and Garrison Areas:* The special privileges obtained by the United States and Great Britain in the Peace Treaty of 1901, such as the Legation Quarters and the right to garrison troops along the Peiping-Mukden

Railroad were relinquished. Governmental and administrative functions in the Legation Quarters, as well as all official property and obligations in these Quarters, were transferred to the Chinese Government.

3. *Concessions:* All American and British Concessions in China were relinquished. Their administration and control, and all official properties and obligations therein were transferred to the Chinese Government.

4. *Special Courts:* The United States and Great Britain relinquished the right to special courts in the International Settlement.

5. *Foreign River Pilots and Other Special Navigation Rights:* America and England relinquished their right to employ foreign pilots in Chinese ports, and the right of their warships to cruise in Chinese territorial waters. Henceforth, the visits of naval vessels between China and these two countries are to be accorded the courteous treatment prescribed by international tradition.

6. *Employment of a British Subject as Chief Commissioner of Customs:* Great Britain relinquished her right to demand that China employ a British subject as Chief Commissioner of Customs.

7. *Coastal Trade and Inland Navigation Rights:* The rights of American and British nationals to conduct coastal trade and inland navigation were relinquished.

8. *Other Matters Relating to China's Sovereignty:* Other matters affecting Chinese sovereignty that were not dealt with in these new treaties are to be settled between China and America and Britain in accordance with the generally recognized principles and practices of international law.

The campaign for tariff autonomy was successful after the Northern Expedition, and the return of judicial rights has now been achieved. Furthermore, since the relations between China and America, and China and Great Britain, have been established on a basis of equality and mutual benefit, there are no relations and no problems that cannot be settled satisfactorily. We need only compare the new treaties with the previous unequal treaties to recognize their great significance. However, there remains a certain cause for regret in connection with the conclusion of these new treaties, namely, the fact that the question of the leased territory of Kowloon, which was originally Chinese territory, was not settled in the new treaty [between China and Britain]. This leaves a stain on the cordial relations between China and England. On the day that the new Sino-British treaty was signed, however, our Government presented a formal note to England, reserving the right to recover Kowloon, which means that negotiations concerning Kowloon can be initiated at any time. What we must recognize is that there exists a definite geographical interdependence between Hong Kong and Kowloon, and that both questions must be settled at the same time. Obviously, this is the reason for the British delay. We are confident, however, that the British Government will not allow the enduring friendship between China and England to be injured on account of this tiny plot of land.

After the Russian Revolution, the Government of the Soviet Union, in the "General Settlement of Cases Pending between China and Russia" [1924], relinquished all special privileges in China. However, at that time, the Nationalist Revolutionary Government was confined to a corner of Kwangtung Province, and it was not possible to conclude a formal Sino-Soviet treaty of equality. Because of the interaction of external dangers and internal disturbances following the establishment of the Nationalist capital in Nanking, the frontier problems between China and the Soviet Union have not yet been satisfactorily settled. But now that the anti-aggression powers are successively relinquishing their special privileges in China, there is no doubt that the various problems between China and the Soviet Union will be equitably and justly settled, since relations between the two countries have been traditionally friendly.

We have already stated that the virtues of the Chinese nation include endurance, responsibility, integrity, and humility. Because of our endurance and sense of responsibility, the Chinese nation, though shackled by the unequal treaties for one hundred years, has been able to achieve a status of freedom and independence. With the determination and strength born of suffering, we have made our state at last a free and independent state, and our citizens have again become free and independent citizens. Because of our integrity and humility, the Nationalist Government regards the independent and free status achieved through the relinquishment of the unequal treaties, and China's future role in the world, not as a privilege, but as a duty and responsibility. Our nation's reaction to the abolition of the unequal treaties is not to seek material gain. The reaction of our nation is a heightened feeling of duty and an increased sense of responsibility. This is a point that I wish to explain clearly to our people.

We must recognize that the relinquishment of the unequal treaties is a preliminary step in the success of the Nationalist Revolution. During the past hundred years, the citizens of the entire country, suffering under the yoke of the unequal treaties, were unanimous in their demand that the national humiliation be avenged, and the state be made strong. Various proposals and movements, however, either failed because of differences of opinion, or collapsed because the time was not ripe, or were not supported by the people, or were eliminated because their motives were wrong. Thus some of these movements appeared on the scene for a year or less, while others lasted for three or five years. Whenever there was a change in the international situation in America or Europe, or when there was a change in the domestic politics of a foreign nation, or when a new theory or philosophy was advanced—each of these caused a disturbance in China. Only the Nationalist Revolution bases its principles on universal justice, its motives on absolute sincerity, and

its spirit on the ancient virtues of the nation. As a result, its
central organization, the Kuomintang, has been able to
unite and centralize the revolutionary elements of the entire
nation. It has been tested by fifty years of countless difficulties
and adversities, and through the development of events it
has been able to win the support of the people at home and
recognition by the foreign powers, and to attain the present
stage of its preliminary success. Viewing the future in the
light of the past, we should be even more vigilant and hard
working.

This preliminary success of the Nationalist Revolution
marks the real beginning of the work of national reconstruction. This task has two aspects, domestic and international.
From the domestic point of view, it is only after China has
attained independence and freedom that she can realize the
ideals of political and economic reconstruction. In other
words, the work of revolutionary reconstruction must progress from the realization of the principle of nationalism, to
the realization of the principles of democracy and the people's
livelihood. In regard to democracy, the activities outlined
in "A Law to Begin the Enforcement of Local Self-Government" constitute the foundation on which we must progress
from political tutelage to the establishment of constitutional
government. Moreover, we must establish China as a strong,
closely knit state in its foreign relations, so that it will not
slip back into a status of pseudo-freedom and so-called liberalism in which the state and the nation would resemble a
pan of loose sand. We must train all our citizens to exercise
their governing power, without favoring any particular class;
making Chinese politics the politics of all the people, and
not class politics. In regard to the people's livelihood, we
must continue the productive reconstruction begun during
the War of Resistance, and prepare to carry out the Industrial Plan [of Sun Yat-sen]. Production must be the work
of the entire nation, so that it will not degenerate into class
warfare, or result in an unplanned economy that would be

unable to survive in the present world of trusts and state capitalism.

Internationally, China's War of Resistance has become part of the World War against aggression. Victory in the War of Resistance and victory in the war against aggression are interrelated and inseparable. After this great war, the peace of the world and the liberation of mankind require the joint efforts of China and the Allied nations. Therefore, in addition to national reconstruction, China must be prepared to share heavy responsibilities in achieving world peace and the freedom and liberation of mankind.

2. *Future Direction of the People's Efforts and Essentials in the Work of Reconstruction*

If the people do not thoroughly fulfill their duty toward the state, the state cannot be established, the nation cannot survive, and it will be impossible for China to participate in world affairs. This is an undeniable fact. As stated in the preceding section, China's future responsibilities will be heavy, and it is obvious that the duties of the people toward the state and the world will also become heavier and more complicated each day.

"There is no easy task in the world; there is no difficult task in the world." The preliminary success of the Nationalist Revolution is the result of the unceasing struggle of the entire nation during the past hundred years, and in the bitter and prolonged War of Resistance during the past five and a half years. From this it may be seen that "there is no easy task in the world." But during the last thirty years, the Nationalist Revolution has been able to overthrow three thousand years of monarchy, three hundred years of Manchu absolutism, and even to cause the relinquishment of the most ruthless and powerful unequal treaties in the world. [Revised edition omits the phrase "most ruthless."] From this it may be seen that if our citizens combine their strength and their plans, with complete faith in the Three People's Principles, and advance along the broad road of nationalist revolution, there is nothing that cannot be accomplished.

Sun Yat-sen said: "A state is a collection of men, and a man is the instrument of the mind. State affairs are the product of the collective mind. . . . If my mind believes that it can do the work, then the removal of a mountain and the draining of a sea, though difficult, can be accomplished. If my mind does not believe it can do the work, then even so easy a task as turning the hand or breaking a twig cannot be accomplished. Mind is the root and source of all events. Success in the overthrow of the Ch'ing dynasty was a success of the mind. Failure in building up the Republic was a failure of the mind." Relinquishment of the unequal treaties today, and certain victory and success in the War of Resistance and national reconstruction in the future will also result from our faithful adherence to the wishes of the Father of our Country. Therefore it can again be said that "there is no difficult task in the world."

The principles of the Revolution are as clear as the sun and the moon in the sky. Its method and strategy have been outlined by Sun Yat-sen in detail. Its achievements have also been proved by present events. Citizens of the country need only adhere to these principles, methods, and strategy; follow the road of accomplishment; master the theories and expand their knowledge; and put their knowledge into concrete practice through energetic endeavor, in order to deal with the unprecedented changes in the world situation, and to share with all mankind the great task of reforming the world. Their ultimate success will be assured.

Thorough understanding and active endeavor must be based on absolute sincerity, free from any falsehood or dishonest conduct as well as from the slightest opportunistic motive. The ancients said: "Sincerity is accomplishment. Insincerity accomplishes nothing." What is sincerity? Sincerity means not to be false or dishonest; it means to work hard for better and better results. Without sincerity nothing in the world can be accomplished, while with absolute sincerity, there is nothing in the world that cannot be accomplished. I often say, whence does sincerity come? Briefly, "Altruism necessarily involves sincerity." The objective of our Nationalist Revolution is to destroy individual selfishness, to save the people from suffering and the state from danger—in other words, an altruistic objective. Therefore, if we wish to carry out our principles, fulfill our responsibilities as members of the human race, and seek the most satisfactory living conditions for mankind, we must base all our actions on absolute sincerity. In this way, the labor and wisdom that we contribute will be creative, constructive, and genuinely beneficial to the state and the nation, as well as truly fulfilling the purpose of our life. Hence we should determine our thinking and our revolutionary course in the light of the Three People's Principles and the philosophy of the people's livelihood, which are based on the principles of altruism and sincerity.

We should make full use of our innate virtues to develop our understanding and act with unity and determination to overcome all obstacles. We must exert ourselves to the utmost, and even if this requires us to sacrifice our lives to attain benevolence and righteousness, we must do so willingly and without fear. The ancient saying: "One should sacrifice his own life to achieve benevolence, but not covet life to injure benevolence," should be the principle of our revolutionary action. Furthermore, it is only by genuine revolutionary action that we can give meaning to the idea of creative work. This is the unique spirit of our revolutionists in carrying out the Three People's Principles for the salvation of the country and the world. In short, "sincerity" is the motivating force for all our activity. With sincerity, one knows only altruism and not selfishness. With sincerity, one works to attain benevolence, with no thought of difficulties or dangers, and with confidence in ultimate success. This is precisely what our Leader's theory of "to know is hard, but to act is easy" means when applied to the revolutionary movement.

I have already stated that the present preliminary success of the Nationalist Revolution marks the real beginning of national reconstruction. In other words, the present stage of the Nationalist Revolution marks the realization of the principle of nationalism, from which we must advance to the fulfillment of the principles of democracy and the people's livelihood. It should be remembered that the revolution's destructive operations cannot be accomplished by chance. Only by determined and unfaltering faith, accompanied by absolute sincerity and spontaneous endeavor, can ultimate success be achieved. Constructive revolutionary work requires that all citizens labor earnestly and humbly, and seek the truth through concrete endeavor. Then there will be results according to plan. Sun Yat-sen once said: "Nothing is more difficult than destruction; nothing is easier than construction." The failure of reconstruction after 1911 was due to the people's neglect of construction and their assumption that revolutionary methods were not necessary for reconstruction. We must not fall into this error again, but must make destruction and reconstruction proceed simultaneously. For reconstruction, we must apply the same spirit and the same methods adopted in the Revolution and the War of Resistance.

Sun Yat-sen divided the process of revolutionary reconstruction into three periods—Military Government, Political Tutelage, and Constitutional Government—but the fundamental task in each of these periods concerns the development of education, military affairs, and economics. These three subjects are inherently interrelated and cannot be separated. It can be said that if progress is achieved simultaneously in each of these three fields, the state will be rich and strong, while if any one of them is weak, the nation will decline. This holds true not only as the basic principle for the building of a modern state, it also accords with the history of the state building activities of China's ancient dynasties. Our present aim is to build a state based on the Three People's Principles in order to survive in the world and to carry out our responsibilities to the world. It is necessary, therefore, that we first achieve the integration of education, military affairs, and economics, before we can complete the total task of national reconstruction. We should base our educational program on the essential principles of China's Six Arts, which means training our citizens for self-defense, so that each citizen may devote his energy to production, and offer his body for national defense; and so that both his hands and his brain may be exercised, and his wisdom and virtue are practiced. In this way, we can correct once and for all the defects of lethargy, weakness, hypocrisy, and boastfulness of the past. Our economic program, based upon the independence and freedom that China has attained, must seek a balanced development of the national economy as a foundation for state planning and the people's livelihood, and must correct the past errors of piecemeal, partial, and unequal development, which undermined national defense and the people's livelihood. In the conduct of military affairs, our national defense and culture must be integrated, and national defense and the people's livelihood must be regarded as a single problem. Only in this way can China become a strong, nationalist organization for defense, able to survive in the world, and to fulfill her responsibility of safeguarding world peace and participating in the liberation of mankind.

The fundamental work of national reconstruction depends upon the integration of education, military affairs, and economics. To complete this fundamental work, it is necessary to draw up comprehensive and detailed programs along five main lines of reconstruction—psychological, ethical, social, political, and economic—and make certain that these programs are actually put into effect. In capitalist countries, politics are affected and even controlled by economics. If we desire to replace our hundred-year-old, restricted, unbalanced, semicolonial economy with a free and independent economy that will satisfy the requirements of national defense, we must employ political power to guide economic development. If we wish political reconstruction to be healthy and effective, we must have social reconstruction to provide a solid foundation for carrying out political measures. For the success of social reconstruction, the negative and passive attitude of the people in the past toward the state and the nation must be corrected. Therefore, psychological and ethical reconstruction are the starting points of all reconstruction. Only when these five lines of reconstruction have achieved results can we succeed in integrating the educational, military, and economic tasks of reconstruction.

In my booklet, *The System and Practical Program of the Three People's Principles,* I have already described in detail the principles and program of national reconstruction discussed above. Here I am going to point out the central aims in these five lines of reconstruction, and indicate certain directions for their achievement. Every adult citizen, according to his profession and position, should have a thorough understanding of one of these central aims in order to promote his work, and every young person, according to his interest and course of study, should select one of these directions as a guide to develop his abilities. Only when each and every citizen does this can the work of national reconstruction be successful and the existence of the state be safeguarded.

1. *Psychological Reconstruction.* The psychological effects of the unequal treaties upon our citizens were loss of self-confidence, servile dependence on and a blind following of others, fear of and subservience to foreigners, hypocrisy, and self-deceit, and the deterioration of China's ancient culture. Now that the unequal treaties have been abolished, all citizens should ask themselves: "Has every one of our psychological weaknesses been corrected?" If the people cannot correct these weaknesses and develop ideas of independence and

autonomy, and begin again to act as free and independent citizens, then it is inevitable that, psychologically, they will remain slaves to foreigners, and that politically they will be vassals and dependents of foreign countries.

Henceforth, therefore, the psychological reconstruction of the people should be based on the development of an independent ideology, in which the greatest emphasis must be placed on a revival of the nation's ancient culture and the cultivation of genuinely scientific knowledge. As to the nation's original culture, its essence is found in China's three far-reaching virtues of wisdom, benevolence, and courage, and the sincerity with which these virtues are put into practice. The teachings of Sun Yat-sen were based on China's ancient culture, and combined with this the most advanced theories of the world in order to formulate China's superior principles of national reconstruction. Among these teachings, his work dealing with psychological reconstruction, "Sun Yat-sen's Theory," was especially applicable to the particular disease that ailed the nation. This work is the most valuable guide for psychological reconstruction, and the movement for the development of an independent ideology should adopt it as a standard. As to scientific knowledge, we must not only adopt Western scientific methods and principles, but also sweep away the century-old habits of servile dependence and blind submission to others, and thus restore the original creative power of our nation. In short, our citizens must become actively creative, must use their own initiative, and must transform their cold lethargy into a warm enthusiasm for progress. In particular, they must transform their present attitude of passivity and depression into positive, determined, and daring action, and cultivate the ancient traditions of neatness, austerity, practical action, and earnest endeavor. Only then can we establish the psychology for revolutionary reconstruction.

The greatest responsibility for psychological reconstruction rests on primary and middle school teachers throughout the country. Because they are the guardians and tutors of the young students' morality, knowledge, and physical condition, their effect upon our future citizens is deeper and greater than that of college professors. The character of young students is not yet definitely molded; their knowledge is still scanty and easily susceptible to outside influence, like a piece of white paper that can be painted red, black, gray, or yellow. If the children are weak or unruly, then the youth will not be easily molded by state ideology and national virtues. If the young people lack self-respect and ambition, how can adults shoulder the heavy responsibility of the building up and rehabilitation of the state? Thus, order or chaos in the state, and life or death for the nation, depend upon the multitude of self-sacrificing, hard-working, "nameless heroes" that teach the primary and middle school students.

It is essential that the guardians of these young people realize that they are responsible for the life of the state; that they are sowing the seeds for the survival of the state and the independence of the nation, so that one or two generations from now there will be a continuous supply of reliable personnel at the disposal of the state. In the political and social fields, it is particularly necessary to recognize the importance of primary and middle school education; to give it special attention, encouragement and advice, so that it can develop on a basis of equality with university education in respect to finance and personnel. When primary and middle school education become more wholesome, psychological reconstruction will automatically succeed. Then the independence and freedom won in the War of Resistance will have a solid foundation, and the psychology of revolutionary reconstruction will become a reality. The young men of today who aspire to devote their lives to educational work should not despise the profession of primary or middle school teaching, but should rather regard it as a task of first magnitude in the service of the state and the rehabilitation of the nation. The greatest contribution to national reconstruction can be made by those young people that aspire to become middle or primary school teachers, particularly those that take up the basic task of primary education; that bury themselves in hard work and devote themselves to cultivating the abilities of their students; and that refrain from seeking fame, social reputation, and lofty careers. Only if there are many in this category will the psychological reconstruction of our people achieve success.

2. *Ethical Reconstruction.* The points set forth in the *Program for General Spiritual Mobilization of the People* call for the development of a spirit of belief and confidence in national reconstruction, with special emphasis on the moral requirements for national salvation. Henceforth, ethical reconstruction should take as its foundation the cultivation of the virtues required for national salvation, which need not be sought abroad. For five thousand years, we Chinese have been able to maintain the life of the nation, preserve the existence of the state, and save the nation and state from dangers, disaster, and chaos, and enable them to rise again because of these virtues of national salvation that have been accumulated and developed by the people. Therefore, to cultivate the virtues of national salvation is but to revive, expand, and glorify our original system of ethics. The most important task is to increase the emphasis on propriety and righteousness, and on the virtues of integrity, understanding, and sense of honor. These virtues are the source of the four basic principles and the eight virtues, which in turn are based on "loyalty" and "filial piety." To fulfill the principle of complete loyalty to the state and of filial piety toward the nation; to be altruistic and not seek personal advantage; to place the interests of the state ahead of those of the family; such is the highest standard of loyalty and filial piety.

We must recognize that an individual can survive and make progress only as part of a state and a nation. Thus the life of an individual depends upon the life of the state and nation. The authority of the Government should be based on the free and voluntary will of the individual. Moreover, the demands of the state and the nation should become the free and voluntary demands of individuals. To avoid or tamper with the law is, of course, not to be tolerated, and the people should not seek to avoid heavy responsibilities. Every citizen that fulfills the principles of loyalty and filial piety must dare to assume responsibility that others do not dare to assume, and must endure suffering that others cannot endure. Only then can the life of the state and nation be maintained and its future enriched and brightened. In particular, the youth of the country should stand in the front lines in time of war, should pioneer in the frontier regions for the development of the country, penetrate into the rural areas for social service, and undertake the basic tasks of the state. They must completely eliminate the present practice of loafing in the cities in peacetime, and hiding far away in the interior in time of war. Only thus can a citizen fulfill his loyalty to the state and his filial duty to the nation. The careers that the youth should follow hereafter are separately explained in this section. Here I want especially to point out one objective as a model of patriotism for our young men. Our forefathers said: "To fight without courage is not filial." In this war, none can surpass the pilots of the air corps in daring and importance. Every young man should make up his mind to be a soldier and an aviator. Then the people's three-hundred-year tradition of cowardice and downheartedness can be broken, and the lofty spirit that has characterized our nation for five thousand years can be revived. Then we can lay the foundation for a new ethics for a modern state, based on the supremacy of the state and the nation. Then we can achieve the personality of free and independent citizens, and the Chinese Republic will forever exist in the world and never again be enslaved or extinguished by any other nation.

3. *Social Reconstruction.* The New Life Movement is the basic movement for social reconstruction, and its object is to modernize the Chinese people. Only when the people are modern-

ized will they be fit to be independent and free citizens, and only then can the state be independent and free. The stimulation of the nationalist spirit and the cultivation of the nation's virtues will cease to be mere empty phrases only when they are evidenced in the daily life of all citizens. The promotion of local self-government and the reconstruction of the national economy must also be based on the daily life of the people. Thus the New Life Movement may be regarded as the combined movement of all five phases of reconstruction, and as the foundation for future social reconstruction. The most important items in its program are training for local self-government and planning for the people's recreation and education.

In regard to local self-government, we must remember that in ancient times the organization of the state began with the relation of the individual to the family; [progressed] from the family to the clan, which was held together by blood relationship; from the clan to the *pao chia*, and then to the village community, the members of which were bound together by the system of mutual assistance and joint responsibility. From the village communities, it extended to the counties and provinces, thus forming the unified organization of the Chinese state. Thus, although the form of the Chinese state was monarchical, the spirit of government of and by the people prevailed. Unfortunately, the established institutions of the village community fell into disuse during the three hundred years of the Ch'ing dynasty.[1] Since the latter part of the Ch'ing dynasty, all thought has been based on foreign theories, and the fact that the rural districts and villages constitute the foundation of the state has been forgotten. The social reconstruction of the rural districts and the towns is essential

1. On the contrary, the *pao chia* system, first introduced in the Sung dynasty, was re-established and strengthened during the Ch'ing dynasty, and was used successfully to suppress opposition to the government. Indeed, the Anhwei and Hunan militia that finally defeated the T'ai-p'ing Rebellion under the leadership of Tseng Kuo-fan (with substantial foreign aid), were largely recruited through the *pao chia* system.

for the development of local self-government. Success in re-constructing the rural districts and towns will ensure a healthy development of self-government. When local self-government is healthy, it will serve as the basis for realizing the principles of democracy and the people's livelihood.

As for measures for the recreation and education of the people, these will necessarily remain activities of the rural districts. Recreation and education, together with the four essentials of clothing, food, shelter, and employment, are the fundamental problems of the people's livelihood. Recreation and education in particular transcend material life and con-stitute the foundation of spiritual life. Universal recreation and education for the people can be achieved only by the independent initiative of the rural districts. Public welfare projects, such as nurseries, maternity centers, social clubs, and public hospitals in the rural districts must be developed by the collective planning and endeavor of the people of these districts. Only then will it be possible to create a new society in which there will be "provision for the aged, occupation for the youth, and support for the widowers, widows, child-less, orphans, cripples, and invalids."

It is clear that the responsibility for social reconstruction rests primarily on the local authorities [village councils] in the rural districts. Only these authorities can shoulder the responsibility of giving guidance to the development of local self-government and, in addition, promote the establishment of recreational and educational facilities. It is to be hoped that all those that are interested in building up the state will recognize that all forms of service to the state should include a period of service with such local authorities; they should practice the work of local self-government, and should recog-nize that the local authorities in the rural districts and the chiefs of *pao chia* constitute the basic occupations in social reconstruction. Do not linger in the metropolitan areas, and do not be lured by empty fame; live a simple and frugal life and engage in the basic work of national reconstruction.

Then each individual may lay the foundation for a life career, and the military, educational, and economic reconstruction of the state will be positively safeguarded.

4. *Political Reconstruction.* *The Program for the War of Resistance and National Reconstruction* contains concrete provisions for political reconstruction which have been carried out one by one during the past five years. But with regard to the political system and judicial and legal regulations, the people must display a spirit of initiative and spontaneous endeavor in grasping their essential points before it is possible for a political system or a legal system to become wholesome and effective. The unequal treaties have now been abrogated, and thus the spirit of initiative and spontaneity is even more essential for the citizens of a free and independent state. I have often said: "Only self-endeavor can bring freedom, and only self-reliance can bring independence." If the citizens of the state do not develop a spirit of self-endeavor and self-reliance, then there will come a day when the position of independence and freedom that we have gained will be lost. The citizens of the state are, therefore, the motivating power in political reconstruction, and the spirit of initiative and spontaneous endeavor must give reality to the foundations of political reconstruction. Only then can China's national structure become healthy, and the administration of the state increase its efficiency. Therefore, future political reconstruction should be based on a vigorous cultivation of the spirit of initiative and spontaneous endeavor, and its most basic aims must be the development of democratic institutions and the building of a strong system of national defense.

It should be noted that China's democratic system will certainly not be patterned on the nineteenth-century democratic theories of individualism and class consciousness of Europe and America. The political reconstruction of our country necessitates laying the foundation for the Five Power Constitution and a total people's government. We must not be fooled by empty slogans or by false appearances, but must proceed gradually and according to specific plans. Only then can China become a modern democracy and attain a position of equality with other nations in the international community.[2] In this connection, I hope that all young men in the country that are interested in political work will determine their objectives and shape their ambitions in accordance with the needs of the state and the trends of the times.

Under the bondage of the unequal treaties, there has been an abnormal development of a few of our metropolitan areas, which have become the centers of population and of political activity. The result is that the rural areas have been laid waste, and the frontier regions deserted, thereby causing the strength of the state to decline and inviting frequent foreign encroachments. Now that the unequal treaties have been abrogated, political planning must henceforth seek to eliminate the one-sidedness and decadence inherited from the past, so that all sections of the country will be evenly developed. The development of border regions should be the objective of the youth throughout the country in deciding upon their careers. It is to be hoped that our capable young men of fine character will revive the spirit of Ma Fu-po [Ma Yuan] and Pan Ting-yuan [Pan Chao] and direct their ambition toward the border areas, devoting their efforts to political reconstruction, submerging themselves in hard work, and becoming pioneers who employ both brawn and brain. Sun Yat-sen taught us "to set our ambition on doing big tasks, and not on being big officials." We must recognize

2. In the revised edition, reference to the Five Power Constitution is omitted, and the passage is altered to read: ". . . laying the foundation for a total people's government during the period of political tutelage. . . . Only then will the constitution to be promulgated in the constitutional period not become a mere piece of paper, and only then can China become a modern democracy. . . ." This omission of any reference to the Five Power Constitution may well be due to the fact that when the revised edition of *China's Destiny* was issued, the Draft Constitution already drawn up by the Kuomintang was the subject of vigorous criticism from all sides for its undemocratic character.

that the settlement of the border areas is a task of first importance in national reconstruction, and that the contribution of a settler in the border areas to the political reconstruction of the state far exceeds in accomplishment and value that of city workers and officials. Young men that desire to accomplish big tasks for the state and to contribute great blessings to the nation must neither look for quick results nor be impatient for immediate credit, but must decide upon this objective as their life career, in order to carry out their obligation to the state and the nation.

5. *Economic Reconstruction.* In the *Program for National Economic Reconstruction*, I have already indicated the essential elements in China's economic reconstruction. This program was based on the essence of Sun Yat-sen's "Industrial Plan" and outlined the basic tasks that must be accomplished in order that China's national economy might be adapted to the requirements of national defense. During the five and a half years of the War of Resistance, China's national economy has been moving in the direction of integrating national defense and the people's livelihood. The abolition of the unequal treaties will further enable China to employ her position of independence and freedom to advance rapidly on the road to economic independence and "rebirth through self-endeavor." Meanwhile, in relation to China's "rebirth through self-endeavor," particular emphasis must be given to industrialization. Our future economic reconstruction must be based on the development of an industrialized economy. In this program, the most important point is to prepare to put the "Industrial Plan" into effect, and thereby complete our basic policy of the equalization of land rights and the restriction of private capital. The scope of the "Industrial Plan" outlined by Sun Yat-sen far surpasses that of the Han and T'ang dynasties, and its aims are synchronized with the changing conditions in contemporary international economics. It is unquestionably the most important guide for China's

economic reconstruction. The preparatory work will naturally be difficult, and therefore all citizens, beginning today, must make up their minds to work actively in carrying it out.

In this connection, there is one point that must be called to the attention of our young people that are interested in economic affairs. The abolition of the unequal treaties has already removed the multiple bonds from China's industry. But Chinese industry from now on must progress with the greatest possible speed, before it can hope to equal the high degree of skill and centralized management that characterize the industries of the advanced nations. Therefore, our young men must aspire to become engineers, to improve their technical knowledge, and to devote themselves to the development of manufacturing industry. They should further seek creativeness and inventiveness through practical work. Only then can China's economic reconstruction be assured of success.

In summary, the scope, the plans, and the determination and ability to carry through these plans, should be derived from the lessons of China's five thousand years of history, and should be determined in the light of China's geographical environment and the evolution of the world situation. As to practical application, it should proceed from small to large-scale tasks, and from what is near at hand to what is distant, and there must be a central point of focus. It should be noted that, if there is no strong will and discipline, and no able management, the main task will be forgotten in the course of working out details. If we do not apply ourselves to immediate tasks, we will find ourselves seeking lofty and distant goals without any firm foundation for our effort. I am therefore going to emphasize the essential points in the planning and execution of the program for national reconstruction, and indicate certain directives that should serve as a guide to the youth of the country in deciding on their careers.

Heretofore, none of the plans for Chinese reconstruction

could be easily implemented because of the restrictions imposed by the unequal treaties. However, now that the bonds of the unequal treaties have been loosened, if reconstruction along various lines does not proceed rapidly, it will be the responsibility of the citizens, who are the masters of the state. If our citizens are to shoulder the responsibility for all the different phases of reconstruction, we must first ask ourselves, have we the ability? Especially should we ask ourselves, have we the confidence? Is there any type of reconstruction that does not require capable and confident personnel? Is China's present personnel capable of shouldering the responsibility for the various phases of reconstruction? Reconstruction plans and their execution must have a point of emphasis and a foundation. Of course, the five phases of reconstruction that have been described should be conducted simultaneously, each one being indispensable. But the emphasis must be placed on economics. Sun Yat-sen pointed out to us that the people's livelihood occupies a place of primary importance in reconstruction, and that the basis of the people's livelihood is economics. Economics is not only the point of emphasis, but also the prerequisite of all phases of reconstruction. Economic reconstruction on the basis of the people's livelihood stems from the principle of "enjoyment by the people" [government "for" the people]. We must adopt a planned economy and social legislation to secure the livelihood and survival of every citizen, and it is imperative that we eventually accomplish the objective of "transforming [all] capital into state capital [nationalization of capital], and transforming [all] enjoyment into enjoyment by the masses," in order to bring about a peaceful and universal revolution according to the principle of people's livelihood.

The criterion of economic reconstruction must be the "Industrial Plan" [of Sun Yat-sen]. If we want to complete the tasks assigned in the "Industrial Plan," we must first have the personnel to carry out the Plan and the material resources for its fulfillment. The following tables show the personnel and material resources needed for the first ten years of practical application of the "Industrial Plan."

TABLE I

Table of work to be accomplished during the first ten years of practical application of the "Industrial Plan." This table deals only with nine items by quantity: civil engineering [construction], machinery, electric machinery, aviation, water utilization, building, textiles, sanitation, and mining and metallurgy. Other items are omitted.

ITEMS	ULTIMATE GOAL to Fulfill "Industrial Plan"	Goal for FIRST TEN YEARS
A. Construction [Civil Engineering]		
Railroads	140,000 km.	20,000 km.
Highways	1,500,000 km.	225,570 km.
Harbors	186,000,000 tons clearance	100,000,000 tons
B. Machinery		
Locomotives	24,000	3,000
Passenger and Freight Cars	352,000	44,000
Automobiles	7,677,210	451,570
Merchant Ships	14,417,400 tons	3,043,300 tons
Power Generators	40,000,000 h.p.	10,700,000 h.p.
Tooling Machines	4,500,000	150,000
Other Machines	7,000,000	1,500,000
C. Electric Machinery		
Electric Power (IncludingHydroelectric)	20,000,000 watts	6,200,000 watts
Telegraph Lines	36,000,000 km.	36,000,000 km.[a]
Wireless Stations	3,000	3,000[b]
Receiving Sets	18,000,000	18,000,000[c]
Telephones	9,000,000	2,250,000[d]
D. Aviation		
Planes for Civil Use	120,000	12,000
E. Water Utilization		
Steamer Routes	30,000 km.	18,000 km.
Junk Routes	500,000 km.	200,000 km.
New River Steamer Routes	5,000 km.	1,000 km.
New Trade Ports	1,200	700
Dikes for Flood Prevention	18,660 km.	18,660 km.
Irrigation	250,000,000 *mow* [6 *mow* = 1 acre]	100,000,000 *mow*
Water Power	10,000,000 watts	2,000,000 watts
F. Building		
Dwelling	50,000,000	10,000,000

ITEMS	ULTIMATE GOAL to Fulfill "Industrial Plan"	Goal for FIRST TEN YEARS
G. Textiles		
Cotton Spindles [e]	10,000,000	3,000,000
Cotton Looms	320,000	96,000
Hemp Spindles [e]	277,000	83,000
Hemp Looms	15,700	4,710
Woolen Spindles [e]	580,000	174,000 [f]
Woolen Looms	16,500	4,950
Silk Spinning Machines	236,700	71,000
Silk Looms	94,000	28,200
Dyeing and Printing Machines		
Type A	114 units	34 units
Type B	280 units	84 units
Knitting Machines	16,560	4,970
Sewing Machines	300,000	90,000
H. Sanitation (Public Health)		
General Sanitation Centers	200	100
County Sanitation Centers	2,000	2,000
Village and Town Sanita- tion Centers	160,000	80,000
I. Mining and Metallurgy (Annual Output after Ten Years)		
Coal	150,000,000 tons	
Mineral Oils	1,774,000 tons	
Iron and Steel	5,560,000 tons	
Copper	25,000 tons	
Lead	13,000 tons	
Zinc	2,000 tons	
Aluminum	11,500 tons [g]	
Tungsten Ore	25,000 tons	
Pure Antimony	20,000 tons	
Tin, Refined	30,000 tons	
Mercury, Refined	500 tons	

[a] In the revised edition, the ten-year goal for telegraph lines is reduced to 9,000,000 km.

[b] In the revised edition, the ten-year goal for wireless stations is reduced to 2,000.

[e] In the revised edition, the ten-year goal for receiving sets is reduced to 4,500,000.

[d] No figures for telephones were given in the first edition.

[e] Some take this to mean bales of cotton thread; similarly with hemp and wool.

[f] In the revised edition, the ten-year goal has been increased to 420,000, of which 274,000 are for foreign style woolen cloth, and 146,000 for beiges.

[g] In the revised edition, the annual output of aluminum after ten years is raised to 55,500 tons.

[In the first edition of *China's Destiny,* no figures were given for production of chemicals. The revised edition gives the

following figures for the annual output of basic chemicals and
other chemical products to be achieved after ten years:]

Sulphuric Acid	2,500,000 tons
Nitric Acid	100,000 tons
Hydrochloric Acid	150,000 tons
Pure Soda	1,230,000 tons
Caustic Soda	625,000 tons
Motor Car Tires	2,000,000
Paper	2,000,000 tons
Cement	63,850,000 tons
Glass	1,500,000 tons
Salt	3,750,000 tons
Sugar	1,500,000 tons
Essential Chemicals	100 kinds

[An even more remarkable omission in the first edition of
China's Destiny was the absence of any figures on agricultural
production. The revised edition gives the following figures as
the goal for agricultural output at the completion of the first
ten-year plan:]

Rice	756,000,000 *shih tan* [Chinese bushel—1 *shih tan* equals 100 liters, or 2.8378 American bushels].
Wheat	882,000,000 *shih tan*
Miscellaneous Foods	1,003,000,000 *shih tan*
Beans	686,000,000 *shih tan*
Cotton	23,000,000 *shih tan*
Hemp	2,000,000 *shih tan*
Wool	1,680,000 *shih tan*
Raw Silk	300,000 *shih tan*
Timber	42,500,000 cubic feet

TABLE II

Table of Personnel of all grades required during the first ten years of practical
application of the "Industrial Plan." This table includes the personnel required
in seventeen categories: railways, highways, aviation, water utilization, locomotives, automobiles, electrical power, mining and metallurgy, harbors and
ports, telecommunications, merchant marine, food industry, clothing, housing,
public health, machinery, and printing.

A. Number of university and technical school graduates:

	First Edition	Revised Edition
Civil Engineering	110,000	90,000
Mechanical Engineering	41,900	same

	First Edition	Revised Edition
Electrical Engineering	12,400	13,700
Mining and Metallurgy	8,600	same
Hydraulic Engineering	12,000	same
Architecture	25,000	same
Chemical Engineering	7,200	19,800
Textile and Dyeing	3,600	same
Navigation	7,000	same
Aeronautical Engineering	7,200	same
Geology and Geography	2,400	same
Medicine	232,500	same
Arts and Sciences, Law, Commerce, Economics, etc.	31,000	same
Agriculture	No figures given	55,500

B. Number of graduates from higher or junior grade vocational school courses:

	First Edition	Revised Edition
Civil Engineering	77,500	131,700
Mechanical Engineering	94,500	same
Electrical Engineering	20,400	27,900
Mining and Metallurgy	23,300	same
Telecommunications	41,200	40,000
Aeronautics	12,000	same
Hydraulic Engineering	25,000	same
Architecture	25,000	same
Chemical Engineering	8,100	30,500
Textile and Dyeing	8,200	same
Printing	17,000	same
Agriculture	—	107,000
C. Graduates from Aviation Schools	43,200	18,000
D. Graduates from General Courses in Senior Middle Schools and Higher Vocational Schools	103,400	same
E. Graduates from Junior Middle Schools and Lower Vocational Schools	186,600	same
F. Graduates of Senior and Junior Schools of Medicine, Pharmacy, and Nursing	1,070,000	same
G. Graduates of Midwifery Schools	225,000	same
TOTAL (of All Categories A–G)	2,481,200	2,704,300

TABLE III

Table showing quantities of principal raw materials required during the first ten years of practical application of the "Industrial Plan." Based on the needs of the following categories of development: railways, highways, locomotives, automobiles, aviation, water utilization, merchant marine, electric power, telecommunications, housing, household utensils, and machinery.

	First Edition	Revised Edition
Iron	7,992,000 tons	9,007,000 tons
Steel	25,883,000 tons	28,466,000 tons

	First Edition	*Revised Edition*
Copper	1,080,000 tons	1,381,000 tons
Lead	1,119,500 tons	1,416,000 tons
Zinc	541,000 tons	542,000 tons
Coal	505,505,000 tons	515,881,000 tons
Gasoline	13,134,200 tons	13,879,000 tons
Fuel Oil	24,824,400 tons	28,815,000 tons
Lubricating Oil	1,073,000 tons	1,184,000 tons
Asphalt	288,000 tons	751,000 tons
Paints and Varnish	283,400 tons	308,000 tons
Cement	56,546,000 tons	70,734,000 tons
Glass	1,977,500 tons	2,736,000 tons
	146,900,600 sq. meters	
	3,390 cu. meters	
Crude Rubber	53,700 tons	no figure given
Rubber Tires	2,709,420	2,710,000
Lumber	39,200,000 pieces	
	245,000 tons	
	494,280,000 cu. meters	511,746,000 cu. meters

The completion of the "Industrial Plan" will require a period of from thirty to fifty years. The above tables list only the work, personnel, and materials required during the first ten years. A first glance at these figures may lead some people to think them too large, and the proposed projects too difficult to accomplish. These figures, however, when compared with China's four hundred and fifty million people and her area of over one billion square kilometers, are in reality too small rather than too large. Take cotton looms, for example: Even when we have fulfilled our quota in this category, production will be only sixteen meters of cotton goods per capita per year, and the quota to be achieved during the first ten year period will be only about ten per cent of that amount, which means only an average of 1.6 meters a year for each person.[3] Again, take automobiles. The complete quota will mean one car for every one hundred and fifty persons, and after the first ten-year period, only ten per cent will be available, or only one car for each fifteen hundred persons. As for personnel, it is certainly not a large number for a population of four hundred

3. This percentage does not correspond with the figures given in the preceding tables where the ten-year goal for cotton looms is given as thirty per cent of the total goal.

and fifty million to supply 2,460,000[4] graduates of various grades of schools in ten years.

Take all the officers in the army at present, for example. Those that have received a general or higher education and are qualified as full-fledged administrators number over five hundred thousand. With a short period of special training after demobilization, these officers would readily become the personnel framework for economic reconstruction. We need only consider this one fact to be convinced that we possess an abundance of personnel, and that what is required is only confidence to carry on with vigor, and all phases of reconstruction will be successful. If our citizens should still be bound by old habits, with the feeling that "it is hard to succeed," it will be due to the lack of a firm grasp of Sun Yat-sen's doctrine that "to act is easy," and the effectiveness of vigorous effort. Three thousand years of monarchical government, three hundred years of Manchu absolutism, and, even worse, one hundred years of unequal treaties, have been overthrown by our people as a result of common confidence and unified effort. If we apply the same confidence to carrying out the "Industrial Plan," there is absolutely no reason for failure.

Comparing China with Japan, I am going to quote a part of Sun Yat-sen's conversation with me on the battlefield of San Ho Pa in the seventh year of the Republic [1918] to prove that the Plan will surely succeed. Dr. Sun said: "Japan's population and territory are eight to ten times smaller than China's; therefore, a project that takes Japan eight to ten years to finish would require only one or two years in China." If we are true disciples of Sun Yat-sen, with faith in his superb words and brilliant theories, why should we be hesitant and afraid of difficulties? The failure of China's efforts to build up the state in the past was due to the bondage and oppression of the unequal treaties. Now that the unequal treaties have been abolished, we need only exert all our

4. Actual total, as given in first edition, 2,481,200.

efforts, and it is my belief that the ten-year plan described in the above tables will not fail because the goals are too large, but rather that these minimum goals will be overfulfilled. If the past experience of other countries is taken into consideration, plus the fact that railways and highways were constructed in the midst of internal troubles and external encroachments during the ten years after the inauguration of our Nationalist Government, then my estimate would be that it will not be surprising if the quotas for railways, highways, aviation, harbor construction, dikes, irrigation, and electric power will be fulfilled by more than one hundred per cent. [Revised edition adds: "And when the reconstruction of the first period shows results, the wealth and power of the people will be increased, improving the power and speed of succeeding periods and enabling the entire program of the "Industrial Plan" to be finished ahead of time."]

As to personnel, the carrying out of the "Industrial Plan" requires the number of college, middle, and other school graduates listed above. Are our present schools sufficient to train such personnel to supply the needs of economic reconstruction? Take our present colleges, technical schools, and senior and junior middle schools. In the five years from 1936 to 1941, graduates from all these schools numbered only 471,739, whereas in the first ten years of the "Industrial Plan" it will require 2,460,000 [revised edition: 2,700,000] excluding those not required for the "Industrial Plan." [In the revised edition, the following was added: "Moreover, mechanical and civil engineering, mining and metallurgy, medicine, and other applied sciences cannot be thoroughly mastered without physics, biology, mathematics, and other natural sciences as their basis. Therefore, beside the training of industrial personnel, the schools must also emphasize natural sciences to provide the basis for applied science."] We must, therefore, in the remaining years of the war, speed up the strengthening of education and expand the schools, in order fully to prepare for adequate personnel. It may be noted here that after the War of Resistance, anyone who has but a single skill will not have to worry about lack of opportunity to offer his ability for the work of building up the state. It should further be noted that persons engaged in all kinds of national reconstruction work should each do the work of two people and each day perform the work of two days, before they can meet the requirements of the state and society. An ancient philosopher said: "Think of emulating the wise man whom you see." A proverb says: "It is better to go home and make a net than to stand by the water to admire the fish."

We have observed the wealth and might of other nations. We must then exert ourselves heroically to make the Republic of China just as wealthy and mighty, and furthermore, to make our people's livelihood even more healthy and happy. In regard to the people's welfare in China's plan of economic reconstruction, we must reach the standard set in the second article of the *Program of National Reconstruction*, drawn up personally by Sun Yat-sen, which reads: "People's livelihood occupies the place of primary importance in reconstruction. In regard to the four great requirements of food, clothing, shelter, and movement for the people of the entire country, the Government should endeavor, in co-operation with the people, to develop agriculture to provide sufficient food for the people, to develop textiles to provide sufficient clothing for the people, to construct large-scale housing to provide the people with comfortable dwellings, and to keep roads and canals in good condition to facilitate the people's movement." This is the primary aim of reconstruction, as well as the first step in realizing the principle of people's livelihood. Since the Republic of China is going to build such a wealthy, mighty, healthy, and happy state, everyone of our citizens should feel that time is too short. Only when a man does not neglect his own duty will he be protected by the state, and only when he exerts himself fully can he urge his countrymen to common endeavor. Therefore, I earnestly expect the citizens of the entire country, each to be self-reliant, to strengthen himself, and to stimulate his fellows to common endeavor. Especially, I hope that the youth of the country will decide on their life careers, hold fast to their determination, and fix their eyes on the objective, and devote themselves to reconstruction in order to fulfill the mission of building up the state—an opportunity that occurs only once in a thousand years.

CHAPTER SIX

FUNDAMENTAL PROBLEMS OF REVOLUTIONARY NATIONAL RECONSTRUCTION

1. The Problem of Establishing a Philosophy of Revolution and Reconstruction

TODAY, with the preliminary success in the Nationalist Revolution and the commencement of national reconstruction, citizens may fall into the errors of "arrogant self-indulgence," and "contentment with a little gain" in regard to the attainment of independence and freedom for the state on the one hand, and on the other, into a psychology of "turning away for fear of difficulties" and "avoiding the heavy and choosing the easy task" in regard to the necessary tasks of the future. I have clearly explained these two problems in the previous chapter. In this chapter I am going to point out several basic problems in building up the state, which are the key to its success or failure, in the hope of arousing the vigilance of our citizens as well as encouraging them. The first things to be pointed out are the lessons from the successes and failures of the Revolution of 1911. If our citizens can absorb these important lessons, the work of national reconstruction will certainly be successful.

We all know that the Revolution of 1911, in a very short period, completely overthrew more than three thousand years of monarchical government and two hundred and sixty years of Manchu absolutism. Thereafter, Yuan Shih-k'ai's monarchic rule and Chang Hsun's restoration of the Manchu throne both ended in failure. From this it would appear that the Revolution was extremely successful. But in the ten years or more after the 1911 Revolution, though the opportunity of the World War was at hand, China was not only unable to become self-reliant and strong, but on the contrary, external encroachments greatly increased and the internal situation grew worse. Must we not then consider the Revolution as a failure? As far as the success of the Revolution was concerned, it was only a success in destruction, while the failure was a failure in construction. That the destructive revolution could be successful was due to the fact that the citizens were heart and soul in opposition to the autocratic Manchu Government, which had been undermining the national sovereignty and humiliating the state. The failure in the constructive revolution was due to the citizens' lack of a clear understanding that revolutionary reconstruction and destruction should proceed together; and even when there was such an understanding there was no unanimity. Thus, as soon as the Revolution of 1911 succeeded [in overthrowing the Manchus], the citizens were misled by the saying that "the success of the revolutionary army means the disappearance of the revolutionary party," and assumed that no revolutionary action was required for reconstruction. This was true not only of the citizens, but also of comrades in the Revolutionary Party. As a result, the warlords and politicians did as they pleased. First, they used the provisional constitution as a mask [to cloak their activities] and then they wrecked it; first they organized political parties and then partitioned the country and became self-appointed regional potentates. During this period of great opportunity for the state and the nation, they lived a life of lethargy, fratricide, and self-destruction. No punishment would be adequate for their sins in ruining and betraying the state. But citizens, especially the intelligentsia, the writers and scholars—oppressed by the warlords on the one hand and confused by the anti-revolutionary propaganda of the imperialists on the other—were unable to understand the aims of the Father of our Country or to have faith in the Three People's Principles. Their attitude toward the Kuomintang was either that of an apathetic bystander or of an active antagonist, and they were unable to recognize the inseparable relationship between the Kuomintang and the life of the state and the people. They should therefore shoulder a very large part of the blame. That was why Sun Yat-sen saw that the basis of the success of the revolution lay in the psychological reconstruction of the people. The essence of psychological reconstruction is to impart the doctrine that "to know is difficult but to act is easy" to all party comrades and to the people in general.

The reason for the success of the destructive part and the failure of the constructive part of the 1911 Revolution was entirely due, as pointed out by Sun Yat-sen, to the people's "knowledge" or "lack of knowledge." He said: "What is the reason for the success of the destructive revolution and the failure of the constructive revolution? It was caused by 'knowledge' and 'lack of knowledge.' In the revolution for destruction, I started ten times and failed ten times, because the majority of the people in China at that time did not know that they had been conquered by the Manchus and thus, in their apathy, they regarded the Revolution as a serious crime. As the revolutionary movement subsequently spread, more and more people realized the necessity of overthrowing the Ch'ing Government and rehabilitating the Han [Chinese] nation, and thereupon they rose and overthrew the Ch'ing dynasty with great ease. They did not know anything about constructive revolution, however, and even the revolutionary party did not know what it was all about. Yet the hardest part in revolutionary work is destruction and the easiest is construction. Why should it be that though the difficult part was accomplished, yet the easy part failed? Because it was easy, the people did not realize the necessity for it and neglected it, thereby causing its failure. Why should it be called easy? Because the completion of destruction meant the disappearance of the forces of resistance, after which nothing was impossible and the people were free to act. That situation was worlds apart from the period of plotting destruction, when the least negligence would be followed by unpredictable disaster. When we knew that the revolutionary overthrow of the Ch'ing dynasty was necessary to save the nation, we challenged difficulty and defied danger to do it. Subsequent to the accomplishment of destruction, construction was regarded as easy and safe—work that could be done in many different ways without necessarily employing revolutionary methods. That is why the work of construction failed."

How thoroughly and how correctly does this statement point out the reasons for the success and the failure of the 1911 Revolution! Unfortunately, the party comrades of that day and the people in general did not fully understand. This was because our people had been seriously harmed by the old precept that "to know is not difficult but to act is difficult," and did not know the philosophical truth that "to act is not difficult, but to know is difficult." Sun Yat-sen said: "This theory was deeply implanted in the minds of the scholars, who spread it among the people, so that the difficult was regarded as easy, while the easy was considered difficult. This caused a decadent China, reluctant to face difficulties, to fear what should not have been feared, and not to fear what should have been feared. Therefore, the people neglected and avoided the easy, and rushed to the difficult. They at first sought knowledge in order to act, but when they could not obtain the knowledge, they became despondent and gave up everything in despair. Occasionally there were some courageous people who spent their whole lives to acquire one item of knowledge, but assumed that it would be even harder to act upon it, so they did not dare to act despite their knowledge. As a result, those who had no knowledge naturally would not act, and even those who had knowledge still did not dare to act. Thus nothing could be accomplished. That is the reason why China became increasingly weak and decadent."

After the 1911 Revolution, the people and party comrades

in general did not realize the necessity of construction nor that construction must be carried on by revolutionary means. Though they had Sun Yat-sen's knowledge as their guide, they still assumed that to know was easy and to act was difficult. They neglected reconstruction, and especially could not understand the doctrine of the people's livelihood. They were contented with the mere form of nationalism and democracy, and thus the constructive revolution failed.

The old saying: "To know is not difficult, but to act is difficult," was not the traditional psychology of China. [In the revised edition, this sentence was altered to read: ". . . was not a fine and profound philosophy of China."] Everybody in society acts according to the laws of nature, but very few understand these laws. Therefore, Confucius said: "The people may be made to follow a course of action, but they must not be expected to understand." Those who understand, of course, act according to the laws of nature, but those who do not understand also follow the laws of nature in their actions. Therefore, Mencius said: "There are many people that act according to the Way [truth] without noticing it, repeat their action without examining it, and follow the Way all their lives without knowing it." The "Doctrine of the Mean" said: "The Way of the superior man is extensive yet subtle; the unintelligent man and woman can share in the knowledge of it, but in its utmost reaches there is that which even the sage does not know. The common man and woman can carry it into practice; but in its utmost reaches, there is that of which even the sage is incapable." It is sufficient to note that it is easy to act in accordance with the laws followed by all things in the universe, but difficult to understand these laws.

The knowledge of the ancients came from generations of experience and lifelong endeavor. Thus I often say: "There can be no knowledge without action." Only the knowledge gained from endeavor is true knowledge; only with true knowledge is it easy to act. Confucius taught the people the

Six Arts, and expected his disciples to acquire true knowledge by practicing those Six Arts. Cleanliness, correct behavior, archery, chariot riding, writing, and arithmetic—all may enable the student to acquire true knowledge by progressing from learning to higher comprehension. Students in later generations looked upon true knowledge, gained by the ancients through generations of experience and lifelong endeavor, as an easy matter. They therefore assumed that it was easy to know and difficult to act. The old saying: "To know is not difficult, but to act is difficult" has as a consequence been deeply implanted in men's minds, resulting in the separation of knowledge and action, and the habit of considering the easy task difficult, and the difficult task easy. Wang Yang-ming's theory of the "oneness of knowledge and action" was intended to correct the spread of this evil of the separation of knowledge and action. But in a scientific age, the philosophy of the identity of knowledge and action is not sufficient as a guiding principle of man's life. According to scientific methods, each man's work must follow the principles of division of labor and specialization of duty. Though those that know and those that act should co-operate, there should still be a division of labor. Therefore only Sun Yat-sen's theory that "to know is difficult but to act is easy" constitutes a true guiding principle for man's life.[1]

The source of knowledge lies in human nature and does not have to be sought from outside. Speaking superficially, in seeking knowledge we must accept the experience and teachings of the Chinese people and study foreign science and

1. There would seem to be an excessive amount of space devoted to this simple concept of the importance of action with or without full understanding. One can only conclude that the author is going to extreme lengths to induce the Chinese people to follow blindly and unquestioningly wherever the Kuomintang hierarchy may choose to lead them. Moreover, Sun Yat-sen wrote at a time when the people of China were dulled into inactivity by decadent court scholars and bureaucrats. That situation is a far cry from today when the Chinese people are politically more awakened than ever before, and are only prevented from building up a genuinely modern state by the oppressive dead weight of an outmoded Kuomintang bureaucracy.

techniques. But in substance, knowledge that is not "self-acquired" cannot be considered as true knowledge. Only "self-acquired" knowledge is true knowledge, and not only is it true knowledge, but also it is easy to practice. Why did the heroes of the Revolution, at the end of the Ch'ing dynasty and the beginning of the Republic, go through fire and boiling water, and regard death as an eternal jest? Since they deeply believed that only revolution could save the state and the people, they energetically practiced revolutionary work with no thought of life or death, honor or disgrace. It was only because their "knowledge" was based on their nature [instinct or character], and their "action" emerged from true knowledge, that they were able to accomplish the great task of overthrowing more than three thousand years of monarchy and more than two hundred and sixty years of Manchu absolutism. After the 1911 Revolution, why could not the party comrades and the people in general continue the accomplishments of our martyrs and accept the guidance of Sun Yat-sen? Because their theories and contentions were merely picked up here and there, copied from what others had said, and were not "self-acquired." Their "knowledge" did not come from complete sincerity, and their "actions" did not come from great courage. Therefore, after the first year of the Republic, society and government were in a state of conflict and confusion for more than ten years. The actions of the warlords, who mismanaged the state and oppressed the people, together with those of the counter-revolutionary cliques, became unbridled and ruthless.

Why were the people still unable to recognize the correct course to be followed after it had been definitely established by past events? The reason was that, from the theoretical point of view, they were neither able to "seek the truth through actual practice" in searching for genuine knowledge, nor to rid themselves of prejudices and admit the truth already proven by events. From the point of view of action, they were unable to free themselves from the habit of pretending to be right while actually being wrong, nor could they follow the guidance of those with real knowledge, and act with energy and decisiveness. In general, theoretical incorrectness was due to the inability to know thoroughly, while the lack of effectiveness in action was due to the inability to act vigorously. Only with the utmost sincerity can one be free from falsity and achieve true knowledge; only with the utmost sincerity can one ceaselessly devote oneself to energetic action. Only with true knowledge and energetic action can one march straight forward without hesitation. The "Doctrine of the Mean" said: "Without sincerity there is nothing." If the psychology of the people and the habits of society do not return to purity, reality, and sincerity, the work of national reconstruction and rehabilitation cannot be successful. Therefore, after the Revolution of 1911, during the period of greatest difficulty and depravity, Sun Yat-sen instructed our comrades and taught the people that the theory, "to act is easy but to know is difficult," is the permanent, basic philosophy for state building and rehabilitation through nationalist revolution. Hereafter, the success or failure of national reconstruction hinges upon whether or not our citizens can comprehend this philosophy. The citizens of the entire country need only to accept the lessons of the Revolution of 1911, understand Sun Yat-sen's philosophy of "to act is easy," and work vigorously in unity. Then the great task of the state, which is the integration of culture, national defense, and economy through the completion of the five phases of reconstruction, will certainly be accomplished according to schedule.

2. The Problem of Reforming Social and Academic Traditions

Previously, the work of national reconstruction could not, under the restrictions of the unequal treaties, be developed freely. But now that the unequal treaties have been abolished and independence and freedom achieved, any failure in the work of national reconstruction will be the responsibility of the citizens of the entire country. [This paragraph was omitted in the revised edition.]

Order or chaos in a state, and the rise or fall of a nation generally depend upon changes in social customs. The influence of the unequal treaties on our social customs had its root in the concessions and was manifested in various kinds of evil and decadent habits. Now that the unequal treaties have been abrogated, and the concessions are no longer in existence, in whose hands will the responsibility for changing social customs lie? If the present social customs are not changed, and if there is not a spirit of earnest endeavor, then the work of national reconstruction will be difficult to complete. Changes in social customs are usually dependent upon the efforts of a few great statesmen and educators. This has been so in history. But the emergence of these few leaders is certainly not attributable to a miracle or to fate. If, at the turning point between order and chaos in the state, and the rise or fall of the nation, there are a few people that are convinced that the rise or decline of the world is the responsibility of every individual; that take the attitude, "to worry before the world worries, and to enjoy after the world enjoys," together with the concept that "the world belongs to all"; that believe that the salvation of the state and the people is their responsibility—they will be the focal point of changes in social customs.

Mencius said: "Every man can be a Yao or a Shun [a sage]." Again he said: "Those that wait for Wen Wang [King of the Chou dynasty] to rise again are ordinary persons; heroes will rise up without waiting for a Wen Wang." These statements show that once the duty of saving the state and the people has been recognized, if we take it as our own responsibility, and proceed to act vigorously and earnestly in accordance with our own ability and intelligence, then social customs will be changed. Sun Yat-sen said: "Those with the greatest intelligence and ability should do their best to render service to millions; those with lesser intelligence and ability should do their best to render service to one person." Regardless of the extent of intelligence or ability, if only there is devotion to the salvation of the people and the state, accompanied by vigorous endeavor, then its application to a single village will change the social customs of that village; its application to a county will change the customs of the county; and if extended to the state as a whole, the result will be the same. Those few persons need only to take the lead in vigorous action and the mass of the people of a village, county, or the entire country will follow their lead as unconsciously and as naturally as grass bends before the wind. Social customs will thus be successfully reorganized.

At every period when the rise or fall, the survival or destruction of the nation has hung in the balance, there have always been a few great statesmen and educators that rose to take the responsibility of reforming social customs. Toward the end of the Eastern Han dynasty, powerful officials and large landlords annexed land, breaking up poor households and depriving the weak of their means of livelihood. The ideology of the time tended toward Taoism and Buddhism, and the literature toward frivolity. With the Rebellion of the Yellow Turban, the Central Plains were devastated, the warlords set up rival governments, and only the region of Shu [Szechwan] on the border of the country was stabilized. Because of the extravagant customs and unruliness of powerful warlords, the situation was even worse than in the period of the Eastern Han.

Chu-ko Liang, premier during two reigns for a period of twelve years, adopted a military policy of defense through attacks [upon the enemy], and an administrative policy that combined tolerance with severity. He stimulated the people's morale through expeditions against the usurper [the Wei Empire] to wipe out the humiliation [of the Han dynasty], and corrected the customs of frivolity and lack of discipline by demanding that the officials act in accordance with their titles. He was therefore able, from the regions of Pa and Shu, which constituted only a corner of China, to resist the Wei Empire of Ts'ao Ts'ao which was then in full control of the Central Plains. [Confucian] scholars of later generations ridiculed him for promoting government by law. It was ignored, however, that Chu-ko Liang's personality was one of simplicity, tranquillity, great altruism, and utmost sincerity, and that his character was far superior to that of these scholars. Division and chaotic rivalry prevailed for more than two hundred years during the latter period of the T'ang and the Five dynasties. Though a unified regime was achieved by the Sung dynasty, through taking over the military power of the feudatory garrison districts, the ideology tended toward Buddhism, the literature was restricted to the style of parallel construction, the literary examinations were confined to commentaries on the Confucian classics, the administrative functions were controlled by clerks [palace underlings], the economy was characterized by extension of landed estates through expropriation, and military power was concentrated in the capital, while the frontiers were indifferently garrisoned, resulting in foreign encroachments and frequent internal revolts.

Fan Chung-yen first wrote the "Four Essays" to correct decadent thinking, and followed these with a memorial [to the Emperor] on "Ten Affairs," proposing the establishment of schools to train economic, administrative, and fiscal personnel, and the reform of the civil service examinations in order to select economists and administrators. In literature at that time, there were men of the type of Ou-yang Hsiu and Su Shih; in classical studies, there were men of the type of Hu Yuan and Sun Fu—men of ability came forward in great numbers, culminating in the establishment of new social customs. The school of reason of Chang Tsai, Ch'eng I-ch'uan, and Ch'eng Ming-tao, and the new administrative program of Wang Ching-kung arose and flourished in succession. Toward the end of the Ming dynasty, the court and the government were under the control of eunuchs, and society became more and more frivolous. The school of Chu Hsi became too eclectic, while Wang Shou-jen's [Wang Yang-ming] school gradually tended toward mysticism and nihilism. Chang Chu-cheng, premier for fourteen years, advocated "practical learning for practical use," reformed official administration by demanding "practice in accordance with titles," and remedied the people's customs by insisting on a "return to fundamentals." The strength of his conviction, the earnestness of his devotion, and the courage of his action, together with his indifference to personal success or failure, and disregard for temporary criticism or praise, surpassed the qualities of Chu-ko Liang and Fan Chung-yen.

During the reigns of Tao Kuang and Hsien Feng in the Ch'ing dynasty, Tseng Kuo-fan, Hu Lin-I, Tsao Tsung-t'ang, Li Hung-chang, and their like also regarded the reform of social customs as their personal responsibility. Tseng Kuo-fan advocated strict enforcement of the law, and in selecting personnel, he preferred men of righteous indignation [literally "hot-blooded"] and talented comprehension. In regard to scholarship and thought, he adopted the teachings of both the Sung and Han periods and restored them to the basis of utmost sincerity. As for his personal conduct and public duties, he based them on the spirit of "moral caution in solitude, respectfulness as the leading [quality], benevolence to be sought after, and diligence to be practiced." Thus the success of the Hunan and Honan armies was not accidental.[2]

2. The "success of the Hunan and Honan armies" refers to the suppression of the T'ai-p'ing Rebellion (1850–63), a great peasant rebellion stimulated by the intolerable economic conditions of the farmers and precipitated by imperialist penetration. The T'ai-p'ings swept northward from Kiangsu and established their power in the Yangtze Valley for a period of eleven years. The land policy of the T'ai-p'ings involved the seizure of large landholdings for division among the farmer-cultivators. The chief Chinese leaders against the T'ai-p'ings were Tseng Kuo-fan, representative of the landed interests, and Li Hung-chang, leader of the new comprador class. They succeeded in preserving the Manchu dynasty only because of Western military and naval aid, their most effective troops being mercenaries trained and led by such men as Frederick Townsend Ward

The transformation of social customs by thinkers in Chinese history has had very great effects on the rise or decline of our inherent culture and the spirit of the nation. During the early period of the Warring States, the ideas of individualism and utilitarianism [profit-seeking] prevailed; "the teachings of Yang Chu and Mo Ti filled the world" and "the world rallied either to Mo or to Yang." Mencius arose and distinguished propriety from utility, and Kingly Ways [conversion by virtue] from domination by force, according to the teachings of Confucius. He clarified the theories of "comprehension of words" and "nourishing the vital spirit," and he explained and developed man's natural sympathies, sense of shame, deference to others, and distinction between right and wrong, as the origins of benevolence, propriety, courtesy, and wisdom, to stress the difference between man and beast. He denounced Yang and Mo to correct the people's thinking. And he thereby established the foundation of China's three thousand years of orthodox ideology.

Subsequent to the declining years of the Eastern Han dynasty, the teachings of Buddha and Lao-tzu flourished, and those of the Confucian scholars were in eclipse. Wang Ch'ung lectured in the vicinity of the Yellow and Fen rivers, condemning the schools of Buddhism and Taoism, and differentiating strictly between the Hsia [Chinese] and the Yi [barbarian, alien] teachings, so that the grandeur of the political system and the flourishing state of studies at the beginning of the T'ang dynasty were also the result of his influence. In the middle of the T'ang dynasty, Han Yu reformed literary style, denounced Buddhism and Taoism, condemned the partition of the country by warlords, and

---

and the British General Charles George "Chinese" Gordon. All students of Chinese history regard the T'ai-p'ing Rebellion as a genuine popular movement and as the forerunner of the Nationalist Revolutionary movement led by Sun Yat-sen. It is indicative of the author's approach to Chinese problems that the social and economic significance of the T'ai-p'ing movement should be disparaged, and that Tseng Kuo-fan should be praised as a great "Confucian" statesman, although he is regarded by liberal Chinese as the arch betrayer of the Chinese people.

advocated centralized power, thereby paving the way for the Confucian school of Tao [the Way] of the Northern Sung dynasty. With the spread of the [Confucian] Tao School, scholars became used to nihilistic concepts of nature and reason, and were shackled by eclectic terminology, so that Wang Yang-ming championed his theories of the oneness of knowledge and action, and the expansion of knowledge by exhausting reason, which gained wide acceptance. By the end of the Ming dynasty, and the beginning of the Ch'ing, the great [Confucian] scholars such as Ku Ting-lin, Huang Li-chou, Wang Ch'uan-shan, Li Ehr-chu, Yen Hsi-chai, and Fu Ch'ing-chu became prominent and all of them condemned mystic nihilism, and advocated practical application, urging the study of economics and administration to save the nation, and the study of human nature and endowment as a guide to thinking. From this time on, nationalist and democratic ideas spread among the people, and after more than two hundred years came the Revolution of 1911, which overthrew the despotic government of the Manchus and established the Republican People's State.

These statesmen and thinkers all made their enduring contribution to the preservation and cultivation of the nationalist spirit of China, and the strengthening of her inherent virtues. They are our models for the reconstruction of the state and the salvation of the world. It is this group that Sun Yat-sen described as "using their few score years of life to establish the immortal foundation of our state." Those of talent and intelligence that wish to emulate these statesmen and thinkers should start with "exhausting reason" and "comprehension of words." What we revolutionists should constantly bear in mind is that regardless of the size of the task we are performing, we should examine it in accordance with the doctrine of "exhausting reason." We should also, with respect to the theories and contentions that are brought to our attention, examine them carefully in accordance with the doctrine of "comprehension of words." "Exhausting reason" means that we should have a clear grasp of realities, analyze the contents of an event, and firmly grasp the focal point of a problem without hesitation or error. "Comprehension of words" means that we should examine the motive, understand the meaning, study the method, and seek factual verification of the results of every theory or contention, without ambiguity or blind acceptance. By so doing, no matter how confused the various arguments, or how ingenious the phraseology, we will be able clearly to determine their truthfulness and merits or lack of them, and whether they will yield benefits or harm, success or failure. We should bear in mind particularly that where theories or proposals are harmful to the state and the nation, the greater the harm, the more ingenious the arguments put forward in support of these theories.

Confucius, seven days after becoming chief justice of Lu, put Shao-cheng Mou to death, and explained: "There are five kinds of evil people in the world and thieves and robbers are not among them. The first are those whose hearts are rebellious and dangerous. The second are those whose conduct is persistently depraved. The third are those whose words are false but unconvincing. The fourth are those whose learning is extensive in undesirable fields. And the fifth are those who are acquiescent and helpful toward misbehavior. A person with any one of these five faults should not escape execution by the superior man, and Shao-cheng Mou possesses them all; his dwelling serves as a gathering place for his disciples, forming a party; his theories serve to beautify unorthodoxy and please the multitude; his stubborn arguments are sufficient to upset the right and constitute a new and independent theory—he is thus a villain among men and must be eliminated."[3]

From this it may be observed that incorrect, superficial and depraved behavior, and unorthodox contentions, have to be

3. This is an interesting illustration of the Confucian political theory that the definitive suppression by the "su-perior man" of all opposition views is not only expedient but virtuous.

concealed with ingenious theories and persuasive phraseology which, however, can never hide their absurdities and evil consequences. Even if every attempt is made to hide them, we can discover their faults and mistakes in the hidden points of argument. Mencius said: "Concealment is seen in sophistry, demoralization is seen in obscurity, deviation is seen in unorthodoxy, and lack of reason is seen in evasiveness. When these arise in the mind they harm the policy, and when they ensue from the policy they injure the deeds." For example, the theories of Nazi-Fascism and of the Internationalists are eloquently phrased and apparently logical in every way. Their words are very convincing. But if we track down the motives that give rise to these doctrines, and examine the actual instances of the destruction of nationalist thought, we will immediately know that to advocate these doctrines in China means "when these arise in the mind they harm the policy, and when they ensue from the policy they injure the deeds."

As to the motives of Nazi-Fascism and Internationalism, Sun Yat-sen said: "Some nations in the world, after their imperialist conquest of other peoples, advocate internationalism, aiming at the subjugation of the entire world, in order to preserve their special position as masters of the world." As to actual instances of the submergence of nationalism, Sun Yat-sen said: "Whenever one nation conquers another, it naturally does not want the conquered nation to have an ideology of independence. For example, Korea was conquered by Japan; Japan is now seeking to change the ideology of the Koreans, so in the textbooks of Korean schools any sentence relative to nationalist ideology is being deleted. Thirty years hence Korean children will not know that there is a Korea or that they are Koreans."

Therefore, in his third lecture on Nationalism, Sun Yat-sen compared those that discard the idea of nationalism and talk about internationalism, to a coolie, who, after winning a lottery, throws away his bamboo pole in which the winning ticket was concealed. From this it may be noted that if we in China talk about Nazi-Fascism or Internationalism instead of about Nationalism, we will be in danger of the destruction of the state and the subjugation of the nation. This single illustration reveals to us the importance of "exhausting reason" and "comprehension of words." What a pity that during the last twenty years, innumerable, intelligent and talented Chinese have been so beguiled by such ingenious theories that they have misused their intelligence and talents and wasted their lives. [In the revised edition, the phrase "by such ingenious theories" was changed to "by such theories, which are contrary to the conditions in the country and opposed to the times."] This has been the greatest loss to the state and the chief misfortune of the Revolution. Let bygones be bygones. It is hoped that all citizens, and particularly the young men that have not yet decided on their careers, will hereafter recognize the importance of "exhausting reason" and "comprehension of words." Success or failure in the careers of youth depend upon this, and therefore they should note this point in relation to their studies. Only by so doing can they clearly chart their course, reach sound conclusions, and avoid the wrong road, so that there will be no cause for vain regrets.

Since the beginning of the Ch'ing dynasty there has been more than two hundred years' accumulation of depraved customs and bad habits. In addition, under consular jurisdiction in the concessions of the big cities, there has accumulated one hundred years of extravagant and immoral habits of life. Under the influence of drugs and disease, the poor were induced to follow dangerous paths and the rich to become bankrupt. Wherever these effects prevailed, the civil officials became greedy for money and the military officials became cowardly. The people regarded the Government only as a den of criminals, and the officials comported themselves as puppets on a stage, making a pretense with documents and courting favor for their advancement. From the end of the Ch'ing dynasty to the beginning of the Republic, such habits grew worse. Up to the present, these patterns have not been basically changed, nor have such officials fully repented. This is unquestionably a great political humiliation for us. To wipe out such humiliation, gain the confidence of the people, and restore the prestige of the Government, the officials in the administration and the commanders in the army should ask themselves whether they are adhering to the testament of Sun Yat-sen, earnestly practicing the instructions to purge the heart, and conducting themselves with a clear conscience. Can they swear that they will not be superficial and seek shallow notoriety, but will be honest and sincere? If they can trust themselves after introspection, they need have no concern for other people's praise or criticism, or for temporary honor or disgrace, which would lead them to concentrate on appearances while neglecting practical work. Otherwise, they must take pains to repent, and to avoid the pitfalls of failure that trapped the warlords and politicians in the past.

We should also realize that although the more we have fought the stronger we have become, and although the unequal treaties have been relinquished, the enemy is still in our territory and it will require our utmost endeavor and the greatest sacrifice to regain our lost territory, liberate our fellow countrymen, and secure genuine freedom for the nation and independence for the state. Since the outbreak of the European and Pacific wars, the international military, political, and cultural situation has been undergoing violent changes. China's future, whether bright or dark, will be influenced by these international circumstances. At the present time, the strength of the Allies has been sufficient to accomplish the change from the defensive to the offensive, and signs of the aggressors' ultimate defeat are evident. The glory of China's victory in this War of Resistance is within sight, and the winning of a position of independence and freedom will increase China's responsibility to the world. It can be predicted that the conclusion of the war will not be deferred beyond two years, and that this year is the decisive, critical stage of the war.[4]

Whether China's position will be that of master or slave, glory or humiliation, survival or extinction, will not be determined, as at the conclusion of the First World War, by a Washington Conference. Frankly speaking, China's destiny of independence or slavery, glory or humiliation, survival or extinction, will not be determined at an international peace conference at the close of the war, but will be decided in the final critical stage of the war, which is today. Whether the whole state, from top to bottom, can be reborn through its own endeavor depends particularly on whether or not social customs and the people's way of life can be cleansed of the old and changed to the new, so that the people may be fully qualified as citizens of the modern age. We must make sure of victory in the War of Resistance and lay the foundation for national reconstruction before we can determine our destiny as well as carry out the Three People's Principles. If we are hesitant, servile, and indolent, as we were at the close of the First World War, then our lost rights may not be recovered, and the rights already recovered may not be retained. In summary, China's destiny will be decided by the ability or inability of the Chinese people to be strong and independent, and to fulfill the mission of the War of Resistance and national reconstruction. To make China strong and independent, it is necessary that all citizens, from the highest to the lowest, must be united in one purpose; that we rouse ourselves for thorough reform, eliminate frivolity by insisting upon honesty, and discourage indolence by upholding active endeavor. Our thinking must be realistic, our living disciplined; our duties must be performed with a sense of responsibility, and our actions must be orderly; and we must seek the truth through practical

4. The prediction that the war would end in two years, and that the current year was the decisive one, was not changed in the revised edition, published about a year after the original.

work, and progressively strive for improvement. Only in this way can the foundations of a modernized state be established, and only in this way can China stand on a footing of equality in the Family of Nations and share the responsibility for permanent world peace and the liberation of mankind.

The change in political customs depends especially upon a change in social customs, in which education is the primary moving force. It should be noted that academic teaching directly affects political change. It is not only ideological reform that influences social and political customs; important results also ensue from cultural reform. There is no lack of historical evidence for the ancient saying: "Change in culture affects politics." During the transition from the Han to the Wei dynasty, painstaking work was despised, while sophistry flourished and academic traditions deteriorated. At the end of the T'ang dynasty and the beginning of the Sung [in the revised edition, this was changed to "in the middle of the North Sung dynasty"], literary standards reverted to simplicity and reality, and the tradition of vigorous effort and practical action was revived. During the Ming and Ch'ing dynasties, thinking was shackled by the "eight-legged" [stereotyped] essays, and officials were uninformed in administrative matters, with the result that the actual authority of the Government was exercised by clerks [palace underlings]. In general, history shows without doubt that the destiny of a state is linked to academic teaching.

Unquestionably, we should recognize that the final result of the present war will be its effect on culture. Therefore, it may be said that the present war is a war of cultures. The success or failure, survival or extinction, of three hundred and fifty years of Nationalism, Democracy, and Socialism in Europe and America will be decided by this war. The rise or fall of China's five-thousand-year-old culture, and her ancient virtues, will also be subjected to the war's acid test. If this war is not lost to the devilish aggressors, the civilization of mankind will emerge greatly refined, and China's culture will be further brilliantly developed. It is earnestly hoped that our academic circles will thoroughly understand that today is the most critical moment for the continuation of China's ancient culture and its development in the future, as well as for its very survival.

Following the reformation at the end of the Ch'ing dynasty, there came in succession the 1911 Revolution, the May 4th Movement, and the Nationalist Revolution. During these periods, academic traditions underwent changes in unison with the changes in academic teachings, and all the ideologies of the nations of the world, such as Liberalism, Nationalism, Communism, and Anarchism, were subject to experimentation. If examined closely, it may be observed that although quite a large degree of progressiveness was diffused in the social structure, a tradition of genuineness, sincerity, stability, and honesty failed to materialize. Scholars did not seek truth through practical effort. Some concentrated on thinking without learning, closing their eyes to facts, and engaging in hollow discourse and setting up rival schools of thought. Others learned without thinking, uncritically selecting a theory here and there. Those that admired Westernization abandoned China's own culture in favor of allegiance to foreign theories. Those that upheld the national culture reverted to an isolationist chauvinism. The scholars were careless and irresponsible in their lectures, uncritically echoing the popular trend in order to court favor with the people. Their concept of "liberty" was based on their own selfish desires, while their theory of "democracy" was based on their desire to advance their own material interests. Observance of the law was regarded as humiliating, and resistance to orders as clever. They took advantage of the ignorance of youth and called themselves "Tutors of Youth." They wantonly spread superficial propaganda and called themselves "Academic Torch Bearers." The ultimate consequences were turmoil in the state and the decline of the nation to the point of extinction. While such trends existed, it was difficult to find many persons that accepted the principle that the rise and fall of the state was the responsibility of every individual. Such being the condition of education and academic teaching, the attempt to reform social and political customs was as futile as climbing a tree to look for fish.

In this period of the Nationalist Revolution, what should educators, professors, and college students do to fulfill their revolutionary obligations? In the section dealing with "Psychological Reconstruction," I have set forth the outlines, urging the scholars of our country to make their studies fit the needs of daily life; to recognize that culture is the foundation of national reconstruction; to appreciate the truth of Sun Yat-sen's philosophy that "it is easy to act," and carry out the revolutionary doctrine of active effort; to give equal emphasis to moral and physical training; to co-ordinate civilian professions and military science; to exercise both brain and brawn; and to integrate knowledge and practice. Only thus can social and academic traditions be fundamentally changed, and the evils of demoralization, pretense, extravagance, and boastfulness be completely eliminated. This is necessary before the inherent virtues, wisdom, and ability of our nation, and the original status of the state can be genuinely restored, and the foundations for national reconstruction be consolidated and strengthened.

Sun Yat-sen stated: "The construction of a house cannot be accomplished with one stroke. This is true in building a state, which requires a spirit of extreme perseverance and supreme patience." Such perseverance and patience will not be developed without an academic tradition of practical action and earnest endeavor, and social habits of simplicity, tolerance, and generosity. The officials are the craftsmen in the building of a state, and teachers ought to supply talented personnel in abundance for the same task. These two kinds of people have a more direct and heavier responsibility in the changing of academic, social, and political customs than ordinary citizens. Only if each official and each teacher develops his sense of duty and strengthens his sense of responsibility, taking upon himself the role of a devotee or scholar in the reform of customs, will the spirit of perseverance and patience for state building ensue, and the great task succeed. Sun Yat-sen said: "By success is not meant that of one man or one party, but that the Republic of China should progress from dangerous instability to safety, and then to glorious development." In order to enable China to pass from instability to safety, it is necessary that education throughout the country focus on the concept of statehood, and place the ideology of nationalism before everything else. The teachers of the entire country should first strive for this, before they can urge the people in general to change the political traditions in order to lay a primary foundation capable of developing and perpetuating the task of national reconstruction.

3. The Problem of Fostering the Concepts of Freedom and Government by Law

In changing social customs, we must fundamentally change the citizen's concept of law and freedom. It is the nature of man to gather in groups. When an individual is separated from the group he cannot survive. Since the beginning of mankind the individual has been born into the group and has grown up in the group, and there has never been a time that he could leave his group and become completely isolated. The life of an individual thus resides in the life of a group. Only when a group develops can an individual develop. Within a human group, the relation between each individual and between individuals and the entire group are naturally governed by rules, so that the life of the group can be preserved and developed. These rules are ethics on the one hand and laws on the other. The organization of men proceeds from the family to the clan, and from the clan to the nation. The more individuals there are, the more closely knit are the ethics and the laws. The safeguard for a belief in ethics is provided by the public opinion in a given society. The sanctions of the law are enforced by the government, which administers public affairs.

Chinese political philosophy analyzes the relation between ethics and law with the greatest minuteness and clarity. Chinese political philosophy advocates the joint application of ethics and law, though distinguishing between them in their order of application. Chia I said: "Etiquette [ethics] prohibits a misdeed before it happens; law prosecutes after the occurrence." Tung Chung-shu said: "Virtue first, punishment afterward." These statements mean that ethics comes before the law, but do not imply that there are only ethics to the exclusion of the law. Sun Yat-sen's Three People's Principles discussed this subject even more thoroughly. It should be noted that the Three People's Principles stem from China's hereditary [orthodox] moral concepts. Briefly, "altruism" is the basic principle of the Revolution, "benevolence and love" are the foundation of world salvation and, in the final analysis, there is nothing more altruistic or beneficial for world salvation than the principle that "the world belongs to all," which is the basic rule for social reform and the highest ideal of revolutionary action in the Three People's Principles. Practical application of the Three People's Principles, however, must be according to law. During the stage of military government, we should rule by means of military law; during the stage of political tutelage we should rule according to the provisional constitution; and during the period of constitutional government, we should rule according to constitutional law. From this it may be seen that the government of the Three People's Principles is based on ethics but carried out by law.

Chinese political philosophy also defines minutely and clearly the relation between rule by man and rule by law. Mencius said that a state must have "legal regulations" and "jurists and assistants," and also that "law cannot be enforced by itself." This means that a state without law is unmanageable, but law enforcement still depends upon man. Wang An-shih's statement that it is law that defines institutions and functions, and it is man that promotes and carries them out, and Chang Chu-cheng's statement, "enforcement of the law rests on man," have the same meaning. The purpose of our Nationalist Revolution is to build China into a state ruled by law, but its foundation must rest on the people's mental ability [public opinion]. Sun Yat-sen said: "People generally say that China's four hundred millions are really equivalent to a pan of loose sand. What should be done to gather these four hundred million loose grains of sand together to form them into an organic whole? A state ruled by law. We must first take a sincere vow to do this. Only then can we expect to discipline the individual, harmonize the family, govern the state, and stabilize the world." Again he said: "That a state is established is due to nothing else but the joint mental ability of the citizen. The power to govern a state, and the persons that exercise this governing power, are constantly subject to the collective mental force [public opinion] of the citizens, which is the master that directs them." This means that the Nationalist Revolution represents the joining together of the citizens' mental force to establish a state governed by law, and the application of that force [public opinion] for the vigorous enforcement of the law.

Chinese political philosophy pays particular attention to the relation between emotion, reason, and law. It holds that justice can be secured only when emotion and reason are in accord with law. Chu-ko Liang said: "Gratitude follows law enforcement." He also said: "My mind is like a scale—it cannot be lighter or heavier in weighing different persons." Chinese political philosophy also maintains that law must be based on emotion and reason before it is suitable for practical use. Lu Hsin-wu said: "Law is enacted on the basis of reason and human emotions." He also said: "Law is the form within which reasoning is applied." Our Three People's Principles synchronize emotion, reason, and law, and give equal weight to each. In my essay, *The System and Practical Program of the Three People's Principles*, I said: "The reason we human beings differ from and are superior to other animals, and are able continuously to seek progress and development, is that we have emotions that can be aroused, and rational natures that can be disciplined by law—each being indispensable for human survival and evolution. In our daily existence, we regard things as satisfactory only when they are in accord with all three—emotion, reason, and law. Let us examine the Three People's Principles in turn. From the standpoint of the principle of Nationalism: nationalist emotion is the most meritorious of all human emotions, because a nation is formed by natural forces, and the consolidation of a nation must depend upon the instinctive emotions of man. From the standpoint of the principle of Democracy, the best legal form of human organization is government of the whole people, which is democratic government, and this depends entirely on a government by law and discipline in order to designate the duties and privileges of each individual. From the standpoint of the principle of the People's Livelihood, the most reasonable form of organization is one in which all the people are economically equal, without oppression or exploitation; in which the interests of the majority are satisfied; in which there is an absence of poverty because of equal distribution, an absence of strife because of harmony, and an absence of instability because of satisfaction." This cannot be achieved by emotion alone, nor by law alone, but must be based on reason, which differentiates right from wrong, benefit from harm. Therefore I say, Nationalism is based on emotion, Democracy on law, and the People's Livelihood on reason. We secure national independence through increased national emotion; we lay the foundation of democracy through the firm establishment of government by law, and we solve the problems of the people's livelihood through the adjustment of the surpluses and deficiencies in the public and private economy according to fair and uniform lines of reason. In this way, emotion, reason, and law are each assigned their proper place. This is how and why the Three People's Principles are comparatively more complete and enduring, and more far-reaching yet easier to carry out, than other doctrines.

It may thus be noted that the Three People's Principles emphasize emotion, reason, and law equally, giving each its proper place. Thus it is clearly an error for some scholars to assume that Chinese political philosophy stresses government by ethics or by men, and is opposed to government by law. Government by law occupies an important position, plays an important part, and possesses important functions in the Three People's Principles.

After the conclusion of the unequal treaties, China's academic and intellectual circles lost their self-confidence and blindly echoed foreign theories. As a result, some quoted European theories of the eighteenth and nineteenth centuries to destroy our people's concept of government by law. [In the revised edition, the phrase "to destroy our people's concept of government by law" is changed to "as the theoretical basis of China's Revolution."] They came across Rousseau's doctrine of "the natural rights of man" and then maintained that China's Revolution and the European Revolution of the eighteenth and nineteenth centuries were part of the same fight for "freedom." They did not realize that Rousseau's theory did not fit the historical facts. Sun Yat-sen told us: "By the logic of historical evolution, the rights of man are not born of nature, but created by the trend and circumstances of the time. If we investigate the history of evolution, there is no evidence of man's natural rights as claimed by Rousseau." But although Rousseau's theory lacked historical basis, it nevertheless flourished in the Europe of the eighteenth and nineteenth centuries as the principal theory of Europeans in the fight for "freedom." This was "because absolute monarchy had developed to its fullest extent in Europe at that time. The people had long been subject to ruthless absolutism and were suffering deeply from the consequences of lack of freedom. Their only solution, therefore, was to fight for 'freedom' in order to eliminate such sufferings, and upon hearing the word 'freedom' they immediately welcomed it."

If we examine the government of China under successive dynasties, it will be observed that it generally adopted a magnanimous attitude toward the people, and that, aside from paying the grain tribute, the people had almost no contact with officials. According to Sun Yat-sen, "The Chinese people had long had great 'freedom' and it was not necessary for them to fight for it." Therefore, he said that the objective of the Chinese Revolution was opposite to that of the European Revolution. "Because the Europeans were in such dire need of freedom, they had to fight for it by revolution. Because of too much 'freedom' China has had no organization, no resisting power, and has become a pan of loose sand, so that she has been subjected to the encroachment of foreign imperialism. . . . To resist foreign oppression, we must curtail 'individual freedom' and form a solid organization, like putting cement into loose sand to make it a solid rock." In other words, our Chinese nation must crystallize into a solid, rocklike body of national defense, and needless to say, no individual may enjoy the "freedom" of a loose grain of sand. To be more explicit, to win the war we must establish a nationalist body of defense, and the same solid organization will be required to safeguard permanent international peace and to secure the liberation of mankind in co-operation with other free and independent nations of the world. Therefore, in the relation between the individual and the state, whether during or after the war, "individual freedom" of the type of loose grains of sand cannot be tolerated.

From the point of view of the relations between individuals, freedom and government by law cannot be separated. China is a state made up of four hundred and fifty million citizens. Our state demands that each of its four hundred and fifty million citizens have "freedom." Therefore, the boundary of the "freedom" of each individual must be drawn, and no individual must be permitted to encroach on the "freedom" of others in the exercise of his own "freedom." Only such freedom can constitute genuine freedom. This concept of freedom must be thoroughly instilled during the period of nationalist reconstruction in order that each citizen can enjoy his right to freedom. Thus freedom as such must be within the confines of law, beyond which lies licentiousness. If everyone is permitted to be licentious, then the strong will bully the weak, and the majority will encroach upon the minority. Only when every person stays meticulously within the confines of the law can each individual enjoy the benefits of "freedom." Only a state in which each person enjoys his "freedom" may be called a state governed by law. Therefore, a state governed by law will never permit a situation in which the citizens are licentious, the strong bully the weak, or the majority encroaches on the minority. In this connection, it must be noted that it will not be reasonable for any individual to ask for the protection of the law if he breaks the law, or to criticize the state for not upholding government by law if he does not observe the law himself. Such an unreasonable point of view can only confuse the people's concept of government by law and strengthen the people's tendency to disregard the law, and if it is not completely discarded, the building of a state governed by law cannot succeed.

The most licentious people in the world are the "gypsies." We all know that the "freedom" of the gypsies amounts to nothing but indulgence and wandering. Internally, they have no concept of law and no sense of national consciousness, and externally they cannot form into an organized body to protect their own safety. Therefore, they have become the lowest and most backward group in the world, scorned and forsaken by others and mistreated wherever they go. We Chinese citizens cannot adopt the free behavior of the gypsies on the one hand, and on the other, talk grandly about modernization and the establishment of government by law. We must recognize that the state is the source and foundation of ten thousand generations of descendants. The War of Resistance is a sacred task, and the reconstruction of the state is a solemn enterprise. We must never entertain any idea of temporizing with or ignoring the law, nor undertake any childish action, but must accept laws, decrees, and orders with a consecrated mind and solemn purpose, and carry them out in a voluntary and active spirit. Dare we put ourselves in the same category as the gypsies?

During the last one hundred years, the existence of the concessions and the foreign garrison areas, together with the feudal partitioning of the country, were the chief causes for the development of a disdain for government by law, and a negligence in its observance in China. Concessions and garrisoned areas could not be reached by Chinese law, and the people there, who were beyond the reach of the laws of their own country, generally became licentious and violated the laws and discipline of the state in words or action. After a long period, they formed the negative habit of irresponsibility and the positive habit of law-breaking. These habits spread to the people as a whole, who not only failed to realize that these habits were wrong, but actually considered them to be right. The feudal partitioning of the country further destroyed the idea of government by law and the custom of law observance. The warlords and politicians, who supported one leader to overthrow another and shifted their allegiances overnight, not only did not comprehend the meaning of government by law, but considered it an honor to break the law and upset discipline. Under such conditions, how could the idea of government of law be instilled? How could the habit of observing the law be formed?

Today the unequal treaties have been abolished, the foreign concessions and the garrisoned areas are no longer in existence, and the feudal partitioning of the country has been gradually disappearing. Our citizens must awake and repent, mutually encouraging each other to regard the observance of law as a virtue and the shouldering of responsibility as an honor. We must never permit individual interest to interfere with the common interest of the state, nor allow individual "freedom" to encroach upon the "freedom" of others. To seek "freedom" we must first understand its intrinsic nature; to uphold government by law we must first form the habit of obedience to law. Our four hundred and fifty million citizens must each be instilled with this idea of freedom and government by law. Only then can China be established as a state governed by law, and only then will it exist as a solidly organized body of national defense, capable of sharing the responsibility for world peace and the liberation of mankind along with other free and independent countries of the world.

CHAPTER SEVEN

THE ARTERY OF CHINA'S REVOLUTIONARY RECONSTRUCTION AND THE CRITICAL QUESTIONS DETERMINING HER DESTINY

FROM the foregoing analysis, it is clear that the success or failure of national reconstruction hinges upon the transformation of social customs and public morale. This transformation depends upon those people in the villages, counties, provinces, and the whole country that have knowledge, will power, determination, and a sense of responsibility. They must assume leadership and cause the people to carry out their mission constantly and unquestioningly, so that the successful reform of social customs may be achieved. It was pointed out in the previous chapters that the youth of the entire country should make it their ambition to undertake work that others dare not undertake and to endure sufferings that others cannot endure; to overcome difficulties and dangers, and become pioneers in frontier and other isolated regions, in order to serve the needs of the state and society and to enrich the life of the state and the nation. If these things are done, the reforming of the state and society will be an easy task.

I want here to carry this discussion a step further. It should be understood that the transformation of social customs and public morale and the practical work of national reconstruction are the most important enterprises in the rehabilitation of the nation, and require constant effort. If a single individual struggles along in isolation, his achievements cannot be great or enduring. Therefore, all adult citizens and ambitious young men in every village, district, province, and the entire country must be part of a common structure and a general organization for national reconstruction and individual effort. Only when each individual works within such a general organization can we accomplish what Sun Yat-sen described as: "Use each individual's few years of mortal life to establish the immortal foundation for the countless ages of the state."

If China's adult citizens cannot unite on a large scale, our unity cannot long endure, and we shall experience the humiliation and shame of being a "pan of loose sand" and be laughed at for our "five minutes of boiling blood." We should recognize that if we cannot unite together, it is because of selfishness, and that in order to avoid selfishness, there is nothing better than to become public spirited. When unity cannot long endure, it is because of dishonesty, and to avoid dishonesty nothing is better than being sincere. A single thought directed toward the public good will enable us to reach the stage of "all men are brothers and oneness with all things." A single thought of sincerity will enable us to see clearly through a project from beginning to end. And only the Three People's Principles are based upon absolute public good and developed from absolute sincerity. Thus the ideology of the Kuomintang is all-embracing, and the activities of the Kuomintang are "a choice of the best and a retention of the original." These facts have already been demonstrated in my discussion of the process of reorganization of the Kuomintang.

The fundamental reason for the great fault in our youth today, their individual lack of accomplishment and wasted lives, is, of course, the fact that education has not fulfilled its proper mission. Because youths do not accept the guidance of their teachers, do not realize the importance of the connection between "organization" and their personal success or failure, and especially do not understand the meaning of "freedom" and "law," their behavior becomes licentious and their thinking is not based upon reality. Upon entering society, they immediately display their lack of ability to take up practical work, let alone the task of reforming society and building the state. Therefore, young people should become

industrious and able to endure suffering, and should undertake heavy and far-reaching responsibilities as leaders in the
reformation of society and the building of the nation, in connection with which their thinking must be trained by science
and their activities controlled by strict discipline. Because of
this, after the beginning of the War of Resistance, I immediately organized the *San Min Chu I* Youth Corps to serve the
urgent needs of the youth of the country, to open a new life
for the Kuomintang, and to serve as the source of a new
motivating force for the Chinese nation.

With regard to the relation between the people of the entire
country and the Kuomintang, Sun Yat-sen clearly stated:
"Every citizen of the country not only has the privilege of
joining the Party, but also the duty to join it." The youth of
the country also has a similar privilege and similar duty to
join the *San Min Chu I* Youth Corps. We must recognize that
revolutionary reconstruction is a great task that must be
jointly shouldered by all citizens. The Kuomintang and the
San Min Chu I Youth Corps are the general directing agencies
for the carrying out of revolutionary reconstruction. Adult
citizens must join the Kuomintang and youthful citizens must
join the Youth Corps—only then will the happiness of the
entire nation be safeguarded, the interest of the state protected, and permanent security for the nation and the state
be assured. Therefore, joining the Party and the Corps is both
a privilege and a duty. At the same time, the Kuomintang
and the *San Min Chu I* Youth Corps have the power to demand
and the duty to urge all ambitious and zealous adult citizens
and youths to join the Party and the Corps. The heritage left
us by our ancestors through hundreds and thousands of generations will be reformed and administered by the Party and the
Corps. The foundation upon which our descendants for countless years to come will depend must also be created and enriched by the Party and the Corps. Our Party and our Corps,
in order to fulfill their responsibility for preserving the past
and building for the future, therefore have the power to de-

mand that all our citizens come forward and unitedly take up the task, and also have the duty to permit them to come forward and unitedly carry on the Revolution.

Although the people of the entire country already understand the movement to avenge the national humiliation and make the state strong, there are still divergent views as to the direction to be followed in national reconstruction and in the establishment of private enterprises. We have today attained the first step in the abolition of the unequal treaties, and the accomplishment of the Three People's Principles and the Nationalist Revolution is now an immediate prospect. I think that, beginning today, patriots of all groups that have the will to revolution ought to think deeply, subject themselves to a thorough self-examination, and then shoulder to shoulder and hand in hand, go forward with faith in the Three People's Principles, join the Kuomintang, and become close and sincere comrades. It should be recognized that the present is an opportunity that occurs "only once in a thousand years," but it is also without question a situation so critical that it may be likened to "an enormous weight hanging by a single hair." Speaking specifically, China's former destiny, her rise or fall, her prosperity or decay, depended upon whether or not the unequal treaties could be abolished. But now that the unequal treaties have been abolished, China's destiny hereafter will depend upon whether or not internal politics can be unified, and whether or not the strength of the state can be centralized. In other words, China's destiny formerly depended upon external affairs, and was controlled by foreign imperialists. But her destiny hereafter depends entirely on internal affairs, and rests in the hands of our entire citizenry. If our internal affairs are unified, if the strength of our state is centralized, and if, in addition, all the citizens can join in a united effort, then China's destiny may be epitomized by the following words: "Be sincere and united, uphold the Government and obey the law"; and in that event, China's destiny will be independence and liberty. Otherwise it will be epitomized

by another set of words: "Cheating, dishonesty, violation of
the law, and chaos," and will be characterized by a return
to feudal warlordism and military partitioning, thus destroying unity and preventing reconstruction. In such an event,
China's destiny will decline and become extinct. China will
not merely continue to be a subcolony, but the descendants
of the Chinese nation for generations to come will be per-
petually enslaved, with no chance to regain independence
and with no hope for revival.

This is the turning point in China's destiny; the decision
will be made during the present War of Resistance within
the next two years. But China's revival has already become a
predestined fact; it cannot be shaken by any reactionary
force. [In the revised edition this sentence was modified to
read: "The fifty years of our National Revolution and the
five and a half years of total resistance have already laid the
foundation for China's revival."] China today is really in
that period which Chinese philosophy has described as "at
the end of misfortune comes prosperity." We all know that
it is one hundred years since the conclusion of the Treaty of
Nanking; that the national humiliation of 1900 is nearly fifty
years old; and that it is already a generation since the failure
of the Second Revolution of 1913. With any nation, so long
as its mind is not dead and its spirit has not perished, then
the law of the universe that "when things are at their worst
they begin to mend," and that "at the end of a revolution
one returns to the beginning" can be relied upon to continue
unchanged. Nevertheless, the working out of this natural law
will still depend upon the degree of exertion and awakening
of our people, particularly of the revolutionary elements.
In other words, "things depend on how men do them."
Nothing can be accomplished by sitting and waiting; no
opportunity can be seized by those that are fearful and weak;
opportunities must be created by ourselves. If we proceed
with courage and exert our full strength, there will be no
natural conditions that cannot be overcome, and no social

conditions that cannot be reformed. Otherwise, by sitting back we shall lose the opportunity, and we shall have "things at their worst" without the possibility of their beginning to mend.

Therefore the rise or fall, survival or extinction of the state and the nation; the success or failure, happiness or misfortune of the group and the individual, still depend upon our own decision and our own choice, and cannot be left to heaven or fate, which would be to neglect our own future and even forget the purpose of life. Therefore, my philosophy of life is, as I have always said: "The purpose of life is to create succeeding lives in the universe. The objective of life is to advance the welfare of mankind." This means that all new life in the universe must be created by man and decided by man. And there is no doubt that the destiny of our state must be created and decided by our entire people. All the unequal treaties signed since 1842, which forced our people into decline and the degradation of slavery, were brought about by our citizens themselves; the present abrogation of the unequal treaties, which has permitted the state and the nation to obtain equality and freedom, has also been achieved by our citizens themselves. The purpose of life is so great, and the force of the people is so immense, how can we fail to have courage, self-respect, self-reliance, and strength? I firmly believe that today there is no doubt about our nation's surviving and our state's becoming rich and strong. Furthermore, hereafter, military partitioning and feudal reactionary forces which violate the interests of the nation and are opposed to current trends will not only have no chance but also no ground for existence. Otherwise, the destiny of the state would be destroyed by them. Can you not see that a country of four hundred and fifty million people in the present great age, with Dr. Sun's Three People's Principles as its guiding revolutionary doctrine, cannot be subjugated?

My Compatriots! With the survival or destruction of the state, and the happiness or misfortune of the nation thus clearly placed before us, we must choose our course now.

The international situation and the trend of the times do not permit us to hesitate and remain undecided. Therefore, our whole citizenry, particularly those revolutionary fighters that wish to serve the state for the sake of independence and freedom for the nation, for the elimination of our humiliation, for strengthening the state, and for the sake of preventing future generations from falling into the tragic condition of slavery, should all join together within the Kuomintang in order to fulfill our responsibilities and duties.

Furthermore, all our country's youth should especially have a correct understanding of the *San Min Chu I* Youth Corps. Hereafter, youths throughout the country, if you really wish to fulfill your great revolutionary ambitions and carry out the great enterprise of national reconstruction, you must join the Youth Corps as the only course and the absolutely essential road to establish your careers and serve your country. After the abolition of the unequal treaties and victory in the War of Resistance, China's only object is to build a new state based on the combining of three factors—culture, economics, and national defense. The basic program of national reconstruction is the "Industrial Plan" personally drawn up by Sun Yat-sen. The vast personnel required by the "Industrial Plan" has been indicated by the few examples given above. These key workers in fundamental tasks are to be chosen from youths now in school or just graduated. Therefore, every minute of study and every minute of training of each youth today is the source of new life and new strength for our state and nation. How lucky are our youths to live during the Second World War! How lucky to be able actually to participate in this unprecedented era of great change! How lucky to be able to participate in this great and incomparable work of national reconstruction and place yourselves on the front page of this history of independence and liberty! You young people who are at the beginning of your careers are already faced with an opportunity that comes only once in a thousand years. You should calmly ponder your personal

future, and fully understand the needs of a modern state, so
that you will not again blindly follow others, as in the past,
and mistakenly fall into the wrong course and ruin your lives
to your everlasting regret. You should understand that the
Three People's Principles are not only the crystallization of
China's ancient culture and the virtues of the nation, but
also represent the inevitable trend of the modern world.
Since the Youth Corps is the unifying organization for youth
under the Three People's Principles, the youth of the entire
country must be directed by the Youth Corps. Only then
can they decide upon a correct course, follow the right road,
and not injure the state by injuring themselves. Only under
the plan of action of the Youth Corps can they follow the
right course and decide their life careers. The training received by members of our Youth Corps is very strict and the
regulations they must obey are very rigid. What it cultivates
is a wholesome life for the nation, and what it preserves is
the interest of all the people. Its task is to arouse the decadent
and aid the crippled; to eliminate humiliation and foster the
rehabilitation [of the state]. The utmost loyalty to the state,
the utmost filial piety toward the nation; to be saints and
sages and heroes; to become the bloodstream of the nation
and the backbone of the state—all these are involved in the
mission of the Youth Corps. Therefore, the youth of the entire
country should not only recognize that their entry into the
Corps is the beginning of their personal careers, but should
also feel that their joining the Corps is the starting point of
their glory. Therefore, the youth of the entire country should
further recognize that the orders of the Youth Corps are the
life of the nation's youth; that the strengthening of the Youth
Corps means the strengthening of the country's youth. Only
the new life and the new motivating power of the state and
the nation created in this way can enable us to fulfill our
mission in this great age. [In the revised edition, this passage
has been rewritten to read: "The youth of the entire country
should recognize that the regulations of the Youth Corps are

what hold together the whole life of the nation's youth; that
the strength of the organization of the Youth Corps is what
makes possible the completion of the common purpose of all
our young people—the reconstruction of the state. The success of our National Revolution for the revival of the nation
is the practical expression of the *San Min Chu I*."]

In summary, the Kuomintang and the *San Min Chu I* Youth
Corps are the organizations to solidify the state and the nation
into one body—a fact that is shown by history and does not
require further explanation. But there is another point that
ought to be repeated to our citizens, namely that the Kuomintang is the principal organization for the building of the state,
to be shared and enjoyed by the citizens of the entire country.

So long as the Kuomintang remains in existence, so long
will China continue to exist. If China today did not have
the Kuomintang, there would be no China. Had the Revolution of the Kuomintang been defeated, it would have meant
the complete defeat of the Chinese state. Briefly speaking,
China's destiny rests entirely with the Kuomintang. If there
was no Kuomintang, or if the Kuomintang should fail in its
task, China would have nothing on which to depend. [In the
revised edition, the passage from "So long as" to "depend"
has been rewritten to read: "If the Kuomintang Revolution
is brought to a successful conclusion, then and only then can
China be independent. If China no longer had the Kuomintang there would be no more China. Briefly speaking, the
destiny of China rests entirely with the Kuomintang. If
by any mischance the Kuomintang Revolution should fail,
the Chinese nation would have nothing on which it could
depend."] Without the Kuomintang, not only would China
not have been one of the four Great Powers in the world, but
she would certainly have been partitioned by the other
powers, and the name of China would not be seen on the
map of the world.

We should all recognize, therefore, that from the standpoint
of the state's organic life, if there had been no Three People's

Principles, China's work of national reconstruction would have lost its guiding principle. Thus, the Three People's Principles are the soul of the state. From the standpoint of the state's organic activity, if there was no Kuomintang, China's work of national reconstruction would have lost its motivating power. The Kuomintang is, therefore, the state's blood stream [artery], and the *San Min Chu I* Youth Corps provides the new corpuscles in that blood stream. If all the revolutionary elements and the ambitious youth of the country really wish to live and die with the state, share the glory and humiliation with the nation, regard the enterprise of the state as their own enterprise, and the life of the nation as their own life, they should, as a body, join the Kuomintang and the *San Min Chu I* Youth Corps. Only then can they fulfill a citizen's supreme responsibility and attain the most well-rounded life. And only then can we fulfill our great mission of jointly building the state.

The above explanation may draw two kinds of reactions from people. One reaction may be that this is nothing but an inducement for the people outside the Kuomintang to join the Party. The other reaction, advancing a further step, may be that this statement is designed to warn other parties and organizations outside the Kuomintang that there is some positive plan for action against them, or that, negatively, obstacles will be put in their path. Toward the first reaction, I frankly reply: I hope the country's revolutionary elements and ambitious youth will join the Kuomintang and the *San Min Chu I* Youth Corps, because they have that privilege and that duty. If they have the will to save the nation and the state, they should voluntarily join the Party and the Corps without any request or advice from me. Toward the latter reaction, I can also give a frank answer: With regard to all other ideologies and organizations I only wish that they should not partition territory and oppose the Revolution; that they should not organize armed forces and sabotage the War of Resistance. If they are really of benefit to the country, the nation, and the revolutionary building of the state, I not only would have no thought of hampering them, but would even hope that they might also develop and succeed.

My opinions regarding the state, the nation, and revolutionary reconstruction are fixed and unalterable. But I have no definite opinion regarding any theory or organization. [The first two sentences in this paragraph are omitted in the revised edition, presumably because they are contradictory.] For the sake of the state and the Three People's Principles, and also for the sake of the people and my friends, whether public or private, I cannot but open my heart and fulfill my divinely ordained responsibility to warn, sincerely and honestly, the followers of all types of ideologies and organizations within the country: First, I must humbly ask to learn from those friends that now hold an attitude of opposition to the Kuomintang: "Do you oppose the Kuomintang because its principles are not good? Or is it because the Kuomintang's policy is unsuitable? If you feel that its policy is right and its principles are good, and that its revolutionary program is beneficial to the state and the nation, but feel that in its actions or attitudes it has made some mistakes, you should then come forward and correct it and remedy its mistakes. But you should not, because of them, oppose it, destroy it, and through its destruction, destroy the entire life of China as a state. Everybody knows that to destroy the life of the state means the destruction of your own life and the lives of your descendants through countless generations—this is a very serious matter!

I believe that if we all take an objective attitude toward the Kuomintang, use the facts of past history as evidence and analyze it in the light of the present changeable international situation, and examine it in reference to the country's future, we shall then realize that in China only the Three People's Principles constitute a comprehensive and profound ideology; that the Nationalist Revolution is the only upright and bright road; and that, furthermore, the Kuomintang was the motivating power that guided the Revolution and founded the Republic, and is now the main artery for the revival of the Chinese nation and the building of the state.

Aside from this, during the period of military rule and political tutelage, those that endeavor to organize armed forces and to partition territory, no matter under what name or with whatever strategy, may be described if not as warlords, then at the very least as feudal.[1] Are those disguised warlords and new feudalists beneficial or harmful to the nation and to the Revolution? Everyone severely condemned those that formerly controlled armies and the territory-grabbing warlords as counter-revolutionary. Can we now call these disguised warlords and new feudalists genuine revolutionaries? If the anti-revolutionary forces based upon the partition of territories by force and feudal warlordism remain in existence for a single day, then for that day the politics of the state cannot be placed on the right track and the period of military rule also cannot be ended. Not only is there no way to inaugurate the period of constitutional government, but the work of political tutelage also cannot be carried out. The hindrance and damage to the state and the Revolution caused by such a situation is immeasurable.

Moreover, the Great Powers—Soviet Russia, Great Britain, the United States, and other nations—all hope that our

1. This is obviously meant as an attack against the Communist-led forces. The more one studies this book, the more one is led to the conclusion that its entire purpose was to provide a plausible basis for this approach to the one opposition group in China that possesses an army. Chiang Kai-shek and the Kuomintang leadership have repeatedly argued that no government can tolerate the existence of an army controlled by a political party. The Communist reply, and a just reply, is that (1) the Central Armies are also political party armies, being controlled exclusively by the Kuomintang, and (2) that they are entirely willing to surrender the control of their armed forces to a democratic Chinese Government that represents all sections of Chinese life. A comparable situation would exist in the United States if the American Army was exclusively controlled by the Democratic Party, and the Republican Party's only chance of existing as an effective political organization lay in its control of its own troops. Under such circumstances, it is not hard to imagine that the Republicans would oppose a demand that they turn their troops over to the control of the Democrats.

nation will be liberated and become progressive; that our state will become independent and free. Therefore, they have voluntarily agreed to relinquish the special privileges and extensive influence that they had enjoyed for the past hundred years under the unequal treaties. How is it then that our own internal parties and groups are not willing to abandon their evil habits of partitioning territory by armed force and give up their attitude of feudal warlordism? How can they still be called Chinese citizens? How can they be spoken of as a political party? In what country in the world is there a political party that follows a policy of armed force and illegal seizure of territory, obstructs the unification of its own country, and prevents the governmental system from entering upon its proper course? [In the revised edition, this sentence was expanded into the following passage: "In what country in the world is there a political party that at the very moment when the government was engaged in resisting foreign aggression and was fighting for the nation's life and the survival of the state would use the opportunity to expand its own military forces and seize fresh territory, and by disobeying government orders ruin the plans for national resistance, create dissension within the country, make unity impossible, and prevent politics from following the right path? It should be realized that the continuation of this situation can only result in our losing our position as a state and the curtailment of our life as a nation, until both state and nation have been destroyed. Is this not tragic?"] Is this not counter-revolutionary? Is it not an obstacle to the Revolution? If such obstacles to the Revolution are not voluntarily withdrawn, will they not ruin the state and harm the nation? They will not only ruin the state and harm the nation, but eventually will ruin themselves by ruining others.

I have always maintained that the Nationalist Government should adopt a lenient attitude toward all various opinions and disagreements within the country, and should seek to harmonize them through reasonable methods. But if there is

no willingness thoroughly to alter the habit of feudal warlordism, and abandon completely the partition of territory
by force of arms, then no matter how lenient our attitude may
be, it cannot produce any result and no reasonable solution
can be found.[2] I believe that we are all patriots who love our
country, and that no matter how much we may have fought
each other in the past, there is no reason why we cannot give
up our personal prejudices and animosities for the sake of
the life of the state and the future of the nation. This would
allow our internal politics to be unified and our Government
to proceed along the right road, so that foreigners would not
look down upon us as a backward nation and inferior people.
We should further hope that the period of political tutelage
may be speedily completed so that constitutional government
may become a reality—that the state may become a democratic and independent one, and every person in it an independent and free citizen. Only then shall we not be ashamed
of being the descendants of the Chinese nation, and only
then can a party achieve the status of a political party in a
democratic country.

We revolutionaries must speak the truth and perform real
work. We should always remember the saying: "Sincere re-
proofs grate on the ears, and good medicine is bitter to the
mouth." You who gather together in organizations that purport to be revolutionary but in fact destroy the Revolution,
that purport to be patriotic but in fact injure the country,

2. It was this thinly veiled threat
and virtual promise of civil war that
aroused the bitterest criticism from
all shades of political opinion, particularly the Communists. It must be
remembered that when this threat
was made, the Central Government
forces were sustaining serious defeats
at the hands of the Japanese, and
that despite these defeats, the Kuomintang bureaucracy was using its
best troops and equipment to strength-
en and enlarge its blockade against
the Eighth Route and New Fourth
Armies, and was openly making
elaborate plans for a full-scale civil
war against these armies. It was this
chapter that received the severest
criticism in a very lengthy Chinese
Communist reply to *China's Destiny*,
written by Chen Pai-ta, which was
published in the United States in the
January, 1944, issue of the *Communist*,
and was incorporated in a book entitled *The Chinese Communists* by Stuart
Gelder, published in London in 1946.

are not only harming the state and the nation and injuring the revolutionary reconstruction of the state, but are also harming your own futures and dooming your personal enterprises to failure. I wish most honestly and frankly to warn everyone again: If you cling to your old habits and maintain your past attitude, you will only obstruct your own future, hinder your own enterprise, prevent the strength of the state from being completely centralized, and the work of national reconstruction from being satisfactorily carried out. This will not be of the slightest benefit to you and will cause incalculable damage to the state and the nation. We should realize that today the destiny of our country hangs in the balance between life and death. Not a single person can be permitted to throw himself away; not a single ounce of strength can be wasted. I hope, therefore, that everyone, for the benefit of the state and the survival of the nation, with one mind and one purpose, will join together with faith in the Three People's Principles, and unite together within the organization of the Kuomintang.

This is because it is the privilege and the duty of us all, and is certainly not because the Kuomintang has any improper or harmful purpose toward you. Everyone should also know that, for the past fifty years, the Kuomintang has never abandoned any of its revolutionary work because of the opposition or obstruction of other parties or groups. That is why today we have achieved the preliminary stage of success [in the Revolution]. Hereafter, the Kuomintang will certainly not delay its revolutionary work because of the opposition or sabotage of other parties, but will determine to continue until success is achieved. We all know that during the past fifty years every party that opposed the Kuomintang was defeated, no matter how big it was and no matter how powerful the military forces it controlled. This was especially true of the warlords and parties that had the backing of Japanese imperialism. [The word "Japanese" was deleted in the revised edition.] We ought to realize that this was not due to any special strength of the Kuomintang, but to the mission entrusted to us by time and history. This mission is something that cannot be opposed or destroyed by any force. The stronger the opposition, the sooner has been the victory; and the more violent the attempt to destroy it [the Kuomintang], the greater its strength has become.

Therefore, I have always said that if the Kuomintang itself contains the seeds of self-destruction, then it will certainly be defeated without waiting for opposition from others. Otherwise, no opposition or obstruction to it can be effective. Thus the opposition of other parties will be unable to damage or halt the revolutionary work of the Kuomintang, but it will, I am afraid, have a bad effect upon China's work of national reconstruction, in which case a most unfortunate blow would be dealt to our position of independence and equality, which has been achieved through the suffering and sacrifice of our entire nation. This would also mean that the able and intelligent people within the country would not be able to work together in the great task of national reconstruction. They might even misuse their ability and intelligence, and miss this great opportunity. For the individual, this would be a most regrettable matter, and for the Kuomintang it would mean that it had not fulfilled its responsibilities or performed its duties toward the people. I cannot help, therefore, but ask the people again and again to work together in unity. I trust all of you will make allowance for the fact that my words are from the bottom of my heart.

CHAPTER EIGHT

CHINA'S DESTINY AND THE FUTURE OF THE WORLD

We know that our backwardness in science and technical skill were the obvious reasons for China's decline and weakness. During the past hundred years, the Chinese people, desiring to study foreign sciences and technical skills, worshiped all foreign civilization and did not understand the innate spirit of the Chinese nation or the virtuous character of the people, both of which have their fine points. China's native political philosophy was especially the product of the nation's innate spirit. China's political philosophy believes that warfare and production should serve men and opposes the idea that man is the servant of war and production. Mencius said: "Like material things but love the people," which means that the state should dispose of material things for the benefit of the people, and should not make the people the servants of material things. The "Great Learning"[1] said: "Where there is man, there is land; where there is land, there is wealth; where there is wealth, there is usefulness." This means that the productive system should be based on the people's livelihood, and that productive skill should not be permitted to dominate man's nature.

For three thousand years, this political philosophy and the economic principle determined the psychology of the Chinese nation, and the virtuous character of the people was affected by and existed simultaneously with this political philosophy and this economic principle. It has been previously stated

1. The "Great Learning" (*Ta Hsueh*) is part of *The Book of Rites* (*Li Chi*) and was used by the Sung philosophers in the thirteenth century A.D. as a source of the later Confucian philosophy.

230

that the inherent virtues of the Chinese people consist of the ability to endure humiliation, accept responsibility, understand thrift, and possess a sense of honor. Because the Chinese people possess these virtues, they are not afraid of strong enemies, and do not take advantage of minorities and the weak, but rather apply their traditional principle of magnanimity, and treat others as they wish to be treated themselves. For this reason they have been for thousands of years the leaders of the people of Asia in "preserving the perishing and sustaining those that might be destroyed," and in "helping the weak and assisting the fallen." As a consequence, there is no historical evidence of economic exploitation or of political domination of the peoples of Asia during the period when China was strong and prosperous; nor was there any imperialism or colonialism. This political philosophy and political virtue was despised and not practiced by modern European nations. Their capitalists subordinated human life to techniques of production and strove for profits. Their imperialists subordinated human life to the techniques of war, and sought to develop colonial possessions. Due to these interrelated ideologies, internal class conflicts and international wars fill the pages of modern world history.

At the close of the First World War, when the human race was painfully reflecting on its past sufferings, war-weary philosophers placed the blame on science, stating that science had improved the instruments of killing and had thereby caused the havoc of war to spread to all mankind. They did not realize that the ending of warfare depends upon eliminating the sources of war, and not in limiting the instruments of war. Mencius said: "Is there any difference between killing a man with a club or with a sword?" If mankind cannot develop its concepts and moral character sufficiently to put an end to war, what difference does it make whether people are killed by bows and arrows or by airplanes and big guns?

The war-weary philosophers also failed to recognize that science is motivated by service to mankind. The misuse of

scientific discoveries causes man to become more cruel as
science progresses, but this is not the fault of science. The
fault rests in the fact that China's exalted political philosophy
has not been popularized, and her profound and eternal
political philosophy has not gained wide acceptance. I feel
that the termination of the Second World War must at the
same time terminate the system and concept under which
man is now subordinated to techniques; only then can permanent peace be established and a step be taken in the
direction of a truly cosmopolitan world. This must be done
if our war against aggression is to have real value and real
purpose.

A political scientist of England once said: "If we do not
end war, war will end us." This is absolutely true. Nearly
three thousand years ago, Lao-tzu made the statement that
"it is a misfortune to have good soldiers." Chinese sages of the
past all maintained that military virtue consisted of "helping
the weak and restraining the strong," and all considered that
"war to end war" was the real objective of war. According
to the ancient doctrine that "it is a misfortune to have good
soldiers," those advocating militarism are certain to bring
destruction upon themselves in the face of the righteousness
and justice of mankind. According to the principle of "war
to end war," and the military virtue of "helping the weak and
restraining the strong," the antimilitarist and anti-aggressor
Allies must, at the conclusion of the present great war, jointly
exert all their efforts to eliminate the cause of the war. If the
cause of war cannot be eliminated, a Third World War will
follow on the heels of the Second World War, exactly as the
Second World War followed the First.

What is the cause of war? Whenever among nations and
states there are any political, economic, or military ideas or
actions of an aggressive nature, or any relations or systems
based on such ideas or actions, there will be a cause of war.
Frankly speaking, the cause of war is imperialism. Therefore,
I believe that the end of the Second World War must also

mark the end of imperialism. Only then can the permanent peace of the world be firmly assured.

China has suffered the longest and the most deeply as an oppressed nation. Therefore, China's demands for national freedom and equality among nations are also the most urgent. When China raises these urgent demands, it does not mean, as those that are suspicious of China claim, that China "wants to lead Asia." It should be noted that for the past five thousand years China's wars with her neighbors have been only "righteous wars" for self-defense and for the "preservation of the perishing and the sustaining of those that might be destroyed," and she has never had "good soldiers" to invade other countries. During the past hundred years, the movement to eliminate our national humiliation and become strong arose from the unanimous demand of the Chinese people. There are two meanings in this movement which we ourselves and all other countries of the world should recognize. First, after China has become independent and strong, she will definitely not wish the sufferings she has endured to be inflicted upon other countries, and furthermore, after the overthrow of Japanese imperialism, she will not even consider assuming the mantle of Japanese imperialism with the idea of "leading Asia." Secondly, the goal of independence and rehabilitation, strictly speaking, means that China must first become self-reliant. In order for China to become self-reliant, she must, spiritually and materially, seek freedom and independence, and she must also seek progress and development in the fields of national defense, economics, politics, and culture. China's desire for independence and strength does not arise from selfishness. In seeking freedom, independence, progress, and development, China's objective is to stand "shoulder to shoulder" with the other countries of the world, and to share with other nations the responsibilities for the maintenance of permanent world peace and the liberation of mankind. In other words, China's desire for independence and strength is motivated by a feeling of duty and responsibility, and not by greed for power and ideas of material gain. Therefore, since China opposes the existence of imperialism in the world, she surely will not follow a policy of imperialism.

During the last hundred years, while experiencing bitter sufferings, China has adhered to her traditional feeling of duty and sense of responsibility, and has observed that the existence of imperialism is the real cause of world war. China, therefore, is forced to give double consideration to the question of freedom and equality for the nations of Asia. Asia occupies a quarter of the globe. Asia's population is more than half that of the world. The nations in Asia have been, on the whole, subjected to bitter sufferings from oppression similar to those of China, and their sufferings have been equally deep and long lasting. If China cannot be free and independent, the other nations of Asia will each fall under the iron heel of the enemy, and world peace cannot have a solid foundation. Therefore, China's independence and rehabilitation are essential for the stabilization of Asia; and freedom and equality for the nations of Asia are essential for permanent peace in the world and the elimination of the causes of war, so that the evil of war will not again be let loose in the world to destroy the security and happiness of mankind.

The principle of self-determination and equality among nations ought to be applied to the organization of international peace after the war. The eventual failure of the League of Nations, formed after the end of the First World War, was due mainly to the ignoring of this principle. The concepts of "World Powers" and "Spheres of Influence" and the system based upon such concepts ought not to be allowed to reappear in the organization of international peace after the Second World War.

The principle of self-determination and equality among nations should, moreover, be applied to the revival and development of post-war world economics and culture. With respect to world economics, the principle of co-operation in [control of] natural resources and freedom of trade should be observed by all nations, but it is even more important for all nations to achieve equilibrium in the development of productive power. The Japanese imperialists hope to put into effect in Asia their ambitious program of "Industrial Japan—Agricultural Asia," and its poisonous effect would be the same as that of Nazi Germany's so-called "Plan for Greater Europe." If the productive power of all the nations of the world cannot be developed equally, then political freedom and equality will be affected by economic differences, even to the extent of being destroyed by economic exploitation.

With respect to world culture, cultural freedom and independence are essential to the freedom and independence of nations and states. The "Pan-Japanism" advanced by the Japanese imperialists and the Nazi "Theory of the Superiority of the Aryan Race" are both concepts that are destructive in world peace. Hereafter, theories of superior civilization and superior races must be forever eliminated from the world if international peace is to be guaranteed.

The aims and ideals outlined above were first formulated when China began her War of Resistance. Since the outbreak of the European War and the Pacific War, the co-operation among the Allies in the military, economic, and diplomatic fields, together with the interpenetration of their cultures and ideas, have caused them [these ideals] to advance to the eve of concrete realization. However, the ultimate realization of these ideals still requires that the entire citizenry of China follow the road of the Nationalist Revolution, adhere to the program of the War of Resistance, and national reconstruction, and continue the bitter and difficult struggle.

CONCLUSION

IN SUMMARIZING the discussion contained in the foregoing chapters, its important theme may be divided into two phases.

1. From the historical point of view, the unequal treaties concluded during the past hundred years aroused the unanimous demand of the people of our entire country for a movement to rid ourselves of humiliations and become a strong nation. The Revolution to overthrow the Manchus occurred because of this, and the War of Resistance and the movement for national reconstruction also occurred because of this. The events that took place during the course of the movement to rid ourselves of humiliation and become strong have proved that the road of the Nationalist Revolution is the most effective and the most correct. Today, the Nationalist Revolution has achieved preliminary success. Hereafter, our Chinese citizens must follow this successful road to attain their objectives in the War of Resistance, and to carry into effect the program of national reconstruction.

2. From the standpoint of the changing international situation: While the Second World War is in progress, it is only through China's War of Resistance that the various nations of Asia can become firm in their opposition to aggression; and victory in the World War depends on the efforts of the Asiatic nations. After the close of the Second World War, the attempts made to secure permanent world peace and the freedom and liberation of mankind must take as their starting point the national freedom and equality of status of the nations of Asia. China's independence and freedom are the forerunners of the liberty and equality of other Asiatic nations. That is, only when China obtains her independence and freedom can Asia be stabilized and advance into the realm of liberty and equality. Asia's stabilization is the guarantee of world peace, and

the liberation of the peoples of Asia will also mean the liberation of all mankind.

China's status of independence and freedom today has been obtained by the abrogation of the unequal treaties. But the proper reaction of the Chinese people to this should be a heightened feeling of duty and a strengthened sense of responsibility. The responsibility of the state and the duties of the citizens will become heavier hereafter. Completion of the work of national reconstruction and the realization of this ideal depend on a vigorous struggle and great sacrifice on our part.

"There is no easy task in the world; there is no difficult task in the world." Our people need only have absolutely sincere confidence in our own state and nation—enthusiastically supporting and actively carrying out the Three People's Principles and the building of the state; unanimously recognizing and jointly struggling for the purposes and objectives of the Nationalist Revolution. Then, even though future difficulties are as great as removing a mountain or emptying the sea, there is no reason why we shall not succeed.

My Compatriots! The unequal treaties have been abrogated! Looking back at the sufferings of the last hundred years, we should be even more eager to carry out the ambitions of our soldier comrades and revolutionary martyrs who gave their lives to the state. We should be eager to perpetuate the spirit that has upheld this country during the last five thousand years; revive our ancient virtues; be determined and practice what we believe; strive to advance from better to best, and sincerely follow Sun Yat-sen's revolutionary philosophy that "to know is difficult, but to act is easy." Each person, according to his profession and position, each according to his intelligence and ability, must aid in the work of reforming social customs, modernizing political practices, and cultivating the concept of freedom and government by law, and must unite in the work of national reconstruction—that is, reconstruction in the five fields of psychology, ethics, society, politics, and economics. We must exert all our efforts to carry out the total plan of reconstruction which combines culture, economics, and national defense, in the hope of sharing with the Allied nations the responsibilities of reforming the world, safeguarding the peace, and liberating mankind.

CHINESE ECONOMIC THEORY

By Chiang Kai-shek

INTRODUCTION

CHINA's economy during the past century was influenced by Western industry and commerce, and in consequence underwent a great change. As a result, many people were inspired to study Western industrial and commercial organization as well as Western economic theory. Orthodox Western schools of economics and Marxist theory have been the most popular with Chinese students. No one, however, is studying China's own economic principles. If, today, one were to refer to Chinese economic principles, he would not be understood. Moreover, there is a type of person that adheres so stubbornly to the principles of Western economics that he is unable to accept or understand the economic principles and theories that are traditionally Chinese.

A study of the real nature of recent economic changes in China, an estimate of future economic developments, and any attempt to work out the objectives toward which our economic development should be directed, all reveal the reasons why current economic theories are not related to the historical economic theories of ancient China. This is because during the past century China was under the bondage of the unequal treaties.

Most so-called scientific thinkers tend to disparage things of their own country and to esteem highly everything foreign. Our economists, moreover, have been influenced by our semi-colonial status and thus have lost their independence and initiative. They lack the spirit of invention and discovery. The most economically developed cities of China are the Treaty Ports, especially the foreign concessions. And the chief objects of study by Chinese economists are these same Treaty Ports, particularly the industrial, commercial, and financial concerns in the foreign concessions. Since these are merely appendages of foreign industrial, commercial, and financial enterprises, our economists have learned nothing except to copy the accepted foreign theories. They have forgotten that China herself has had a long historical development, her own special geographical environment, and her own economic laws and principles, upon which the country developed. This tendency is very regrettable. We have now lived through fifty years of National Revolution and six years of sacrifice in our War of Resistance. We have been successful in abolishing the unequal treaties. If all our people will maintain their firm stand and continue their determined efforts to defeat Japanese imperialism, China will become a free and independent country. Our economic development can then be based on independent and free plans, which must be worked out now. And still more important, we must establish our own free and independent economic theories as the basis for these plans.

We must bear in mind that current economic theories are merely imitations of those accepted in the West, which are based on economic conditions in the West. And these conditions constantly change. The most important recent change occurred at the beginning of the twentieth century when free industrial and commercial competition in Europe and America was transformed into monopolistic concentration. This change was particularly apparent after the First World War— the late Father of our Country [Sun Yat-sen] called it the "Second Industrial Revolution." Today, twenty years later, the Second World War is being fought on a larger scale than the First. It will result in even more radical changes. World economics has again come to a sharp turning point. At this time, we must reconsider both Chinese and Western economic theories to find the right path for our own economic development and for world economic reform.

CHAPTER ONE

DEFINITION AND SCOPE OF CHINESE ECONOMIC THEORY

FROM the standpoint of the relations between men and material things, Chinese theory defines economics as "the study of managing men and adjusting things." As for the relations between the parts and the whole, economics is defined as "the study of national planning and the people's livelihood." The basic principles of Chinese economics are therefore the management of human activities and the adjustment of goods, and the study of national planning and the people's livelihood. In more simple terms, economics is the study of how to make the nation rich and strong—to build a nation into a wealthy, powerful, healthy, and contented state. In essence, it is the study of national development. From this it is clear that the scope of Chinese economics is much broader than that of Western economics.[1]

There is a reason for the creation and existence of everything in the universe. The *Book of Odes*[2] states that "God

1. It is difficult to translate many terms from Western languages into ideograph languages such as Chinese and Japanese without distorting or restricting their meaning. This is particularly true of scientific terminology. Throughout this book, "economics" is expressed by the Chinese ideographs, *ching chi*, which mean literally "management and supply" and which are used by the author in their literal sense. Such a definition of "economics" is in no sense comparable to the content and methods of modern economic science as developed in the West. Management and supply were the chief if not the only problems in China's ancient agrarian feudal society, but they are far from constituting an accurate definition of the scope of modern economics. From such a restricted definition of "economics" it is easy to deduce the need for a paternalistic government centered in a self-perpetuating bureaucracy. In Hitler Germany, such theorizing led to the Nazi regime; in China it can lead only to a feudal-fascist bureaucratic system.

2. See *China's Destiny*, footnote, p. 31.

created men and for everything created, there is a reason."
Since man was created, there is a reason for his existence,
and that reason lies in man's nature. Like all other creatures,
man wishes to live, but unlike other creatures, he can reason
and think. This is the special characteristic of man's nature.
According to the *Book of History*,[3] "Man is the cleverest among
creatures." This refers to his thinking and reasoning powers.
Chinese economic theories, whether Confucian or Legalistic,[4]
all base their discussion of the relation between men and
things on the rational nature and wants of mankind. The
Confucianists wished to develop man's rational nature, while
the Legalists advocated the control of man's desires. Confucianist theories were therefore based on benevolence and
love, while the Legalist theories were based on rules of law.
This is the distinction between the two schools of thought.
The benevolence and love advocated by the Confucianists
are predicated on man's rational nature, while the legal
restrictions of the Legalists are primarily concerned with
human desires. Both schools, however, are in reality concerned
with man's rational nature: one aiming to develop it and the
other to control it. Thus the basis of Chinese economic theory
is man's rational nature—not his wants.[5]

Everything in the universe fulfills the purpose of its creation.
Each has its own place. If this law is recognized, we can enable
everything to attain its own proper place. This is what is
meant by the statement in the Doctrine of the Mean: "All

3. The earliest literary source for
Chinese history, comprising ancient
documents and speeches. Only part
of the book has survived, and there
is considerable debate over the au-
thenticity of the present text.

4. The Legalistic School (also
known as the Juristic) developed in
the fourth century B.C., in opposition
to the idealistic teachings of the Con-
fucians. The Legalists rejected the
idea of government by "morality"
and "benevolence" as impractical,

and wished to replace it with government by law as a more efficient way
of maintaining the authority of the
state.

5. This is merely one of many illustrations of the wholly unscientific
character of "Chinese economic theory" as developed in this book. To
start from the premise that man is
"rational" and from this deduce the
answers to all social and economic
problems is completely contrary to
the methods of modern social science.

things will flourish when equilibrium and harmony have been achieved, and when heaven and earth are in their proper positions." This is the traditional Chinese philosophy, based on the idea that men are not individual separate entities, not each a single "I," but each a part of the plural "We." Similarly, things are not divisible; each thing constitutes a part of the whole. The relations between men and things should therefore be studied and controlled from the standpoint of the whole. Thus Chinese economic theory does not base itself on the individual or single unit. It is based on the study of mankind and society as a whole. This is quite different from the theories of all Western economists.

According to Western economists, capital, labor, and land are the three chief factors of production. They therefore devote themselves to the study of these three factors. Chinese economic theory, on the other hand, begins its study of the important factors of production with man himself. The "Great Learning"[6] states: "Where there are men, there is land. Where there is land, there is money. Where there is money, there is use for it." This simply means that manpower and land are the two important factors of production. If manpower is used to develop the land, there will be goods and money. Goods are of two kinds: the agricultural and mineral products that are taken directly from the land, and the products of agriculture and mining to which labor has been added to make manufactured goods. Money is not regarded as an essential factor of production in Chinese economic theory. Chinese economists regard goods as the products of manpower and the land, and money simply as a medium of exchange.

To return to the central theme of our discussion: man is man because he wishes to live and has the ability to think. Man differs from other creatures because he is able to use his mind and his rational nature to guide his activities in making a living. Manpower comprises both physical strength and

6. See *China's Destiny*, footnote, p. 230.

mental power, or wisdom, which guides physical strength. Human skill in production is characterized by uninterrupted progress, while the productive skill of all other creatures is limited to their claws and teeth. Ancient man's bow and arrow for hunting, his hook and net for fishing, and his plow and harrow for farming, and modern man's steam and electric machinery and tools for industrial use are all the inventions of his wisdom. These inventions, and the natural science that produced them, constitute an important factor in man's ability to increase his productivity.

Secondly, men are able to form groups. They do not have claws or teeth like other animals, but because they have this social nature, they have conquered all other animals and are able to live on a much higher level. The reason that men are capable of living together peaceably in large groups is their ability to think and their rational nature. The highest and most important grouping of men is society or the nation. The strength of the nation-society is much greater than the sum total of the strength of each individual member. Each individual's strength can be best employed only as part of the unified strength of the nation-society. Separated from this society, man as an individual cannot exist—much less utilize his mental and physical powers to increase production. The organization of this nation-society, and the rules established for its preservation, thus constitute another factor in man's ability to increase his productive power.

If man ignores the laws of nature and of society, he will not only be unable to exist, but will also lose the special characteristic of a human being. The way of living in accordance with the laws of nature and society is called "culture." Other animals do not know these laws, and are thus unable to improve their livelihood. Only man knows these laws, and knowing them, can take steps to improve his way of life. These steps constitute cultural development and result in continuous progress.

All inventions are based on natural laws. The ancient emperors, kings, sages, and wise men, venerated by the Chinese, were all capable of understanding the laws of nature, and hence of making inventions and discoveries that improved man's livelihood. It is for this reason that the Emperors Fu Hsi and Shen Nung, who invented nets, plows and harrows, and Emperor Huang Ti, who invented bows and arrows and Chinese characters, have been worshiped for five thousand years.[7] These inventions were all designed for the improvement of the people's livelihood and the attainment, in successive steps, of the ideal state. Because of this, these inventors are still honored by the Chinese of today. To speak of culture without reference to clothing, food, shelter, and transportation, to think that there is such a thing as culture apart from these, or to believe that only such arts as literature constitute culture, is seriously to misunderstand the term. In Chinese economics, culture and the people's livelihood are inseparable. There is no culture apart from the people's livelihood, and no people's livelihood apart from culture.

As stated above, the nation-society is the highest form of human grouping. In ancient times, production in China depended solely on handicraft industry and agriculture, and communications depended on human and animal power. Nevertheless, China grew into a great nation and a unified country, because of the great knowledge of the ancient sages and wise men in "managing men and adjusting things" and in "national planning and the people's livelihood." The ancient statesmen and economists took great care to distinguish

---

7. These "Three Sovereigns" of legendary Chinese history are credited in the Chinese classics with being the inventors of all the arts and crafts. They were supposedly divinities with the bodies of serpents and human heads. However, according to Ssu-ma Ch'ien, who compiled the first general history of China in the first century, B.C., Huang Ti was not one of the "Three Sovereigns" but the first of the "Five Emperors"—a human ruler who, with his four successors, Chuan Hsiu, Ku, Tao, and Shun, were the founders of Chinese civilization. The period of the "Five Emperors" is known in the Chinese classics as the "Golden Age" when the government of the world was perfect. The last of the "Five Emperors"—Shun—was succeeded by Emperor Yu, who according to orthodox Chinese tradition founded the first dynasty, the Hsia, in 2205 B.C.

between man's rational nature and his wants, to adjust and balance the relations between the government and the people, and to co-ordinate the civil and military services. Their most important discussions and theories emphasized that national planning and the people's livelihood must be considered as a single problem.

According to Chinese economic theory, the government's duties are to support the people on the one hand and to protect them on the other. National plans for the support of the people are plans for the people's livelihood. But since this livelihood must also be protected, plans for livelihood become plans for the national defense. The people's livelihood and national defense are thus inseparable. From the Chinese standpoint, therefore, Western economics is merely the study of private enterprise or of market transactions, whereas Chinese economic theory is not confined to private enterprise or market transactions, but is a combination of the people's livelihood and national defense. It may thus be said that there is no national defense without the people's livelihood and no people's livelihood without national defense.[8]

In summary, it may be stated that the principles of Chinese economic theory are to study and administer the relations between men and goods and to enable man's rational nature to improve his livelihood. These principles allow for both the possibility of war and the fundamental unity of all races and nations. In the light of these principles, we can understand the dictum: "Where there are men, there is land; where there is land, there is money; where there is money, there is use for it." We will then have a clear knowledge of the objectives of economics.

Chinese economists regard manpower and land as the im-

8. This is an example of the unscientific and inexact reasoning and terminology that characterize this book. Culture is identified with the people's livelihood, and the people's livelihood with national defense. Therefore, culture equals national defense—a concept that perhaps satisfies the military mind, but can hardly be regarded as the product of scholarly or scientific analysis.

portant factors of production: the former develops the latter and produces goods. The aim of economics is to make the most efficient possible use of manpower, land, and goods. The late Father of our Country said: "Men should develop their ability, land should be made to produce to the limit of its productivity, things should be used to the fullest, and goods enabled to move freely." This means that we must make the best possible use of manpower, land, and goods, and to achieve this aim, there are certain laws, methods, and objectives.

Laws: We must recognize the reasons for the creation and existence of all things. The reason for the creation and existence of a particular thing may be termed the nature of that particular thing. In order to make the best use of manpower, land, and things, we must abide by the natural laws of men, land and things, because before we can make use of anything we must understand its true nature. Thus, in Chinese economic theory, it is maintained that in order to exploit manpower and the utility of things, we must first understand their nature.

Methods: We know that the principles of Chinese economics begin with men and then turn to things. Mencius advocated "kindness to man and regard for things." The Doctrine of Mean states that only after man's nature is thoroughly understood can we understand the nature of things. If we wish to make full use of the fertility of the land, we must first understand man's nature and make the best use of it. The two most important ways to understand and utilize man's nature are: First, to preserve the inherited ethics of the nation and restore its traditional wisdom and ability; second, to master the advanced science of the West and introduce the newest Western technical skills. This is essential if we are to exploit the nature and utility of things.

Objectives: On the basis of our traditional culture coupled with modern science, we must aim, in the shortest possible time and with the least possible effort, to make the best use of our manpower, land, and goods to improve our livelihood and strengthen our national defense. In other words, the two objectives of Chinese economics are to support and to protect the people. Western economic theory is based on wants, especially personal wants, but if this theory is carried out in practice, the techniques of production and national defense would not serve the people's livelihood—on the contrary, they would enslave men and even destroy man's nature. Chinese economic theory is different, in that it takes the people's livelihood as its objective. All economic systems and policies must be in accord with man's nature and of service to the people's livelihood. Mencius's saying, "kindness to men and regard for things" means exactly this. We must love and cherish things and expand their utility for the sake of man. The people need the support of the nation, and the nation should therefore, as quickly and easily as possible, make the best use of manpower, land, and things, in accordance with its traditional culture and modern scientific methods, in order to achieve its economic objectives, namely, the people's livelihood and national defense.

CHAPTER TWO

DIFFERENCES BETWEEN CHINESE AND WESTERN ECONOMIC THEORIES

1. Economic Theories of Ancient China

THE objectives of Chinese economics are derived from the principles common to the theories of all Chinese economists. All sound economic theories must conform to the nation's natural, geographic, historic, and climatic conditions, and to its racial spirit and social phenomena. Theories differ in different countries and at different times. The ancient sayings, "find reasons according to things," "suit the time, suit the place," mean that theories and policies should conform to the time and circumstances and must be flexible. For this reason, the economic theories in ancient China were both varied and flexible.

Thirty centuries ago, during the Chou dynasty, people migrated from the upper reaches of the Yellow River to the valleys of the Yellow, Huai, Yangtze, and Han rivers, and agriculture, industry and commerce flourished. During that period, China produced a great economist—the Duke of Chou. There are disputes over the date and text of the Chou *Book of Rites* [*Li Chi*], but the greater part of the book is confirmed by the Chou dynastic annals. Other sources are the *Book of Odes*, especially the chapter entitled "Seventh Moon" and the poems, "Ta Tien" and "Pu Tien," and the comments of Confucius and Mencius concerning the Chou dynasty. All these sources indicate that the Chou dynasty developed the "well-land" farm system as the basis of conscription, government, and taxation.[1] The foundation of the state on this merging of culture, the people's livelihood, and national defense was originated by the Duke of Chou. During the next five hundred years, Chinese agriculture and commerce made considerable progress, but each influenced the other and this gave rise to certain problems and differences in economic thought. These issues were discussed by Kuan Chung, Chi Jan, and Pai Kui of the Ch'un Ch'iu period [722–481 B.C.], and also by economists during the period of the "Warring States" [481–221 B.C.]. The most important point about these discussions was that both the Confucianists and the Legalists regarded agriculture as the basic economic activity, although they differed with regard to commercial policy. Mencius and Hsun Tzu [Confucianists] advocated the supervision of trade without the imposition of taxes—a *laissez-faire* policy—while Kuan Chung and Shang Yang [Legalists] urged the control of trade and the stabilization of prices—an interventionist policy. It was not until the period of the West Han dynasty [206 B.C.–A.D. 6] that a detailed chronological record [of these economic discussions] was kept—the "discourses on Salt and Iron," which is comparable to the disputes among European economists eighteen centuries later concerning the relative importance of commerce and agriculture.

Following the period of the West Han dynasty, Chinese economic theories, systems, and policies were gradually unified in accord with the teachings of the Confucianists. But

---

1. The "well-land" system (*ching-t'ien*) derived its name from the fact that the land was supposed to be divided into square units, each unit being divided into nine equal squares, the inner boundary lines resembling the shape of the Chinese character *ching*, meaning "well," (similar to the diagram for the game, tick-tack-toe.) The eight outer squares were cultivated by eight individual families, who jointly cultivated the central, or "public" square. The system was first described by Mencius (372–289 B.C.) and elaborated on by later writers in the *Chou Li*, a book compiled during the Han dynasty, purporting to give a detailed account of ancient Chinese society. Though it presumably never existed in such an artificially perfect form, modern scholarship accepts the fact that some such system formed the basic administrative and economic unit in ancient China.

the Confucianists themselves divided into two groups: one emphasizing nature and reason and the other stressing "merits and gains." The former group included Chang Tsai, Cheng Hao and Cheng Yi of the Northern Sung dynasty [960–1125] and Chu Hei and Lo Chiu-yuan of the Southern Sung dynasty [1125–1280]. In the latter school of thought were Su Hsin, Su Shih, and Su Che of the Northern Sung, and Chen Tung-po (Chen Liang) and Yeh Ping-hsiang (Yeh Chih) of the Southern Sung dynasty. Other economists combined certain features of all these schools—nature and reason, merits and gains, and the common ideas of the Confucianists and Legalists—into theories of their own. Fan Wen-Cheng (Fan Chung-yen) and Wang Chiang-kung (Wang An-shih) of the Sung dynasty and Wang Yang-ming (Wang Shou-jen) and Chang Chiang-ling (Chang Chu-cheng) of the Ming dynasty [1368–1644] were important economists of this type who were noted both for their theories and for their success as practical administrators.

These various schools of thought can be illustrated by a few examples. Among the kingdoms of the Ch'un Ch'iu period, the kingdom of Ch'i was noted for the prosperity of its fishing, salt, ironware, cocoon raising and silk industries. Its commerce therefore exercised a dominant influence on the livelihood of the farmers within the kingdom and also monopolized the market in other states along the Yellow River. In the economic writings of Kuan Chung[2] there is a detailed discussion of the relation between agriculture and commerce, and the system of conscripting farmers. Kuan maintained that manpower and land were the only important factors of production, and that the first was the more important because it was the basis of production. In his *Eight Viewpoints* he stated: "People cannot eat unless there is grain; grain cannot grow unless there is labor; land cannot produce without men; men cannot make a living unless they work—so whatever heaven creates is created by the use of manpower." This thesis is identical

2. Premier of Ch'i under Duke Huan, who ruled from 685–643 B.C.

with: "Where there are men, there is land; where there is land, there is money; where there is money, there is use for it."

Kuan endeavored to solve the question of prices from the standpoint of the relations between agriculture and commerce. He argued that gold is useful to the people only in business transactions, whereas grain is a necessity of life. The more gold there is, the lower prices will be, and vice versa. Similarly, the more expensive grain is, the cheaper other commodities will be, and vice versa. Low prices discourage the production of goods, and a scarcity of gold hampers trade. High prices for grain causes popular suffering, and cheap grain causes loss to the farmers. Kuan maintained that the government must stabilize the price of gold and grain before it could stabilize prices in general, and that to do this it was essential to prohibit hoarding and facilitate the transport of goods. Supplies of gold and grain must be controlled by the government and kept out of the hands of the nobles. If prices rose, the supply of gold should be reduced. If grain became costly, the supplies in government granaries should be sold at reduced prices. Such a policy would facilitate the free circulation of all goods.

Kuan also advocated that to build up the power of the state and prevent the people's livelihood from being controlled by the nobility, the government should monopolize salt, iron, and the products of mountains and rivers, and should also control foreign trade. These monopoly and control policies exercised considerable influence in later centuries. Kuan's most famous policy, however, was that relating to the conscription of farmers. His theory was to "use civil government to cover up military orders." With the disintegration of the "well-land system," the distribution of land had become unequal and farmers had become distinct from soldiers. Kuan's policy was to organize the farmers and give them military training, and by this means he made the entire population of Ch'i potential soldiers. The people's livelihood and national defense were thus provided for simultaneously. The "farmer-soldier" policy of Shang Yang was based on this policy of Kuan's, and was used in the kingdom of Ch'in, whose troops ultimately succeeded in conquering all other kingdoms [in 221 B.C.]. Of all Kuan's theories, this policy exercised the greatest influence in later centuries.

From the foregoing, it is clear that as early as 600 B.C. China possessed an outstanding economist in the person of Kuan Chung. In subsequent generations, other famous economists emerged and economic systems and policies varied from time to time. In the first century A.D. China was reunified after a period of feudalistic division lasting well over two hundred years. Problems such as the concentration of land ownership, commercial prosperity, financial difficulties and aggression from abroad were far more serious and complex during the Sung dynasty than in the Ch'i kingdom of the Ch'un Ch'iu period. At that time, Fan Chung-yen was the first to urge that the educational and civil examination systems be reformed in order to train the youth in economics. Wang An-shih[3] followed Fan's lead and revised the laws. Wang

3. As prime minister during the reign of Emperor Shen Tsung (A.D. 1068–85), Wang An-shih instituted various reforms known as the "New Laws." Wang's aim was to improve the lot of the peasantry, curb usury, and revise the system of administration, which he considered wasteful, inefficient, and needlessly oppressive. Though a Confucianist, he did not believe that the Confucian virtues were sufficient to ward off foreign invasion or to relieve peasant discontent. He revised the most oppressive features of the system of tribute, by which grain and other produce had to be transported to the capital from distant provinces; instituted a system of state loans to farmers to free them from dependence on local money-lenders; substituted a system of graded taxation for the former system of forced labor on public works—the proceeds of the tax being used to hire labor when needed; revised the land tax laws; established state pawnshops; and instituted a system of official price fixing and limitation of profits on the sale of property. All these measures were violently opposed by powerful vested interests among the landowning and official classes, who denounced Wang as an "unorthodox Confucianist." Their enforcement was also hampered by the lack of an efficient civil service capable of administering them, and they were eventually repealed in 1086.

Because of his emphasis on the need to improve the lot of the peasantry, Wang is often called a Socialist statesman, but this description is misleading. Wang believed in the accepted form of government—autocratic monarchy. His reforms were inspired by the need to counteract the threat of peasant uprisings, and were based on a return to the au-based his economic theories on the doctrines of Confucius and Mencius. He stated: "The ways and means set forth in the classics were meant for the management of practical affairs. But present-day scholars are mostly incompetent, so they regard the classics as no longer applicable to such management." Wang held that the classics were studies of economics, but that economic policies should conform to the "changes of circumstances and trends"; that people in later centuries might follow the principles set forth in the classics, but should not slavishly copy the methods for carrying them out. His views thus differed from those of the ordinary Confucianists who emphasized the economy of consumption; Wang was more interested in increased production. He wrote: "With the world's labor we earn the world's money, and with the world's money we meet the world's expenditures." His policy was based on agriculture and water conservancy. He urged economy and thrift, the prevention of further land concentration, equalizing taxes and services, and furnishing rural credit in order to enable everyone to develop his resources. With regard to domestic trade, he prohibited the organization of centralized firms and broker shops and established the so-called "marketing administration" and "brokerage exemption" so that the market could not be monopolized and goods were enabled to move freely. His views also differed from those of the Confucianists with regard to foreign trade. At that time there was an embargo on coins that limited foreign trade along the sea coast and the borders [of China]. In spite of opposition, Wang removed the embargo and encouraged imports and exports. With respect to national defense, he urged

---

thoritarian concepts of the Ch'in and Han dynasties. It is significant that he instituted the *pao chia* system to curb internal disorder and to serve as a basis for military conscription of the farmers—a system based on the theory of strict authoritarian control. Wang was in reality a Confucianist "reformer," and it is interesting to note that the present leaders of the Kuomintang have reinstated the *pao chia* system (see *China's Destiny*, footnote, p. 134) and that Wang's theories are singled out for special mention in this book.

the conscription of farmers and established the *pao chia* system[4] to ensure that all the people would receive military training.

By the middle of the sixteenth century, the laws of the early years of the Ming dynasty were largely ignored. The land [of the poor and weak] had been annexed [by the rich and powerful], taxes and service had become unequal, the cultivation of land by the frontier garrisons was inadequate, and foreign aggression was an increasingly serious threat. At that time, another great economist emerged, Chang Chiang-ling. His economic theories involved the study of both the laws of nature and of merits and gains, and included both Confucianist and Legalist principles. He wrote: "Study that fails to study the doctrines of life is not study; doctrines other than economic are useless." He held that practical studies are necessarily of practical use, and require a thorough knowledge of the laws of nature and the economics of existence, the management of men and the adjustment of things. The chief features of Chang's policy were: "Doing things right, listening to no unconfirmed reports, encouraging the good, punishing the evil, distinguishing the genuine from the bogus, discovering the facts after hearing reports, and correctly giving rewards or inflicting punishment." His objectives were to increase the country's wealth and build up a strong army.

The Confucianists for the most part criticized Chang's policy as that of "might." In reply, he stated: "Confucius, in discussing government, spoke first of adequacy of food and soldiers. Emperor Shun [last of the legendary 'Five Emperors'] instructed his twelve administrative assistants to take steps to produce foodstuffs. Duke Chou in his political writings emphasized military power. People today are not familiar with these fields of study and, instead of pursuing concrete studies, indulge in vague discussions in high-sounding terms. They take such terms as 'faith' and 'sincerity' and call them 'right,' and regard anything connected with 'wealth' and 'strength'

4. See *China's Destiny*, footnote p. 134.

as 'might.' They do not realize that the distinction between 'right' and 'might' and the distinction between 'faith' and 'gains' depend on human nature and not on ways and means. We must recognize that 'benevolence' and 'faith' are steps to 'wealth' and 'strength'—they are basically interrelated. To become wealthy and strong by acting in conformity with man's nature is 'right:' to do so by using measures contrary to man's nature is 'might.' That which is based on 'faith' is 'right' and that based on 'gains' is 'might.' So I say that the distinction depends on man's nature and not on ways and means." On the basis of this theory, Chang achieved notable success in preventing further concentration of land ownership, surveying farm land, equalizing taxes and services, developing trade and reorganizing the military system.

The theories of the aforementioned economists differed, but their origins and objectives were similar. None was based on man's wants—particularly on the wants of any special individual or individuals. All were based on man's nature and all their objectives were national planning and the people's livelihood. To attain these objectives all of them centered their efforts on economic planning and control. They revised their policies as conditions changed, but these revisions did not alter the theories on which their policies were based. Their policies centered around the land problem, and the methods proposed for solving the land problem were all thought out from the standpoint of agricultural-industrial and agricultural-commercial relations. The monopoly of the market by merchants and the annexation of land by the rich and powerful were interrelated—each being the cause of the other. The concentration of land holdings not only affected national finances and the people's livelihood, but also conscription, the military system, and national defense. For this reason, Sun Yat-sen proposed the "Equalization of Land Rights" policy during the time of T'ung Meng Hui [5] [United League of Revolutionaries]. The foregoing is sufficient to demonstrate

5. See *China's Destiny*, footnote p. 50.

that the land problem occupies a central place in the economic problems of China, and that land policy is basic in our economic theories.

2. Western Economic Theories

Western economic theories may be divided into several categories. Natural resources, geographic setting, climatic conditions, historical background, racial spirit, and social phenomena vary in different countries, and their economic theories differ in consequence. The medieval agricultural economics of Western Europe developed into modern commercial-industrial economics during the seventeenth and eighteenth centuries, and this gave rise at different times to different theories, some giving more importance to commerce and others attaching greater weight to agriculture. Those who believed that commerce was the more important urged the government to intervene for the protection of trade and the development of industry. Those who emphasized the importance of agriculture advocated a *laissez-faire* policy and concentration on agriculture as the only productive enterprise. The former were concerned with money, while the latter stressed the importance of products. During the eighteenth and nineteenth centuries, the Industrial Revolution occurred in Western Europe. At that time, the English economist, Adam Smith, wrote his *Wealth of Nations* [1776] in which he discussed both commerce and agriculture. The book won wide popularity in Europe, and for a considerable period individualistic and *laissez-faire* economic theories were widespread. Toward the middle of the nineteenth century, however, German economic thinking developed into an independent system. Friedrich List, in his *System of National Economy*, opposed Smith's individualism and advocated a nationalist approach. He also urged a protectionist policy in opposition to Smith's theory of free trade. By the beginning of the twentieth century, as a result of [Othmar] Spann's *Foundation of Economics* and other similar works, German economic theory began to concentrate on [national] self-sufficiency in every respect.

Though American economic thought had the same origin as English, American economic theories advocated protectionist policies with regard to foreign trade and tended toward planning in the domestic economy—a tendency that was particularly marked after the First World War. Great Britain alone continued to adhere to the theories of Adam Smith, though these also had undergone many changes. During the nineteenth century, David Ricardo's "theory of economic rent" exercised a greater influence than the *Wealth of Nations*, and early in the twentieth century, the theories of mathematicians like [Alfred] Marshall[6] displaced those of Adam Smith and Ricardo, while the welfare economics of J. A. Hobson also gained popularity. The economic theory of Karl Marx, although he himself considered it to be a branch of orthodox economic theory, is the product of German idealism and differs in origin from English economic theory. Lenin's theory was based on that of Marx, but his political and economic theory and policies differed radically from those of Kautsky. Before and after the Russian Revolution, the disputes between Lenin and Kautsky represented the disagreement between the proletarian politicians and the social democrats among the Marxists, and indicated the fundamental differences that existed between the Marxists of Germany and of Russia.

Although Western economic theories differed, their origin was similar. All of them sought to explain existing economic phenomena in terms of human wants. When the *Wealth of Nations* was published, the disputes among economists centered on the problem of value. Adam Smith maintained that society is a collection of individuals, each of whom produces goods for their exchange value on the market; the exchange

6. Alfred Marshall was not a mathematical economist; he was the last and one of the greatest of the utilitarian classical economists.

value and the freedom of exchange of these goods being maintained by the market. He also held that money is only an expression of the exchange value of commodities; that economics is the study of these exchanges and transfers; and that economics, therefore, is the study of values or of exchanges among a great number of people. Marx's *Das Kapital* opposes the theories of the *Wealth of Nations*, but it too starts with an analysis of the value of commodities. Marx regarded capitalist economy in terms of the sum total of commodities, and the commodities themselves as a synthesis of the contradictions between use value and exchange value. Thus his theories, too, did not extend beyond the scope of the theory of value.

There are different views about the origin of "value" in Western economics, but every school believes that it derives from human wants. At the end of the nineteenth century, the Austrian economists began to discuss "marginal utility" on the theory that value depends upon human wants. For example, to a hungry man, the first bowl of rice is more valuable than the second and third, and successive bowls will approach "marginal utility" as their value decreases with each additional bowl. This theory became popular in the United States, and at the beginning of the twentieth century, the American economist, J. B. Clark, expanded it to explain the phenomena of interest, wages, and rent. Karl Marx's labor theory of value is contrary to the "marginal utility" theory and derives from the classical theory of value. According to this theory, commodities possess use value because they are able to satisfy human wants, and exchange value because they are the products of a measurable amount of labor. For example, five pieces of cloth are exchanged for one picul of rice; this means that the amount of labor represented in five pieces of cloth is equivalent to that contained in one picul of rice. Even today, the Communists maintain this rigid theory of value with little if any change. Although these two theories are opposed to each other, their point of origin is the same—human wants.

During the nineteenth century, the newly industrialized states that were competing with the advanced industrial nations of Western Europe adopted a protectionist trade policy. Though American economic theories had the same origin as those of England, the United States pursued a protectionist policy contrary to the free trade policy of Great Britain. This tendency exercised a strong influence on the development of economic theory. The German economist, Friedrich List, was apparently influenced by American protectionism when he wrote his *System of National Economy*, and with the end of the nineteenth century and the beginning of the twentieth, the basis of industrial and commercial organization in American and European countries shifted from free competition to monopoly and concentration. Following the First World War, this trend became even more pronounced, and the economic theories of various countries underwent similar changes.

During this period, the American economist, Thorstein Veblen, strongly criticized both individualism and Marxism and endeavored to formulate rules for the economic development of mankind based on human nature. He stressed the unselfish characteristics of mankind, such as the love of parents and the willingness to serve, as the basis for social progress and racial existence. Lester Ward, the American welfare economist, like Spann of Germany, criticized economic theories that emphasized materialism and profit-seeking. He argued that the value theory only pertains to problems of personal property, and that the highest goal of economics can be attained only on the basis of social welfare theories. Similarly, Hobson, the English welfare economist, criticized the post-Ricardian economists for their preoccupation with the production, accumulation, exchange and consumption of wealth. In his view, such economics was merely the science of commerce, and he argued that the objectives of economics should not be limited to the increase of wealth; that emphasis should also be placed on the rational control of labor and the equitable distribution and consumption of commodities, in order that society might gradually attain optimum welfare.

From the foregoing analysis, it is clear that the most recent trend in Western economic theory is to seek an understanding of human nature over and above mere human wants, and an understanding of social organization over and above private individuals. The scope of economics has thus risen above the value theory, and the objectives of economics have similarly transcended profit-seeking. I am confident that the present World War will strengthen this trend, and that after the war, Western economists will abandon their selfish individualism and materialism and, starting from human nature and aiming at the people's livelihood, will strive to attain the same goal as that prescribed in the economic theories of ancient China.[7]

7. All students of modern economics will recognize the total inadequacy and striking inaccuracy of this "analysis" of Western economic theory and Western economists. It does not indicate even a grammar school acquaintance with Western economic thought. It is a complete perversion of the true facts in order to reach a conclusion that suits the author's own purpose. As for the comments on individual economists, it is worth special note that the author comes closest to accuracy in considering Othmar Spann a "praiseworthy" critic of materialism and profit-seeking. Spann is generally regarded by Western economists as a "clerical Fascist" who derived his theories of the complete subordination of the individual to the state from the romantic medieval concepts of Adam Müller, an extreme German nationalist of the early nineteenth century. Spann's "universalism," with which he sought to oppose the "individualism" of current economic theories, is based on the idea of authoritarian control by a feudal state, translated into modern terms of "National Socialism" or Fascism.

CHAPTER THREE

ECONOMIC DUTIES OF THE STATE IN ANCIENT CHINA

THE principles of Chinese economic theory were not merely the discoveries of a few scholars and great economists. They also formed the basis of activity of great men of the past who used their abilities and wisdom, and even sacrificed their lives and property to put these principles into practice.[1] In addition to studying the economic theories of ancient China, we should pay particular attention to the actual constructive economic activities of various dynasties, in order to understand thoroughly the principles of Chinese economics. The economic duties of the nation are twofold—to support the people and to protect the people. Let me explain the constructive eco-

---

1. This seems as appropriate a place as any to include a general comment on the author's discussion of "Chinese economics." In the first place, it is based on quotations from the classics and ancient dynastic histories, arbitrarily removed from their historical context and applied to modern conditions of which their authors were naturally ignorant. The dictums of Confucius, Mencius, and other ancient sages, no matter how pertinent to conditions in a feudal, agrarian society, can hardly be regarded as appropriate guides to the solution of modern economic problems. In fact, it is impossible to avoid the conclusion that this glorification of the wisdom of "ancient times" is designed to obscure the real nature of the present agrarian problem in China, and the urgent need for democratic reforms in the oppressive system of landlord-tenant relations and for the development of industry free from the strangling restrictions of bureaucratic control. Secondly, the fact that individual Chinese scholars and statesmen commented on or dealt with the specific economic problems of their day does not support the conclusion that there exists a Chinese "school of economics" superior to modern or "Western" economic theory, with its systematic and scientific analysis of economic data. Here, as in *China's Destiny*, the main object appears to be to glorify "ancient China," with its autocratic government and feudal agrarian economy, together with the political and social concepts of Confucianism, which provide an ideal philosophical base for a feudal-fascist state.

nomic activities of ancient times from these two standpoints.

Men desire to live and thus have wants which give rise to demands. There is a limit to the things that men need to exist, but there is no limit to their wants and demands. Since it is impossible to satisfy unlimited wants and demands with a limited supply of goods, human conflicts develop. The land problems of an agricultural community and the disputes between capitalists and workers in industrial centers are examples of such conflicts. Is there any way to end such conflicts? Yes. Since human nature is naturally benevolent and loving, there must be principles and methods for stopping them.

As an individual, every man wishes to listen to pleasing sounds, look at beautiful colors, eat good tasting things, wear comfortable clothing, live in a good house, and ride in good vehicles. If he subjects himself to the "wants" and "demands" of his ears and eyes, he is serving and is controlled by material things. This is what the *Analects* of Confucius mean by saying: "The mind of the small man is fixed on advantages." It is also what is meant by the statement in the "Great Learning" that "unkind men procure riches by bodily health," which means the same as "sacrifice one's life to gain possessions." We recognize that money and possessions are necessities of life, but it is extremely "unbenevolent" to die for possessions or riches simply because our ears, eyes, mouth, and body have been attracted by them. Appetites must be controlled by the mind, which is able to think, to consider, and to make distinctions. A man should consider his wants: which cannot and which should not be satisfied. He should also consider material possessions: which are not obtainable, and which it is not desirable to obtain. Furthermore, he should learn to differentiate between the things that should be consumed and those that should be saved, and between those that are for the good of the public and those that are private and harmful. If a man does all these, his activities will be well planned and he will be able to save money and use it to expand his enterprises.

In any group of men, personal demands will, unless limited, result in disputes. Hsun Tzu[2] in his "Chapter on Rites" stated: "Everyone from birth has wants. If he fails to satisfy them, his desires persist. If there is no fixed limit to personal wants, strife will arise. Fighting will disturb order and in [the course of the] disturbance, commodities will be scarce. The late King, fearing that such disturbances might occur, enacted rules for the distribution of things in such a way as to satisfy wants, meet demand, prevent the government from exhausting [the supply of] goods, and protect goods from being the slaves of individual wants, in order to balance the two [demand and supply]." This explains clearly how a group of men should be organized. The mind should control the appetites, and there should be rational machinery to enable each individual to sustain his life. A government, therefore, should be organized to satisfy the people's wants on the one hand, and to restrict them on the other. Once such rules are established and the necessary limitations made clear, the people will no longer find it necessary to resort to fighting to satisfy their wants, and society will not be impoverished for failing to satisfy the wants of individuals.

Aside from meeting or restricting human wants, there is a need for a government that manages the people's affairs. This is the basis of the philosophy of national economics. European *laissez-faire* economics holds that the government ought not to interfere with the people's economic activities, and advocates economic freedom and lack of restraint. The Marxists, on the other hand, believe that the government must be controlled by the proletariat to eliminate personal

2. Hsun Tzu was a philosopher of the Chou dynasty, living in the fourth century B.C., who differed with Confucius and Mencius in believing that the principle of authority should be based not on human "morality" but on the legal power of the state. Hsun was thus the forerunner of the Legalist school, which believed in a government of law rather than a government by "benevolence." The fact that Hsun Tzu's teachings are emphasized, together with those of Wang An-shih and Chang Chiang-ling, supports the conclusion that the author has selected classical sources that justify the doctrine of authoritarian control.

economic freedom. From the standpoint of Chinese economic principles, neither is right.[3] If a government does not impose restrictions on, or devise plans for the people's economic activities, and if it allows the people to drift into conflicts, the result will be social disorder and national poverty. If the government fails to control the people's wants and to protect their livelihood, it does not fulfill its duties; the people will not be able to live a comfortable life and there will be no increase in production. The following paragraphs discuss concrete activities to be undertaken by the government to meet or restrict the people's wants.

1. Satisfying the People's Wants

Confucius advocated: "Adequacy of food," and "first satisfy, then enrich." Mencius stated: "In the control of property, they should be able to support their parents, wives and children, to enjoy a happy year without fear of hunger, and to avoid death from starvation in years of poor harvest." Hsun Tzu said: "Everything under the sun and on the earth should be best used to support the people and make them happy." From this it is clear that the economic theories of ancient China considered the duties of the government to be of a positive nature, on the basis of which the governments of ancient times developed comprehensive economic plans and policies, of which the following are some of the most important:

Land Holding: The production of the farmers depends on land. The economic theory current in ancient China was that

3. This conclusion appears over and over again in all current Kuomintang literature. *China's Destiny* frequently points with pride to the fact that China's future does not lie in imitating either the West or the Soviet Union. Even such a liberal Kuomintang leader as Sun Fo often repeats this shibboleth, as if there were something magic and decisive about not being like something. Aside from the fact that the characterization of *laissez-faire* economics and the theory of the Soviet State is inaccurate, the conclusion that follows from this reasoning, as throughout the book, is for the adoption of a system of benevolent autocracy.

everybody should have land to cultivate. Mencius repeatedly said: "Five *mow* of house, a hundred *mow* of farm land." A land allotment system was enforced by the government, of which examples are the "well-land" system of the Ch'un Ch'iu period and the "equal-land" system after the Wei and Tsin dynasties [220–420]. After the T'ang dynasty [618–906], the "equal-land" system gradually disappeared, but certain features of the land allotment system continued.

Water Conservation: Irrigation is necessary for farming. To irrigate all the farm land requires planning and construction on the part of the Government. Emperor Yu [legendary founder of the Hsia dynasty in 2205 B.C.] was the first and greatest economist in ancient China, and his major contributions were water conservation and construction [of irrigation works]. Confucius said: "I cannot but laud Yu. He maintained a poorly built palace and gave all his energy to water conservation." Since the days of Yu, Chinese history contains a long record of conservation works and irrigation control. Why should water conservation and construction activities related to it be undertaken by the Government? Conservation plans must aim at the benefit of all farmers and not merely that of a limited number of persons—especially, they should not be solely for the good of one or two wealthy gentry.[4] Unless consideration is given to all farmers in the area, the building of dikes and the demarcation of farm land to be included will inevitably cause the soil and sand to block the river, or to accumulate on the river bed, thus causing a flood in the lower reaches. With streams containing a limited quantity of water, the distribution and storage of water requires control by dams. Since fishing and irrigation are apt to come into conflict, there must also be rules to restrict fishing in order to facilitate irrigation and vice versa. Also, since the

4. The author fails to note that the primary purpose of these "benevolent" water-conservation plans was to enable the bureaucracy and the wealthy gentry to collect their unearned tribute of grain.

needs of irrigation and transport sometimes conflict, there must be a system to preserve enough water in the rivers to permit transportation and also to restrict transportation to facilitate irrigation. This has been the practice among the people, and there have also been detailed ordinances and laws enacted by the Government. But [present-day] students of economic principles and policies have been confused by Western theories and are unable to understand practical economics, much less to further these basic economic principles. This is very much to be regretted.

Granary Storage: To support the people, it is essential to accumulate savings. The *Book of Rites* advises: "Save one year's crops from every three years' harvests." The ancient sages also said: "Kings rely on their people, and people rely on food." The governments of the various dynasties of China, therefore, devoted much thought to the storage of grain, and the national wealth was determined by the amount of grain stored in granaries. This theory is opposed to the economic theories advocating free trade. The free-trade economists consider the export of surplus products and the import of money as national wealth. Not until the present time have foreign nations understood the necessity of developing and saving resources as a means of increasing national wealth.

Communications: Agricultural products must be exchanged for other commodities, and this exchange depends on transportation. China is a continental country and her mountains and waterways run mainly from west to east. There is no natural waterway between the south and the north. On the plains north of the Huai River, communications are hampered because the Yellow River is easily flooded. Under these geographic conditions, the construction of transport facilities and the care with which communications were systematically protected must be attributed to the greatness of our ancient rulers. This has enabled China to become a great and unified nation. The roads built during the Ch'in, Han, Sui, and

T'ang dynasties began at the principal cities and spread in all directions like a spider's web. During the period of the "Warring States," human labor was employed in digging the Grand Canal, which was connected with the Yangtze, Huai, Yellow, and Sze rivers during the Sui and T'ang dynasties. The canal is still the most famous engineering project in the world, and we cannot but praise our ancestors for the achievement of such a great work by an agricultural society.

Climate and Soil: In ancient times, the preparation of the calendar was an important task. We know that agricultural work must proceed in accordance with weather conditions, and in the past, the governments not only supplied the people with calendars but also prepared agricultural books giving the farmers directions for each season. We also know that soil conditions are a relatively new field of study in Western countries. But if we would only read the writings of Emperor Yu and Kuan Chung, we would realize that detailed soil research was carried on in ancient China. The governments of various dynasties taught the farmers how to select crops according to the productivity of the local soil. All these facts can be found in our historical records.

2. Restricting the People's Wants

In addition to advocating "adequacy of food," Confucius also urged the equalization of wealth, saying: "I am not worrying about shortage; I am worrying about unequal distribution." Similarly, Mencius advocated "support for the people" on the one hand and "economic supervision" on the other. According to him, "good government must begin with economic supervision." Since that time, the scholars of various dynasties have constantly discussed the demarcation and distribution of land, and the governments have issued various ordinances connected with this problem. The most important points in this connection are as follows:

Equalization of Property: The equalization of land holdings was enforced on numerous occasions in ancient China.[5] Whenever the concentration of land ownership occurred on a large scale, there was always a movement for the equalization of property. History teaches us that the equalization of land holdings by compulsory means is certain to fail, e.g., the "land order" of Wang Mang[6] and the "farm land system" of the T'ai-p'ings[7] both failed when an effort was made to carry them out. A detailed study of history reveals that the land problem cannot be solved by distributing the land by force. We must first support the people, for unless and until the farmer's livelihood is improved and farm production increased, no policy for equalizing property will be successful. The statesmen of ancient China therefore adopted the following measure.

Equalizing Taxes: The ancient rules and ordinances with regard to the tax system in China called for the allotment of land to male citizens and the collection of taxes according to the number of allotments. In subsequent periods, the land was not allotted in this way, but taxes continued to be levied on the basis of the number of persons. The equalization of taxes therefore required that farm land be surveyed. In the late years of the Ming dynasty, the tax system was changed, and taxes were computed on the basis of the area of farm land. This also required a land survey. The methods used for surveying land were "owners' evidence" in the Han dynasty, resembling the present day "applicant's report;" Wang An-

5. It would be more accurate to say that land was periodically redistributed, as a result of antidynastic upheavals, changes of dynasty, and the emergence of a new ruling bureaucracy.

6. Wang Mang, a member of the Empress's family, usurped the throne of the Han rulers during the period A.D. 9–25, but failed to found a dynasty. The "land order" referred to was an attempt to restore the ancient "well-land" or *ching-t'ien* system by limiting landholdings to 900 *mow* for a family with eight or less male members, on the grounds that the ancient *ching* for eight families consisted of 900 *mow*. Wang ordered that all families owning more than 900 *mow* should give the surplus to neighbors or relatives, but this action was opposed by all the wealthy and powerful families, and he was forced to rescind the law and decree that land could once more be freely bought and sold.

7. See *China's Destiny*, footnote, p. 194.

shih's "square land" calculation, similar to the present "land survey"; and the method developed by Chu Hsi[8] which was comparable to the current method of checking applicant's reports with the survey reports of local officials. These various methods have both advantages and disadvantages, but can in no way be compared with the Father of our Country's method of equalizing land rights which is excellent in every way.

Transport: The collection and distribution of agricultural products depend on merchants, but if the merchants are allowed to manipulate prices, this will harm either the farmers or the people. To prevent this, there was developed in ancient times the method of equalizing supplies by transport. The general theory was to transport goods from any locality where prices had dropped because of a surplus, to places where prices had risen because of shortages. This method was successfully adopted by Liu Yen in the T'ang dynasty, whose theory was to "facilitate the transport of goods as a fundamental principle, and to use the government's power to devise a general plan for the distribution of goods that would deprive the merchants of all power and opportunity to manipulate prices."

Government Monopolies: An agricultural community endeavors to be self-supporting, but there are certain commodities that cannot be produced everywhere. Salt, for example, is a necessity that can only be made by using sea water in the southeast or the water of the salt wells in the northwest. If salt is marketed by merchants, the farmers will be subjected to extortion. The salt laws have been changed many times since ancient days, but have always returned to the principle of government monopoly. Similar monopolies were also established for iron and tea.

Rural Credit: If the financing of agricultural production depended on the merchants, it would involve high interest rates. Ancient laws, therefore, placed strict restrictions on the rate

8. A leading Confucianist scholar and statesman of the Sung dynasty.

of interest on loans, and many statesmen and scholars discussed the theory that the Government and not the merchants should provide rural capital.

In summary, the economic duties of the Government are twofold: to satisfy the people's wants and at the same time to restrict them. The former involves positive support, and the latter precautionary control. The former may be regarded as an act of "benevolence" and the latter an act of "justice." It is thus clear that benevolence and justice were not vague teachings in ancient times. The application of these principles in social, political, and economic organization will result in correct systems and policies.

3. Protecting the People

The economic duties of a government are to support the people—the people's livelihood—on the one hand, and to protect the people—national defense—on the other. The people's livelihood and national defense are a single problem. In actual practice, the ancient land system was in itself a system of conscription—a very important point that should be clarified. Confucius repeatedly stated: "Adequacy of food and sufficient soldiers;" Mencius declared: "In economic control no reference is made to conscription," meaning that the land system was the conscription system. The *Book of Rites* provides a very clear explanation of the imperial policy with regard to this question. To combine soldiers and farmers has been a traditional ideal in Chinese history but the motives may differ. There is the kingly way or the tyrant's way. Hsun Tzu said: "To cherish the people is the way of the king; to cherish the soldiers is the way of the tyrant." This means that to support the people with land is "right," while to support soldiers with land is "might." The Confucianists advocated the former, while the Legalists supported the latter theory. If the people are supported with land, this will protect the farms by making all the people themselves soldiers—the way of "right." To support the soldiers with land will enable them to fight vigorously, but will inevitably impoverish the people—the way of "might." Mencius on several occasions stated that "benevolence is invincible," and that "good government must start with economic supervision." Economic supervision was the foundation of conscription. Once economic supervision is established, all the people will become soldiers and will be able to "take up arms to beat the soldiers of the Ch'in and Ch'u kingdoms" [a metaphorical phrase signifying any strong enemy]. These ancient teachings are very direct, very definite, and not mere abstract generalities.

Since ancient times, these concrete systems and policies have been discussed. The "well-land" system, though it had its strong supporters, was never adopted after the Ch'un-Ch'iu period. Those who tried to reinstitute it failed. Now that China, an agricultural country, wishes to become an industrialized country, our agricultural policy is to equalize land rights and improve agricultural techniques. Plows and harrows should be gradually replaced with farm machinery and the present small, parcelized farms should be consolidated into collective farms in order to save labor and increase production. There are already co-operative organizations of various kinds in China, as well as the custom of labor exchange during the busy seasons [one man with special skill doing the work for another, and vice versa], and it should be easy to develop such co-operation still further. It is not necessary to go back to the "well-land" system, but the collective farm [9] system might easily be adopted in its place. With regard to national defense, the farmers of each unit of nine farms [under the "well-land" system] made up a military unit in ancient times. In the future, the farmers of each collective farm could be considered as a group of soldiers assigned to cultivate the

9. It must be noted the term "collective farming" is not used in the same sense as it is in Soviet Russia, nor does it correspond to capitalist or co-operative farming in Western countries. It signifies purely and simply a modernized version of the ancient feudal system of economic-military village units.

land. Thus, a production unit would also be a military unit. This combination of the land and conscription systems could be realized by the adoption of a system for its practical enforcement.

The interrelation of national defense and the people's livelihood is obvious from the foregoing explanation. History teaches that the combination of the two makes a country strong and their separation makes it weak. That this has always been true is demonstrated by the following analysis of three periods: (1) The conscription system of the Han dynasties [207 B.C.–A.D. 221], though not precisely an enforcement of the principles of "supporting the people," was an ordinary militia system. Every subject was compelled to do military service for a period of two years. "Even the premier's son must do garrison duty on the national frontier." Since most of the people were farmers at that time, the soldiers were chiefly farmers, and the government was very successful in military conquests. (2) The Southern and Northern Empires [A.D. 316–589] and the Sui and T'ang dynasties [A.D. 589–907] adopted the "equal-land" and "farmer-soldier" systems, but the characteristic features of these systems had already altered. After the middle of the T'ang dynasty, the army was composed chiefly of the sons of noble families, who enlisted to escape paying taxes and performing public services, with the result that pride, idleness, and slackness developed in the ranks. Ever since then, the farmer-soldier system of China has been a failure. The military conquests of the early years of the T'ang dynasty and the division of the empire by high-ranking military officers in the later years of the T'ang illustrated the results of combining and of separating the farm and conscription systems. (3) After the Sung dynasty, the mercenary soldier system was adopted, and the farmer-soldier system disappeared. The old system of training the people as soldiers did not endure because land ownership had become too concentrated, despite efforts to restore it [redivide it] by Wang An-shih, T'ai Tsu [first Emperor of the Ming dy-

nasty, 1368–98], and Chang Chu-cheng [Minister of the
Ming dynasty]. The fact remains, however, that the recapture
of Linchow by Wang An-shih, the defeat of the Japanese invaders by General Wei Chi-kuang [commander of the Ming
armies that defeated Hideyoshi in Korea, 1592–8], and
the suppression of civil war by Tseng Kuo-fan[10] were accomplished chiefly with the aid of farmer-soldiers. But with social
economics and national defense economics separated, the
country was inevitably weakened and was subject to constant
aggression from abroad.

Since modern wars are fought by the entire nation, we
must re-establish the system of combining soldiers and farmers.
Only in this way will there be an ample supply of recruits and
reinforcements. Only in this way will the people realize that
they are fighting for the protection of their own homes. Only
in this way will we be able to fight a prolonged and extensive
war. Henceforth, we must strictly enforce this system, not
only to correct the mistakes made in the Sung and Yuan dynasties, but also because this system is essential to enable the
nation to fight a modern war.

10. This reference is to the T'ai-p'ing Rebellion. It is incorrect to refer to Tseng Kuo-fan's troops or those of Wang An-shih and Wei Chi-kuang as "farmer-soldiers" in the sense of farmers trained as military reserves, since this system had not existed since the early T'ang dynasty. Furthermore, as noted previously, the mercenaries that were primarily responsible for the defeat of the T'ai-p'ings were foreign-led.

CHAPTER FOUR

ECONOMIC PRINCIPLES OF THE "MIN SHENG CHU I"—THE PEOPLE'S LIVELIHOOD

THE traditional economic principles of former dynasties may be summarized as follows:

Supporting the People: The basis of economics is human nature and its fundamental purpose is to support the people. Sun Yat-sen said: "The Principle of the People's Livelihood is designed to support the people, while capitalism seeks profits." He also said that "social progress should be measured by the people's livelihood and not by material production." In other words, the basic principle of Chinese economic theory is that commodities are valued not for their own sake but for the sake of the people. This is what is meant by the saying, "be kind to men and have regard for things," which also refers to the people's livelihood.

A Planned Economy: Inasmuch as economics is based on human nature, it calls for "supporting wants and supplying demand" on the one hand, and on the other, for developing man's rational nature and mental powers so that he may distinguish between and restrict his wants. Economic development must therefore be planned, and that planning must rest on a basic theory. The basic theory of the Principle of the People's Livelihood is to develop national enterprises and aid the people in order to improve their livelihood, while at the same time controlling private capital and equalizing land ownership in order to prevent the capitalistic control of the people's livelihood. Chinese economic principles are not those of *laissez-faire*, nor of promoting the class struggle. They call

277

for economic plans to "nationalize capital for popular enjoyment"—to realize the ideal of [government] "for the people,"
whereby China may become a wealthy, healthy, and happy
state.

Combining the People's Livelihood and National Defense: Since
the basic purpose of economics is to support the people, the
Government should develop natural resources, improve transportation, and accumulate national wealth, and at the same
time, make certain that the farmers and the wealth of peace
time will be transformed into soldiers and military supplies in
time of war. Only if a program of economic development is
based on the people's livelihood will it suit the needs of national defense.

1. Laissez-faire and Marxism

Only if China's economic reconstruction is based on these
three principles will she achieve success. There are some who
do not understand the principles contained in the Principle
of the People's Livelihood, and who have proposed different
plans in accordance with Western economic theories. Without
exception, their proposals are unsuited to the present needs
and social structure of China. The most important defects and
disadvantages in their proposals may be summarized as
follows:

The *laissez-faire* economists propose that China should be
industrialized according to the *laissez-faire* policies and free
trade doctrines of Western Europe, on the ground that only
in this way can industrial progress be facilitated. They fail to
realize that the *laissez-faire* theory is based on a system of free
competition such as developed in Western Europe after the
First Industrial Revolution. At that time, the industries of
England, France, and other countries enjoyed markets both
at home and abroad, and as a consequence, English and
French manufacturers supported the policy of free competition and free trade as the best means of achieving industrial

prosperity. Subsequently, Germany and the United States became strong industrial powers and began to compete with the Western European nations. As this competition became more and more severe, free trade was replaced by protection. In order to strengthen their competitive power abroad, the entrepreneurs combined the strength of individual factories producing similar goods by forming trusts or cartels, and even centralized this power through government operation of industry. This trend has been called the Second Industrial Revolution. And today it may be said that there is basically no reason for *laissez-faire* economics.

Because she has been subjected to the bondage of the unequal treaties and is industrially backward, China cannot compete with the advanced industrial nations. She must therefore adopt a protectionist policy with regard to foreign trade, and a policy of economic planning with respect to her industrial development. Private capital alone will not be sufficient to operate on a large scale, or to compete with the trusts and government-operated enterprises of foreign nations. This is the great weakness of *laissez-faire* economic theory, and it is this that makes it unsuitable for China. Having long ago recognized this defect, the Father of our Country said: "The tendency of modern economics is to substitute economic concentration for free competition." His plan for dealing with this situation was: "In China, two revolutions must be launched simultaneously: the replacement of hand labor by machinery, and unification under government-ownership." Only if this policy is adopted can Chinese industry hope to achieve unimpeded progress.

The Marxists advocate the overthrow of the capitalists by class struggle and the organization of a Communist society. This theory is based on a belief in class selfishness—a fundamental error. In pointing out this error, Sun Yat-sen said: "In the past and present, man devoted his energies to the sole purpose of maintaining existence. Since man seeks uninterrupted existence, there must be unceasing social progress. Thus the established rule of social progress is the effort of mankind to maintain existence, which is the real reason for such progress. Class struggle is not the cause of social progress, but a disease arising in the course of social progress. The reason for this disease is the failure of certain men to maintain their existence, and for this reason wars occur." On the basis of this analysis, Sun Yat-sen described Karl Marx as a social pathologist rather than a social physiologist.

Marxists consider labor the only important factor in production. [They hold that] all value is produced by labor, and that profits and land rent are surplus value produced by labor. They do not recognize that manpower and land are basic requirements of production, and that manpower includes mental as well as physical strength. Industrial goods are not only the product of the labor of factory workers, technicians, and managers, but also of the inventors and manufacturers of the machinery used in the factories concerned. Similarly, the profits of industry are not only due to the labor of the workers, but also to the management of the enterprise, the blueprints of the technicians, the transport of the commodities by rail or highway, and the activities of commercial houses. Each step in the process of the production and consumption of goods is a source of industrial profit. Sun Yat-sen declared: "The surplus value of industry should not be attributed solely to the labor of workmen in the factory. All members of society possessing usefulness or ability have more or less, directly or indirectly, contributed to production or consumption." We must recognize that each man's activities are only a part of the activities of all members of society, and that the production of each article is the result of the activities of all members of society. In view of this, Sun Yat-sen stated: "Social progress is due to the harmony of a majority of economic interests in society and not to their conflict. The harmony of economic interests in society works for the good of the majority of the people. Only if the majority of the people receive the benefit will there be social progress."

As for wars among mankind, the greatest wars are those between nations and not between classes. In the First World War, the workers of the European countries rejected the resolution of the Second International and fought for their respective countries. In the present World War, not only are the workers of Britain and the United States fighting for their own countries, but Soviet Russia is co-operating closely with Britain and America. Thus conflicts between capitalism and socialism have not harmed the united front among various nations because every man naturally wishes to protect his own existence, and the existence of an individual is insured by and depends on the strength of his nation. This may be explained from two standpoints, as follows:

First, from a political point of view, if one nation is conquered by another, the laborers as well as the capitalists suffer the fate of national destruction and racial extinction. This explains why [government] "of the people" precedes "for the people." No matter what theories the workers or the labor parties of various countries may claim to have adopted, they are all aware of this point. Therefore they abandoned the class struggle and joined forces [with the capitalists] when their countries were at war. Furthermore, in the countries defeated and conquered [by Germany] during the present European War, the workers, like the capitalists, were enslaved by the "Fascists." To engage in class struggle at such a critical time simply means the destruction of one's own country. Only a fool would think that it is unnecessary for a nation to use all its energies to lay the basis for economic reconstruction while it is fighting for national existence, or that the proletariat can, after national destruction, seize the opportunity to fight a revolution for the attainment of proletarian government.[1]

Second, from the economic point of view, the industrial development of a country enables the capitalists to make

1. It would be interesting to know how the author would reconcile this statement with the Russian Revolution of 1917.

profits, increases employment opportunities, and improves the people's livelihood. If industry does not progress, or if it declines, or is completely destroyed, not only will the capitalists have no factories to operate, but the workers will have no factories in which to work. Today, industrially backward nations are suffering because of their undeveloped industries, while the industrially advanced nations are threatened with the danger of total industrial destruction. If a nation is defeated in war, all industries will be destroyed by the enemy. The workers will have no work to do; they will be unemployed and unable to earn a living. For this reason, all workers regardless of their nationality, fight for their own countries. This is a definite, self-evident fact. Karl Marx failed to understand this basic feature of human nature and saw only temporary defects. His theory is a medicine that does not suit the disease, and Chinese who believe in his theory suffer from the symptoms of an imaginary ailment.

China is suffering because her industry is undeveloped. As Sun Yat-sen said, the economy of the nation consists of poor and poorer people. No real class struggle can exist between the poor and the poorer. In future, after the abolition of the unequal treaties and the achievement of a free and independent status, if industry in China should develop according to *laissez-faire* principles, it is probable that industrial development would be followed by class conflicts or even class struggle. But China does not intend to adopt *laissez-faire* principles. She has adopted an economic system based upon the Principle of the People's Livelihood, which aims at the simultaneous achievement of the social and industrial revolutions. The Principle of the People's Livelihood is based on human nature and its objective is the people's livelihood. On the one hand, national industries must be developed, and on the other, private capital must be brought under control. Thus there will be no real motive for class struggle, since the workers will only enjoy increasing opportunities for employment and the improvement of their livelihood, and will not suffer from capitalistic oppression. The industrialization of China can succeed without suffering from the effects of the "class struggle," as the Communists call it.

Another important feature of the Principle of the People's Livelihood is the equalization of land rights. This is the correct way to solve the land problem, which has a long history in China. Chinese history teaches us that the land problem cannot be solved by force, and that efforts to solve it by force or compulsory means are bound to fail immediately. Chinese economic theory regards man as basic. "Where there are men, there is land" means that land has no value by itself, and that its value is created by adding manpower to it, i.e., farming or cultivation. In sparsely populated areas, everyone has sufficient land and no land problem arises, but such areas will gradually diminish in China. In densely populated areas, or in areas where industry and commerce are prosperous, agriculture will be seriously affected by industry and commerce. Because of that effect, there is a natural tendency toward the sale and purchase of land. Rich men invest their money in the purchase and sale of land, thus causing an unequal distribution of land ownership. Since the feudal system of China was destroyed several thousand years ago, the unequal distribution of land is not inherited from feudalism, but must be attributed to the influence of industrial and commercial economics. Unless attention is paid to the relations between agriculture and industry, and between agriculture and commerce, any forcible equalization of land ownership will not last long. After a short period, the distribution will again become unequal. Will not a poor farmer who kills a rich farmer today become rich tomorrow? Such [forcible] methods misinterpret the nature of the land problem, because they are based on material conditions and not on human nature. If such a policy is followed, a repetition of the failures of history is certain.

Why should the land problem be considered in terms of agricultural-industrial relations? The characteristic feature of the ancient Chinese economy may be expressed by the saying: "Men cultivating, and women spinning." In every family, agricultural and industrial production were combined, and this combined agricultural and industrial economy was self-supporting. With the exception of salt, iron, and other commodities of a special nature, farmers did not have to buy goods originating outside the locality. For this reason, the monopoly of the sale of salt and iron was an important economic problem in ancient China. In modern times mechanized industry has gradually affected the [self-sufficiency of the] farms because many forms of industrial production have been taken over by factories in the cities. The self-supporting economy of the rural districts has been gradually destroyed, and in order to buy goods from outside, the farmers have found it necessary to sell their products. Thus the commercial economy has tended to dominate the rural economy. As mentioned above, many economists of various dynasties studied the relation between agriculture and commerce and worked out policies to deal with this problem. What must be emphasized here is that Chinese commercial capital has always been invested in land. The more prosperous the commercial market, the more land has been concentrated in the hands of a few individuals. Instead of investing in industry, commercial capital has continued to be invested in land. In cities, the accumulation of capital results in hoarding of goods; in rural districts, in the acquisition of land.

The land policy embodied in the Principle of the People's Livelihood starts with the stabilization of land values. It prohibits the investment of commercial capital in land and this prevents land from being an object of speculation. The inability of rich men to invest their money in land will automatically equalize land ownership and will prevent these equalized land rights from becoming unequal. In addition to enforcing this policy, the Government should also take the necessary measures to finance agricultural production, adjust the prices of farm products, and improve agricultural techniques and the farmers' livelihood. In this way, the land problem will be solved.

Once the land problem is solved, commercial capital will no longer be invested in land, but will be invested in industry instead. The industrial policy expressed in the Principle of the People's Livelihood is to "abandon hand labor for machinery, and to unify industry under Government ownership." Government-owned industry will need the raw materials produced in the rural districts and will also need the rural districts as markets for manufactured goods. Thus the prosperity of large-scale Government-owned industry and the development of agriculture are interrelated and not contradictory.

To summarize the foregoing analysis, we may say that the land problem should be considered in terms of agricultural-industrial, and more especially of agricultural-commercial relations in order to achieve a real solution. The solution of the land problem will not only put an end to commercial profiteering and the enlargement of land holdings, but will also facilitate the industrialization of China and lay a foundation for national defense and future constructive enterprises related to the people's livelihood.

Sun Yat-sen commented in detail on the economic theories of *laissez-faire* and of Marxism. Everyone should study this question thoroughly and ponder it carefully. The above are only a few of the more important points.

2. Sun Yat-sen's "Industrial Plan"

Since the people's livelihood is the basis of all our economic thinking, economic planning and the identification of the people's livelihood with national defense are fundamental features of the Principle of the People's Livelihood. To develop this statement in greater detail: Sun Yat-sen adopted the essence of the industrial, social, and economic theories of the West, corrected their errors, remedied their shortcomings, and transformed them to suit the principles of Chinese economics, so that they emerged as the ideals of the Principle of the People's Livelihood. On the basis of these ideals, Sun Yatsen wrote his great and all-inclusive "Industrial Plan," which is the basis of the national-defense economic plans of China. It is highly regrettable that he only drafted an outline of the Ten-Year National Defense Plan and was unable to complete the text of the plan itself for our guidance, but the principles and measure of national-defense economics may be deduced from his "Industrial Plan."

The scope of the "Industrial Plan" is more extensive than the highway and water-conservation plans of the T'ang and Han dynasties, and its outline is more detailed than the economic laws and ordinances of those dynasties. Unfortunately, there seem to be very few people who really understand the essence of the Plan, so I wish to make some simple explanations at this point.

In the first place, the basic idea of the "Industrial Plan" is to formulate measures for the economic development of China, with her vast land area as a base and with prosperous sea harbors as outlets for exports. Foreign trade is to be carried on via the seaports [while trade in the products of] agriculture and mining should be conducted overland. In time of peace, trade with foreign countries is to be carried on through the seaports, while in time of war the inland area will serve as a base for [military] operations. The basic idea of combining the people's livelihood and national defense is especially evident and important in the Plan. And if one reads the Plan from the standpoint of this combination, one will find that each section and each category contain measures of far-reaching importance.

Second, the "Industrial Plan" considers communications, agriculture and mining as the basic economic enterprises. People in general refer only to industry when they discuss the industrialization of China. They fail to recognize that in order for China to become industrialized, it is first necessary to develop the resources of the interior, carry out rural economic reforms, improve the farmers' livelihood and make the rural districts a market for industrial products. In order to develop the resources of the interior, it is necessary to build railways and increase the number of waterways throughout the country. In order for China to become industrialized, it is necessary to develop agriculture and mining, since these are the main sources of raw materials for industry. Once communications, agriculture, and mining have been developed, there will be raw materials for industry and a market for finished products. Naturally, economic conditions will then be improved.

Third, the "Industrial Plan" emphasizes the equal distribution of the population. The trend toward the concentration of the population in the southeast during the past century is much more serious than it was during the Sung and Ming dynasties. The "Industrial Plan" calls for the emigration of the people in the southeast to the northwest and southwest in order that the population of the country may be equally distributed. Special emphasis is given to the necessity of increasing the population in the northwest and southwest in order to make these areas the bases for armed resistance and national development.

Fourth, the industry to be developed under the "Industrial Plan" should of necessity be distributed among the farms and mines. According to the Plan, the interior should not only possess modern means of communications and prosperous agriculture and mining, but industry should also be distributed equally. Chinese industry, in order to be near the areas producing raw materials, to find markets for finished products, and to meet the needs of the people, should be located at inland centers. From the standpoint of national defense, industry scattered throughout the interior will develop the potential material strength of all parts of the country. As far as the people's livelihood is concerned, cities and rural districts will be brought into equilibrium, and will not be separated or radically different, as is the case with the present gap of one or two centuries between living conditions in the coastal cities and those in the rural districts of the northwest and southwest.

Fifth, the "Industrial Plan" calls for the equal development of China, both in the interior and on the coast, and also for the equal development of all localities. The various chapters of the Plan reveal that the late Father of our Country considered every district of China and wished to utilize each one to the best possible advantage. During the Sung, Ming, and later dynasties, the activities of the government were on a reduced scale. Even during the Han and T'ang dynasties, when the scope of government activities was extensive, the central provinces were overemphasized and the border regions were neglected. The "Industrial Plan," however, is sufficiently broad in scope to enable China to become a strong nation.

The "Industrial Plan" is extremely complex, and the above are only some of the most essential points. A study of the full text of the Plan, after grasping these central points, enables us to understand not only the truth contained in the Principle of the People's Livelihood, but also the validity of the general principles of national-defense economics embodied in Sun Yat-sen's Ten-Year National Defense Plan.

CHAPTER FIVE

CHINA'S FUTURE ECONOMIC IDEALS

WE HAVE discussed the most important, present-day economic principles of China, but these are still not the ultimate ideals of China. The ancient scholars studied the truth embodied in the economic principles that Sun Yat-sen understood so clearly. During his lifetime, he discussed both policies and methods, and he praised the chapter, "The Great Harmony," [*Ta T'ung*] in the *Book of Rites*, which embodies the final economic goal of the Three People's Principles, i.e., the economic ideals that China should strive to realize.

Though world development cannot be foreseen in detail, its abstract principles should be thoroughly understood. The same holds true for economic development. No one can foretell the details, but everyone should understand the principles. Some of these principles have already become facts, while others have not yet been translated into practice. But these principles are not altered simply because all of them have not yet been put into effect. The ancient wise men of China understood all the principles of economic development, and the chapter "The Great Harmony" in the *Book of Rites* pictures a world in which all these principles are actually enforced.

In the world of the "Great Harmony" when human nature is developed to the highest point, no one will be able to earn a living by sitting idle and none will be unable to find work. All adults should work, and the social system will be such as to provide every adult with the opportunity to fulfill his obligation. This is what is meant by the saying: "Adults shall be of service." Moreover, everyone should strive to earn a living for mankind and not for himself. Thus the "Great Harmony" states: "It is regrettable if one does not work. What he does is not necessarily for himself."

The people's livelihood as described in the world of the "Great Harmony" is entirely satisfactory. All resources must be developed for the people's use, and the failure to develop these resources is a fault. The development of production will result in surplus products, but these should not be privately owned or used for satisfying private wants. Hence the statement: "It is regrettable if any resources are not developed. Such resources when developed are not necessarily for personal use."

The economic activities proposed in the world of the "Great Harmony" provide a most satisfactory basis for progress. The producers produce for the welfare of mankind and the distributors distribute according to the needs of each individual. The people as a whole have the responsibility and ability to support those who have passed or have not yet attained working age, as well as those who are unable to work. This is what is meant by the statement: "Old enabled to work, minors enabled to grow, and widowers, widows, orphans, and disabled given support."

The economics of the world of the "Great Harmony" are based entirely on the people's livelihood. In this ideal world, there are no punishments because no one commits crimes. There is no war because no nation adopts an aggressive policy. Thus the book states: "No plots, no robbers, no thieves, no rebels, and consequently no doors necessary." As explained in the *Book of Rites*, economic policies based on the people's livelihood constitute the only correct road to the "world in harmony." There is no other way to realize our economic ideals.[1]

1. This passage on the "Great Harmony" is perhaps the most striking example of the book's attempt (1) to portray the ancient sages of China as omniscient guides to the principles of economics, and (2) to assert the superiority of all things Chinese over all things Western. The author blandly ignores the fact that the authors of the "Great Harmony" had

Although the economic ideals set forth in the *Book of Rites* cannot be attained at an early date, I am confident that the present war will advance world economic theory to a point nearer such ideals. This war will mark the life or death of the policy of economic aggression. That policy is bound to fail. All nations may, by their own spiritual and material strength, achieve equality and freedom. The aggressors brought about the calamity of war because they failed to use science and technology to serve men according to human nature and, instead, allowed science and technology to control men. Unless this mistake is rectified, mankind will be doomed to total destruction. The aggressors may, by an extravagant use of science and technology, achieve temporary victories, but the final result will be either the destruction of the world or their own destruction. Science and technology are the products of human effort and are developed for the sake of mankind. The principles of Chinese economics are "true virtue," the utilization of resources, and increased production. They are based on human nature or the people's livelihood, and their objective is that commodities should serve and not enslave men. This basic point has long been understood by the Chinese people, and the Three People's Principles have won nation-wide support because they are based on this highest ideal. Today, men everywhere have experienced suffering and have begun to realize the validity of this ideal.

After the present war, all peace-loving nations and races will surely reform their economic systems and theories, and will make certain that the development of science and technology will serve mankind. Only when this is done will the post-war world have advanced one step nearer to our eco-

---

no knowledge of the problems of a modern industrial society. Their theories were formulated at a time when China was divided into numerous feudal states, and thus expressed simply the desire for greater centralization or federation. They did not even recognize the existence of foreign nations as coequal to China; much less think in terms of world organization. The term "foreigner" was used to denote Chinese from other Chinese feudal states. All non-Chinese were regarded as uncivilized barbarians.

nomic ideals. Adherents of the Three People's Principles and all Chinese citizens that have understood this truth should not only work for the further development of Chinese economic principles, but should also strive to realize China's economic ideals.

Commentary on

CHINA'S DESTINY

and

CHINESE ECONOMIC THEORY

By Philip Jaffe

COMMENTARY ON "CHINA'S DESTINY" AND "CHINESE ECONOMIC THEORY"

IT IS assumed that the reader of the following commentary will bear in mind the points already made in the numerous footnotes included in the texts of *China's Destiny* and *Chinese Economic Theory*, as well as in the introductory essay on "The Secret of *China's Destiny*."

A noteworthy feature of both *China's Destiny* and *Chinese Economic Theory* is that they appear to have been designed particularly to reach and influence the students of China. Great emphasis, for example, is placed on the important role of the *San Min Chu I* Youth Corps, and on the duty of all young Chinese to join that Corps. This intensive effort to win the support of Chinese youth is easily explained by the fact that, more than in any other country, the students of China participate actively in politics. For the past twenty-five years, they have taken a prominent part in the movement to free China from her semicolonial status and to modernize her social and economic structure. At critical times, the entire Chinese student body has flared up in open revolt against repressive or reactionary Government policies. In 1919, in the years from 1923 to 1927, again in 1934–36, and once again in 1946, the students of China broke the bonds that tied them to the ruling bureaucracy and took the lead in organizing great mass protests and demonstrations.

Because the Kuomintang regime is well aware of the potential power and influence of the student movement, its leaders have carried out a rigorous system of "thought control," under which both the activities and the "thoughts" of students and teachers are closely supervised by the various secret police organizations. Independent thought and teaching are banned in favor of blind adherence to "orthodox" Kuomintang doctrines, such as those expounded in *China's Destiny*. In view of the vigor and ruthlessness with which this "thought-control" program has been pursued in recent years, it is easy to see how a young Chinese student, living under the "protective custody" of the Kuomintang and kept in ignorance of the true history of modern China, would find it difficult to judge the validity of the conclusions reached in *China's Destiny* and *Chinese Economic Theory*.

It is undoubtedly true that a certain percentage of students, as well as other sections of the Chinese population, have succumbed to the emotional spell of these two books. Nevertheless, most observers of the Chinese scene believe that the majority of students are critical of the theories and conclusions expressed in these volumes, and that they are deterred from openly voicing their criticism only by a knowledge of the dangers involved in such action. It is significant that since V-J Day, the Chinese student movement has again become articulate in its opposition to the ruling regime, and that such cities as Kunming, Chengtu, and Shanghai have become the centers of what may prove to be another great student uprising. The Chinese student movement today is opposed to civil war and selling out China to foreign powers. It is opposed to foreign aid to a regime that is openly bent on civil war. And it is particularly vehement in its opposition to the corruption of a regime that even goes so far as to convert UNRRA supplies, intended to feed starving millions, into personal profits for a few strategically placed bureaucrats. Chinese students have demanded the immediate formation of a democratic coalition government free from foreign domination, and the substitution of a democratic constitution for the undemocratic one proposed by the Kuomintang. In general, the student movement supports the position and program of the Democratic League—the combination of "little parties" that has so far successfully withstood the efforts of the Kuomintang's secret police to destroy it. Under these

circumstances, it is not difficult to understand why the Kuomintang leaders should try desperately to persuade China's
youth to accept the views and policies advocated in *China's
Destiny* and *Chinese Economic Theory.*

No one that has followed the course of recent Chinese
history would deny that the views expressed in these two
books represent the political and economic aims of China's
present rulers, yet there is the danger that a casual Western
reader may fail to recognize their significance. He may come
to the erroneous conclusion that the ways of the Oriental mind
are hopelessly mystifying, and that to make a serious effort to
follow what he would term the "Chinese" lines of reasoning
in these books would be a purely academic exercise and of
no particular relevance to his life. If this is the way the Chinese
nation decides to live, an unwary reader might ask, why
should it be a matter of concern to anyone else, so long as
China is not an aggressor nation and does not seek to foist this
philosophy on other peoples against their will?

It is this commentator's contention that such a detached
attitude is not valid on the following grounds: (1) that the
philosophy expressed in these books is not mystifying or pe-
culiarly "Chinese," that it is not the natural outgrowth of
China's past, and that the Chinese people can be made to
accept this philosophy only by the repressive methods of a
police state; (2) that for the past twenty-five years the Chinese
people have vigorously opposed the imposition of such a
philosophy upon their economic and social lives; (3) that the
Chinese Government's attempt to impose an oppressive political and economic philosophy upon its citizens by force has
subjected China to disunity, civil war, and general demoralization; and (4) that such a China has been and will continue
to be an object of penetration by outside forces, thus promoting aggressive ambitions among imperialist powers and
constituting a serious danger to world peace. If these contentions are correct, then every peace-loving non-Chinese
as well as Chinese in the world has a stake in China's future,

and the struggle of the old against the new in China, so clearly illustrated in these two volumes, becomes a matter of vital concern to all.

Both *China's Destiny* and *Chinese Economic Theory* paint a seriously distorted picture of Chinese history—a picture particularly notable for its glaring omissions. *China's Destiny*, for example, almost completely ignores the struggles of the Chinese people against the oppression of their own rulers. The author is lavish in his praise of the "Confucian" virtues of such statesmen as Tseng Kuo-fan and Li Hung-chang, who enlisted Western military aid to preserve the foreign Manchu dynasty against the native T'ai-p'ing Rebellion. He also portrays the ancient Chinese society as an example of ideal social organization that was only undermined by the impact of the West. But he does not explain why, if ancient China was so perfectly organized and her people so harmonious and content, she succumbed so easily to Western imperialism, or why so many of her officials readily became the lackeys of foreign interests and co-operated with them in suppressing the spontaneous uprisings of the Chinese people.

As far as the treatment of more recent Chinese history is concerned, the bitter and bloody struggles that China experienced in the years from 1931 to 1936 are dismissed in the following sentence: "Again, during the period from 1931 to 1936, there was continuous war and disaster in southern Kiangsi, eastern Honan, western Anhwei, southern Honan, western Hupeh, Szechwan, and Shensi." There is not a word about the extensive and costly military campaigns conducted by the Kuomintang against the forces of a resurgent revolutionary movement as well as bitter armed struggles between Chiang and many of his Kuomintang generals, and no mention of the most dramatic incident of that era of civil strife—the kidnaping of Chiang Kai-shek at Sian in December, 1936, by a group of his own Kuomintang followers.

Another example of the calculated omissions that characterize *China's Destiny* is its treatment of the May 4, 1919, Movement. The author criticizes the May 4th Movement sharply for encouraging the spread of "the ideas of Liberalism and Communism." He attacks its leaders for "losing their confidence in Chinese culture" and for worshiping foreign theories that were "opposed to the spirit of China's own civilization." And he declares that this "copying of Western theories" only caused "the ruin and decay of Chinese civilization." Yet it was this great student and intellectual rebellion that gave a powerful impetus to the struggle for national independence and democracy. It was this movement that made it possible for the Kuomintang to become the leader of the Chinese Revolution from 1924 to 1927, and that gave Chiang Kai-shek himself the opportunity to become the leader of the Northern Expedition.

In this connection, it is pertinent to recall that the T'ai-p'ing Rebellion (1850–63) was the earliest manifestation of the Chinese people's revolt against both alien subjugation and the rule of the landed gentry. This great peasant uprising established its government in the Yangtze Valley for a period of eleven years, and though its leaders inevitably came into contact with foreign interests, they never concluded any "unequal treaties." The T'ai-p'ings were finally crushed chiefly as a result of the armed support given to the Manchu dynasty by the Western powers, which intervened actively to prevent the overthrow of a regime that had proved so amenable to their demands. Many Chinese believe that if the T'ai-p'ings had succeeded in maintaining their power and overthrowing the Manchu dynasty, the Western powers would never have succeeded in obtaining such extensive concessions and special privileges in China. They therefore regard the suppression of the T'ai-p'ings as a critical defeat for the Chinese people and a notable victory for foreign imperialism. Yet the man who played the most prominent role in the suppression of the T'ai-p'ings, Tseng Kuo-fan, is praised in *China's Destiny* as a great statesman and patriot.

It is significant that *China's Destiny* analyzes the 1927–28 period in much the same manner as it deals with the T'ai-p'ing Rebellion. One would never gather from *China's Destiny* that the split of the right-wing Kuomintang from the left wing, and the establishment of a right-wing government at Nanking, was followed by one of the greatest campaigns of repression in modern history, second only to Hitler's campaign to destroy every vestige of liberalism, intellectual freedom, and labor organization in Europe. The author of *China's Destiny* also sees fit to explain the 1927 split entirely in terms of Wang Ching-wei and the Chinese Communists. With exceptional "modesty" he omits all reference to his own leading role in winning the battle of reaction against the Chinese people. The story of the Shanghai massacre of April 12, 1927, which Chiang Kai-shek organized in co-operation with Tu Yueh-sheng, the gangster leader and opium czar, and with foreign powers, has been so fully told that it need not be detailed here. But it is important to recognize that the use of foreign gunboats in the "Nanking incident" preceding the Shanghai affair, the use of foreign munitions obtained from the French Concession's chief of police in staging the Shanghai massacre, and the financial support given by both Chinese and foreign bankers to Chiang Kai-shek in his campaign to block the domestic effects of the revolution, bear a significant resemblance to the circumstances surrounding the suppression of the T'ai-p'ing Rebellion. As described in *China's Destiny*, the heroes in both instances are the suppressors of the people's movement, and the villains are the people.

From 1931 to 1936, there was increasing organized resistance to the Kuomintang Government's policy of appeasing Japan. But the author of *China's Destiny* dismisses this movement with a contemptuous reference to "militant radicals" that had no appreciation of the "needs of the National Government," and he insists that the Kuomintang was actually doing everything possible to build up China's powers of resistance. He also argues that the Kuomintang could not explain its policy to the various opposition groups because this would have entailed revealing its plans to the Japanese. Actually, the Central Government armies were considerably strengthened during this period as a result of substantial aid from the United States and Great Britain. But these armies and their foreign-supplied equipment were expended in a series of costly and ineffective civil war campaigns, while the Government went on yielding to the successive demands of Japan. Chiang Kai-shek may argue that it was necessary to keep the Government's plans a "secret," but they were no "secret" to the thousands of Chinese that were killed during these years by Central Government troops.

Moreover, the "militant radicals" to whom Chiang Kai-shek so scornfully refers, comprised men and women of all classes of Chinese society, including students, intellectuals, industrialists, bankers, and even important sections of the Kuomintang Party membership, all of whom joined in demanding an end to civil war and the beginning of united national resistance to Japan. This opposition movement reached its climax in the December, 1936, kidnaping of Chiang Kai-shek by Kuomintang Generals Chang Hsueh-liang and Yang Hu-ch'eng and the troops under their command. The last straw that precipitated the Sian kidnaping was Chiang Kai-shek's order to these troops to attack the Communist-led forces in Shensi, at a time when it was obvious that Japan was making final preparations for a full-scale invasion of China. Both Chang Hsueh-liang and Yang Hu-ch'eng are still in jail, more than ten years after the kidnaping. Furthermore, there is not a word in *China's Destiny* about the fact that Chiang Kai-shek's release from Sian was conditional upon his verbal promise to end the civil war, a factor that soon led to the formation of an anti-Japanese united front. Although this united front was broken by the Kuomintang early in 1939 even this brief period of unity enabled the Chinese people to offer heroic resistance to the Japanese, and was chiefly responsible for the organizing of millions of guerrillas behind the Japanese lines who, in the long run, proved the decisive factor in preventing Japan from consolidating her conquests in China. It is easy to see why Chiang chose to omit any discussion of these eventful months.

As presented in *China's Destiny*, the story of China from 1928 on is one of important constructive activities by a "new and revivified" Kuomintang. The author is certainly correct when he emphasizes the changed character of the Kuomintang. But when he expresses regret that the Chinese people were unable to understand or accept the leadership of the Kuomintang, he fails to give the true reason, namely, that the Kuomintang had ceased to be the broadly inclusive and progressive movement that it had been in the 1924–27 period. The dominant influence in the Party after 1928 was exercised by the landed gentry, the Shanghai bankers, and other reactionary elements. This period witnessed the growth of the Blue Shirts, a secret terroristic Government organization that was later transformed into the secret military police headed by General Tai Li. The main job of Tai Li's operatives, who numbered some three hundred thousand and whose network extended not only throughout China but also to all Chinese communities overseas, was to discover and wipe out all forms of opposition to the Kuomintang regime.

The years following 1928 were also notable for the growing influence of the ultra-reactionary "CC" clique, headed by the Chen brothers, Chen Li-fu and Chen Kuo-fu. This clique exercised complete control over the Kuomintang Party machinery and was responsible for the system of "thought control" and surveillance by the Party's secret police that inaugurated a reign of intellectual terrorism throughout Kuomintang China. Another important development during this period was the establishment of the *San Min Chu I* Youth Corps, which Chiang Kai-shek praises so highly. This organization, bearing a marked resemblance to the Hitler Youth, is the principal means by which the Kuomintang hierarchy seeks to impose its doctrines and its control on the youth of China, and also to ferret out any tendencies toward "unorthodox" thought in student circles by means of Youth Corps spies and informers.

Behind all these various developments was a highly organized effort to restore the Confucian doctrines of political and social organization as the basis of Chinese society. In 1936, the *pao chia* system was reintroduced as a means of military and labor conscription, and also as a method for checking "subversive" activity by means of the undemocratic principle of collective responsibility (see footnote, page 134). After 1938, the system of forced conscription for military and labor service became so pernicious and corrupt that it constituted a national scandal and even precipitated large-scale rebellion in three provinces.

As a popular movement to instill in the people a respect for the "ancient virtues" of frugality, cleanliness, and a pure and simple life, the New Life Movement was launched in 1934. This movement was at first received by the average Chinese with respect, but by 1936 it had become a general laughing stock, as the people saw that its protagonists were leading far from pure and frugal lives. It was well known that the same officials who wore cheap cotton gowns in public and ordered "frugal" meals in restaurants, led very different lives in private, where they dressed and dined luxuriously and squandered huge sums on gambling and other amusements. Even before the outbreak of the war, it was clear that the New Life Movement had failed to win the respect and support of the Chinese people. Yet its sponsors continued their efforts to get the people to take it seriously. During the war, when the country-wide devastation made it inevitable that the people lead a life of the utmost simplicity and frugality, there was hardly a need for such a movement, but from time to time the New Life Movement would reappear with its wholly unnecessary decrees forbidding permanent waves, dancing parties, and other features of a frivolous and extravagant life. To the homeless and destitute millions of China, such moral precepts seemed little more than a mockery. Certainly, they failed to evoke the desired loyalty to the "ancient virtues" or to divert popular attention from the demand for democratic government and economic reform.

One cannot help noting in this connection that the Japanese made use of much the same tactics in their efforts to subdue the Chinese people. Not only did they adopt a form of the *pao chia* system in Manchuria, but they also selected the *Analects* of Confucius as their principal weapon of psychological warfare in China, and made every effort to revive the Confucian system of social ethics in the areas under their control, in order to encourage unquestioning obedience to authority. In their view, Confucian principles had proved themselves the ideal method of combating nationalism and democracy.

After Japan's invasion of China on July 7, 1937, a new factor began to play an important part in China's political life. With the spread of the war, the Chinese were not only driven back from the industrial centers along the coast, but were even forced to abandon the embryonic industrial enterprises that had been begun in the Yangtze Valley provinces of Hunan, Hupeh, and Kiangsi. By the end of 1938, Japan's advance to the line of the Peiping-Hankow-Canton Railway had resulted in the loss of virtually all of China's industrial plants and compelled the Chinese Government to rely more and more upon feudal barons. This loss of China's industrial centers caused a sharp decline in the economic power and political influence of the native Chinese industrial and banking class, which had absorbed some Western ideas of industrial progress and was, in some respects, a relatively progressive-minded group. As a result, the feudal-minded landed gentry, whose power depended on maintaining China's backward and oppressive agrarian system, became the undisputed leaders of the Kuomintang. And as the power of this "sedan chair" gentry grew, so grew the repressive character of the Kuomintang regime.

The climax of the reactionary policy of this new Kuomintang hierarchy was the wartime blockade of millions of Chinese in the guerrilla areas and the open preparations for civil war at the earliest possible moment. The landed gentry of Kuomintang China were deeply alarmed by the growing popular support for the agrarian reforms and democratic electoral procedures that had been introduced in these guerrilla areas, and they were determined at all costs to prevent the spread of this program to the rest of China, since this would inevitably spell the end of their own monopoly of power. Their preparation for the destruction of this growing popular movement even included a close alliance between the Kuomintang Government and several hundred thousand Chinese puppet troops serving under the Japanese. These puppets were encouraged to go over to the Japanese, ostensibly to maintain as much Chinese control as possible in the occupied areas. Actually, there were two reasons for this Kuomintang strategy. In the first place, the puppet troops joined with the Japanese in fighting the Communist-led guerrilla forces. The second and more long-term objective was to ensure that there would be Kuomintang military control in these areas following Japan's defeat. The whole strategy of these "Chungking-planted" puppets became clear following V-J Day, when Chiang Kai-shek called upon the puppet troops to "maintain order" in the occupied areas pending the arrival of Central Government troops, and refused to permit Communist-led Chinese forces to accept the surrender of Japanese troops. It was at this point that the puppets suddenly became known in official Chinese statements as the "underground," although for years there had been nothing "underground" about their activities as instruments of the Japanese.

The Kuomintang excuse for the military blockade against the most active defenders of Chinese soil—a blockade in which the Central Government employed its best troops and equipment—was that the guerrillas were Communist-led. But, as everywhere throughout the world, the use of the term "Communist" to identify all opposition has been employed assiduously as a shield to cover the suppression of all people's rights. If Chiang Kai-shek explains the blockade as an anti-Communist move, how does he explain the suppression of all minority parties within Kuomintang China, the suppression of all civil liberties, the suppression of those groups within the Kuomintang itself, that opposed the policies of the ruling hierarchy, the suppression of students and teachers, of the more progressive-minded industrialists and bankers, and even of some important Kuomintang military leaders that dared to advocate a unification of all China's fighting forces? Such actions can be explained only on the ground that the Kuomintang bureaucracy was the arm of a landed gentry that had become all-powerful and that used both force and propaganda to preserve and enhance its power—the force consisting of an elaborate network of secret police organizations, and the propaganda involving both "thought control" and intensive efforts to revive the Confucian philosophy of government by a privileged feudal elite.

In an effort to make his analysis of the history of the past one hundred years plausible, Chiang Kai-shek blames virtually all of China's trials and difficulties on Western imperialist penetration. Unquestionably, he paints a vivid and damning picture of the havoc wrought by Western imperialism on China's civilization and economy. This is perhaps the section of *China's Destiny* where history is least distorted, a judgment that must be tempered by the knowledge that *China's Destiny* was written at a time when it suited the purposes of the ruling bureaucracy to attack the Western powers (see p. 20). The story Chiang tells constitutes only half the history of that period. A full account would have to include a description of the corruption and decay of China's economic and social structure that made her such an easy prey. The author does criticize the Manchu Government for its yielding to foreign pressure, but his criticism is more in the nature of deploring the unwise actions of a blood brother than a recognition of the fact that the Manchu dynasty represented the final era in a long period of decline of a feudal and oppressive social system. This decline was part of a historic process in which an unhealthy and repressive autocracy finally gave way before the rising strength of popular opposition. As Sun Yat-sen himself declared, "the former weakness and decline of China was due to the harsh oppressions of absolutism." It is significant that this statement is not one of those chosen for quotation by the author of *China's Destiny*.

Much criticism has been leveled against *China's Destiny* for the racial theory expounded in the first chapter, in which the author seeks to prove that all the peoples of China share a common blood stream. This idea of a national blood relationship is similar to that expounded by Hitler, though, in its outward manifestation, it has no important resemblance to Hitler's doctrine, which was used as the basis for the literal destruction of other peoples and as a tool of aggression. There is no such implication in China's case, except insofar as this theory governs the Kuomintang's attitude toward China's national minorities. But the theory itself is certainly one to arouse the scorn of all modern historians, who can hardly accept the thesis that the Chinese, the Mongols, the Tibetans, etc., are really branches of the same racial stock because they are all descended from the same legendary emperor.

As pointed out in the footnote on page 40, this racial theory completely distorts Chinese history, since it would mean that all the bitter wars fought by the Chinese against the Mongols, Tartars, Manchus, and other invaders were really not wars for national independence but merely internal struggles within a single nation. One can only conclude that the author's purpose in elaborating so unconvincing a thesis was to instill in the Chinese people a belief in the "unique" quality and vast superiority of Chinese civilization over all "foreign" cultures, so that they might accept everything about their past as valid and admirable. It would not suit Chiang Kai-shek's purpose to recognize that China's history was a process of constant struggle and adjustment, and that the social ethics and political organization advocated by China's ancient sages did not produce a golden world of complete harmony. But if it were possible to secure widespread acceptance of the thesis that ancient China was virtually perfect, that all the peoples of China were really one, and that the authoritarian doctrines of the ancient sages provided the correct answer to all problems of social and political relationships, then of course the present ruling clique would find it far simpler to secure popular acceptance of the thesis that its "paternalistic" control over the lives of the Chinese people is based on hallowed historical precedent.

Although *China's Destiny* is the book intended for popular consumption, Chiang Kai-shek's more fundamental book is *Chinese Economic Theory*, for this purports to give a theoretical basis for the conclusions reached in both books. Like *China's Destiny*, one of the most notable features of *Chinese Economic Theory* is its strongly paternalistic and feudal outlook. The social and economic concepts that it develops can, in fact, best be described as Fascist theory applied to a semifeudal agrarian economy. Individuals and individual "wants" are treated with "benevolent" contempt. The whole emphasis is on the subordination of the individual to a paternalistic and authoritarian government "which manages the people's affairs." There is nothing in the book to support the allegedly democratic aims of the Kuomintang program. On the contrary, the character of the government that is envisaged in *Chinese Economic Theory* seems to differ very little from the autocratic landed bureaucracy that ruled feudal and imperial China.

Chinese Economic Theory also resembles *China's Destiny* in its strongly chauvinistic tone. There is a repeated emphasis on the vast superiority of the ancient Chinese civilization over "Western" culture, coupled with fulsome praise of the wisdom of China's ancient sages. The book even goes so far as to credit

the wholly legendary "Five Emperors" with being the inventors of the major arts, crafts, and social policies.

The thesis that there is a system of "Chinese" economic
theory, distinct from and superior to "Western" economic
theory, is wholly incompatible with modern scientific thought,
which regards economic science as a system of analysis that
can be applied with equal validity to the specific economic
problems of every country, with due regard for the differences
in the levels of their development and their historical and
political backgrounds. As for the alleged superiority of "Chinese" over "Western" economic theory, this claim is made
solely on the basis of morality or ethics. The author contends
that Western economic theory is materialistic and based on
profit-seeking, and that it is therefore inferior to the teachings
of the ancient Chinese sages who were concerned with far
higher ethical values. But even if he had provided adequate
proof for his contention that China's ancient economic theories were less materialistic than those of the West, which he
does not and cannot because it is not true, there would still
be no basis for his conclusion, because the validity of an economic theory obviously cannot be judged solely in terms of
ethics or morality. The inescapable conclusion is that the
book's emphasis on the ancient moral virtues of feudalism is
deliberately designed to provide a philosophical justification
for preserving the traditional social structure of ancient China,
with its monopoly of wealth and power by the ruling bureaucracy, and its emphasis on authority and subservience as the
basis of social order and harmony.

It is difficult to appraise the specific economic policies advocated in *Chinese Economic Theory* because they are phrased
in such vague and ambiguous terms. In general, the book
advocates economic and political control under a centralized
feudal-fascist government, based on the traditional system in
which the village formed the basic economic and military
unit. Its main arguments apparently favor a protectionist
tariff policy, an emphasis on armaments and strategic com-

munications, the development of a few large-scale modern industries under bureaucratic control, and the wide decentralization of small-scale industry in order to prevent any serious disruption of the present agrarian system.

Chinese Economic Theory lays great emphasis on what the author terms "national-defense economics" and on the subordination of private enterprise to bureaucratic control. Foreign observers of Chinese economic development during the war were unanimously agreed that such bureaucratic centralization in an industrially backward country like China served only to obstruct economic progress and to stifle much-needed private initiative. It was generally recognized that the restrictions, regulations, and bureaucratic red tape to which private industry was subjected in Kuomintang China during the war were largely responsible for the fact that the few industries that China possessed operated at only a small percentage of their full capacity, and that private capital was reluctant to invest in industrial enterprises—confining itself almost entirely to speculation in land and commodities. And what was true during the war will remain true so long as the dominant class in Chinese society is feudal minded and therefore opposed to an industrialization program that would free large numbers of peasants from the land.

Perhaps the most discouraging passages in *Chinese Economic Theory* are those dealing with the land problem. As noted in the footnote on page 274, the suggestion that "collective farms" may provide the solution to this problem means nothing more or less than a return to the feudal system of village units as the basis for labor and military conscription, and the enforcement of the *pao chia* system of collective responsibility. Though the book makes a general reference to the need for prosperous "rural districts" as markets for industry, and an equally general comment on the evils of "land annexation" in ancient times, there is no comment whatsoever on the rapid concentration of land ownership during the war, nor on the other serious economic problems confronting present-day

China. The reader will search in vain for any mention of measures to deal with the immediate need for agrarian reforms, and for the control of inflation, speculation, and hoarding. The Kuomintang's agrarian policy, if judged by *Chinese Economic Theory*, would seem to consist solely of references to an ideal past and a still more ideal future, coupled with a complete disregard for the grim realities of the present.

In general, *Chinese Economic Theory* may be regarded as yet another contribution to the systematic campaign that has been waged in recent years by the Kuomintang to assert the superiority of the ancient Chinese "way of life" over everything "Western," i.e., liberal. The proponents of this thesis make no attempt to prove their unsound and historically inaccurate contentions. Their tactics consist solely of reiterating the claim that all Western culture is "materialistic" and that the ancient sages of China understood all the "true principles" of economics and social organization.

Though Tao Hsi-sheng, the "co-author" of both *China's Destiny* and *Chinese Economic Theory*, is apparently one of its leading "theorists," the real master-minds of this campaign are Chen Li-fu and Chen Kuo-fu, the leaders of the "CC" clique. Though their official positions have shifted from time to time, the Chen brothers have retained their control over the Kuomintang Party personnel and the secret Party police, and their main activity has been to ensure the acceptance of orthodox Kuomintang doctrine by all Party officials, students, teachers, editors, etc. Thanks to their all-pervading influence, the teaching of Western liberal doctrines and democratic principles has been virtually banished from Chinese schools and universities. And in accord with their theory that only the technological achievements of the West have any value for China, students selected for study abroad are compelled to confine themselves strictly to technical subjects.

This type of nationalism is deeply disturbing to all genuine scholars and liberal thinkers in China. They are contemptuous of the distorted version of Chinese history presented in such books as *China's Destiny* and *Chinese Economic Theory*, and disagree completely with the disparagement of the contributions of Western culture. They recognize that modern Chinese political and social thought has drawn inspiration from Western liberal doctrines as well as from China's own cultural heritage, and they are fully aware of the dangers inherent in the type of chauvinistic nationalism promoted by such men as Chen Li-fu and Tao Hsi-sheng.

Thus, despite the machinations of a gestapo-like system of secret police, recent Chinese history is filled with instances of courageous opposition on the part of the Chinese people. Imprisonment, torture, and even assassination have failed to halt the increasingly vigorous criticism of the Kuomintang regime. The leaders of the Democratic League and men like Dr. Ma Ying-chu, China's leading economist, have literally taken their lives in their hands to voice such criticism. Lest this statement appear to be an exaggeration, it may be noted that although Dr. Lo Lung-chi, head of the Democratic League and a prominent Catholic editor, was still alive in the autumn of 1946, two important members of the League— Professors Li Kung-po and Wen I-to—were assassinated in Kunming in July, 1946. Both Li and Wen had been outspoken advocates of a coalition government, and their deaths were regarded in Chinese intellectual circles as proof that the advocates of civil war were resorting to organized terrorism in their efforts to prevent a peaceful settlement of internal political issues.

One of the most daring and persistent critics of Chiang Kai-shek and the regime of which he is the leader has been Professor Chang Hsi-jo, head of the Political Science Department at China's famous Southwest Federated University in Kunming. Professor Chang is a Kuomintang member of many years' standing and one of the few Chinese professors

Southwest Federated University is composed of three universities— Tsinghwa, Peita, and Nankai—which migrated from Peiping and Tientsin after the Japanese occupation of those cities.

that are members of the People's Political Council. Early in
1944, he was removed from his post for having made the
"revolutionary" statement that a system of law without democracy is an empty shell, but was restored because of his tre-
mendous following among the student body. Undaunted,
Professor Chang again made serious charges against the Kuomintang regime in a speech delivered before a large student
assembly on November 24, 1944, in which he accused Chiang
Kai-shek of subordinating China's welfare to his personal
ambitions and to building up his personal political machine
—the Kuomintang—of seeking to deify himself before the
Chinese people, and of attempting to regiment thought and
stifle criticism.

But perhaps Professor Chang Hsi-jo's most important
speech, not only because of what he said but because of the
circumstances in which he said it, was made on January 13,
1946, before an audience of some seven thousand students and
visitors. At a time when students and professors were being
arrested en masse, Professor Chang boldly expressed for the
students and intellectuals of China what the vast majority of
them had believed for many years. His speech so ably ex-
emplifies the all-inclusive opposition to the Kuomintang
regime and to the philosophy embodied in *China's Destiny* and
Chinese Economic Theory that the full text is included herewith:

"It is not easy to see through political difficulties. But it is
the duty of all who study and teach in universities to stick to
the truth. In discussing how China's problems can be solved,
I am going to state the truth without consideration for the
vested interests of any party, or the 'face' of any person. A
solution for our political problems is tied up with a solution
to our social problems. Society frequently becomes sick. In
cases of serious sickness a doctor must be called, prescriptions
written, and medicine taken. This is the situation that China
is facing today. China is suffering because political power has
been monopolized by an extremely reactionary and exceedingly despotic political faction, dominated by a group of

stupid, corrupt ignoramuses. This conglomeration is the Kuomintang, the Nationalist Party. I do not say that the Kuomintang has always been such a body. It has developed into such a body, and today thinks only of its own interests. It shouts high-sounding slogans such as 'for the nation and the people.' It professes to 'bring happiness to the nation and welfare to the people.' But these are mere words, and it really plunges the nation into ruin and the people into misery.

"The Kuomintang still claims that it is a 'revolutionary political party,' but in reality it has long since become something to be revolted against. Its members still talk about revolution, but their words are mere parrot's mimicry. They do not know what they are talking about. How does this political faction continue to exist? The Kuomintang claims that it is the legal government. That is correct, but legality is not enough for a government. It must have the support of the people. Legally, the Kuomintang can be said to be a government. Morally, it is simply a bandit. The Kuomintang holds political power by force and guns. It is charitable to call its members bandits, for when one meets a robber one can call the police. What can one do when one meets these people? They have the law on their side. They are legally recognized bandits. This was clearly demonstrated in the November 25th and December incidents in which one professor and four students were killed. It is unfortunate for China's future that power has been monopolized by an ignorant, stupid, corrupt, reactionary and despotic group. It is also unfortunate for the future of the Kuomintang itself. We honor Dr. Sun Yat-sen as 'the Father of the Nation,' but his principles have been exploited for selfish gain. How his spirit must protest this cruelty and shame!

"The conclusions that I have drawn may be profoundly disturbing to some people. These conclusions are supported by facts, but some people see these facts and others do not. Still others see them and then, not liking them, turn away and pretend that they haven't seen them. I ask you to let the facts speak for themselves.

"1. *The Three People's Principles:* The Kuomintang talks about these day and night. In the May 6th Draft Constitution [1936] it is provided that 'China shall be a Republic of the Three People's Principles.' The first of these principles is nationalism, which means to help each national group to obtain independence and freedom. But the only positive achievement of the Kuomintang has been to recognize the independence of Outer Mongolia. The second principle is that of the people's rights. But the people have no rights. The only right the people have is the right to attend the weekly Kuomintang memorial meetings, to bow to the Kuomintang flag, and to read Kuomintang principles. They have nothing else. I need not talk about the Principle of the People's Livelihood. The streets are filled with beggars. The soldiers live worse than the beggars. The streets are filled with them for everyone to see.

"2. *Limitation of Capital and Equalization of Land Ownership:* The Kuomintang has been talking about this for twenty years. But look at the war profiteers! Did anyone ever try to limit their capital? How do they propose to equalize ownership of land? Maybe they are waiting until the peasants can no longer afford to plant their crops because of the heavy land tax. Not only has nothing been done, but when I asked the Chairman of the Kuomintang and other responsible people about it they all said that they do not yet have any plan.

"3. *The Period of Tutelage:* It has always been said that this period is intended to train the people for the assumption of their political rights. Who has heard of any training being done? The real purpose of 'tutelage' is to postpone constitutional government indefinitely.

"4. *The People's Assembly:* So far we have heard only about the construction of buildings for the Assembly. Dr. Sun's will, which called for the convocation of a People's Assembly 'in the shortest possible time,' was written in 1925. 'The shortest

possible time' is already twenty years. No wonder that foreigners complain that the Chinese idea of a unit of time is
very long.

"5. *Thought Control:* This is the only thing that can be said
to have been a really successful undertaking.

"6. *The Two-Year Plan:* At the beginning of the War of
Resistance, the Government suddenly became energetic and
every ministry published a plan. But there was no co-ordina-
tion among the different ministries. The Ministry of Communications wanted to build railroads, the Ministry of War
an army, etc. No one stopped to ask if the Ministry of Finance
would be willing to foot the bill. Now no one knows what
became of these plans. In the second year of the war, I at-
tended the People's Political Council at which the Government produced a new three-year plan. I asked the head of
one of the Yuans whether this three-year plan included the
foregoing two-year plan, or was to be started after the two-
year plan was concluded. This Government official replied:
'You're asking me. Whom shall *I* ask?' Then he added: 'Professor Chang, why be so particular?' The plans were nothing
but a display of 'intentions' by the Government to impress the
People's Political Council.

"7. *Military Affairs First: Victory First:* These Government
slogans were correct for the war period, but they did not correspond to actual practice. Newspapers boasted that 'the
more our army fights, the stronger it becomes.' But as late as
the summer of 1945, the moment our armies were attacked
they started to retreat. Was this a sample of their increased
strength?

"8. *Those with Money Give Money; Those with Strength Give
Strength:* This was one of the popular Kuomintang war slogans.
Those with strength certainly gave strength. They could not
do otherwise when guns were held over them. But those with
money became profiteers. When victory came, the Government appropriated several billions of dollars to subsidize them.
But when better treatment was asked for soldiers and higher

pay for white collar workers, the Government replied that 'it was difficult to get funds and it just couldn't be helped.'

"9. *Administration in Formerly Occupied Areas:* The scandal of the taking over of Shanghai was excused by the Government on the grounds that Japan surrendered so suddenly that it had not been possible to make proper preparations. But there was plenty of time to make plans for the taking over of Peiping and Tientsin; yet conditions were exactly the same. Officials arriving from Chungking entered these areas like conquerors, confiscating money, automobiles, gold, and women. Newspaper reports from Peiping said that the local authorities prohibited people from telling these stories to Chiang Kai-shek when he visited the city.

"10. *'Victory' Decorations:* So many of these were awarded that it took the papers several days to complete publication of the list. Only one person received a First-Class Decoration— Chiang Kai-shek. First in the Second Class was Ho Ying-chin, former Minister of War, who was followed by a number of officers and commanders. In the Third Class were members of the Central Committee of the Kuomintang, headed by Wu Chih-hui. The Seventh Class consisted of women, headed by Madame Chiang Kai-shek and Madame Kung. I only know a few of the people named. What these ladies did for resistance only their husbands know. And what their husbands did, I suppose is known to those who happened to be their wives. Those who fought and won victories in Burma, such as General Sun Li-jen and General Liao Yao-hsiang, were not mentioned in the Victory Medal lists. They were only given Chung-chin medals (Chung—loyalty; Chin—industriousness). This is an excellent example of Kuomintang bureaucracy. Titles but not men count; rank but not deeds. This accounts for the fact that some of those who ran away and spent the eight war years in the United States received Victory Medals. Apparently our gallant soldiers who fought at the front and our munition workers in the rear are without merit.

"11. *'Turn the Government Over to the People; the Army to the*

Nation!': This is now the most loudly shouted slogan. But the words are empty. To whom is the Government to be turned? What is meant by the people? If the 'people' means Chiang Kai-shek and the two Chen brothers, of course it could be done. If 'turning the army over to the nation' means turning it over to Chiang Kai-shek and the Chen brothers, it also could be done. Slogans pleasing to the ear are one thing; what is done in practice is another.

"12. *The Massacre of Kuoming Students:* This was a good example of the Kuomintang Government which 'is filled with good words, but has not done one good deed.'

"What can be done? First, we must abolish one-party rule so that the whole attitude of the Government can be changed. I will suggest concrete steps that might be taken. For the sake of our country and for his own sake, I advise Chiang Kai-shek to resign. If I were to meet Chiang Kai-shek I should say to him: 'You are responsible for all our evils. You should be punished. The lightest possible punishment is to ask you to get out and make way for good and worthy people.' For many years, Chiang Kai-shek has been exceedingly presumptuous. Isn't it right to ask him to be unpresumptuous for once? Here is his chance to act nobly and resolutely: to resign before the day of his downfall. Not only should Chiang Kai-shek resign, but also all his lieutenants. They bear their share of responsibility and should be punished. A coalition government should be formed which might include enlightened and liberal-minded Kuomintang elements. When formed, the coalition government should call a convention to draft a constitution for the nation.

"The above would be the ideal solution. However, I realize that it might not be practicable and so I suggest the following: To abolish one-party rule and tutelage, but to allow Chiang Kai-shek to stay. This does not mean that we want him, but merely that since he will not get out, we will suffer him under certain conditions: (a) The 'Supreme Leader,' 'Chief of State,' or 'President' must come within the law. This means that Chiang Kai-shek must abide by the law, shall have no part in legislation, and cannot change laws at will. (b) Policy making must be removed from Chiang Kai-shek and given to the policy-making body. Chiang Kai-shek could participate, but he would have only one vote. If this is not done, the Political Consultative Council will be impotent. (c) The responsibility for putting agreed policies into practice must be vested in a group and not in one man. Only when this is done will ministers become responsible officials. (d) The number of posts held by Kuomintang members must be limited to twenty-five per cent of the total or at most thirty-three per cent. This is necessary because of the poor record of Kuomintang officials in the past, and because the Kuomintang is badly in need of a purge. If this were done, there would not be many members left qualified to hold official posts.

"I realize that the Political Consultative Council might think it impossible to put these suggestions into practice. What then would be the future? If the despot [Chiang Kai-shek] refuses to accept these demands, all non-Kuomintang members of the Council should resign en bloc immediately. They would be better off at home taking care of the babies than sitting at such a conference. Sun Fo has suggested that a few members from parties other than the Kuomintang be added to the present Central Political Committee. There are at present about a dozen or so members of this committee, and in the past they have never held a meeting. But members were entitled to rice subsidies and free automobiles. The present suggestion is merely an attempt to satisfy the popular demand for a coalition government without giving up one iota of power.

"It has been suggested that a few ministers without portfolio be appointed under the Executive Yuan. A few unwanted ministerial positions will be doled out! The ministers so appointed would be handed over to vice-ministers who would spy on them and block anything they tried to do. Could this be called a coalition government? The Kuomintang and its spokesman Sun Fo are just trying to set a trap to entice members from other parties to nominal participation in the present Kuomintang Government, so that they can loudly proclaim that they have formed a coalition. They are seeking for a deceptive solution to our problems. With regard to the National Assembly, delegates must be elected by the people under a coalition government. The present delegates were appointed by Chiang Kai-shek and the two Chen brothers, and cannot be recognized. After the coalition government is formed, it should promulgate an electoral law, and the new delegates should be elected according to that law.

"In conclusion I want to tell you a story. General Kuan Lin-cheng once told me that Professor Ch'ien Tuan-sheng was a Communist. I asked him how he knew this. He replied that in one of his speeches, Professor Ch'ien had referred to Chiang Kai-shek as Mr. Chiang instead of 'The Leader' and had described him as 'senile.' If this makes Professor Ch'ien a Communist, I do not know what I shall be called after this speech. But we who love our country and the truth, and who do not wish to be slaves, must not hesitate to speak up. Our consciences, our education, and all that our great teachers have taught us, leave us no other course but to speak loudly in this time of serious national crisis."

No appraisal of *Chinese Economic Theory* can fail to point out that if the theories expressed in this book remain the directives for China's future development, the Chinese economy can only become a duplicate of the pre-war economic structure of Japan. Japan also limited her "borrowing" from the West to the technological field, and succeeded in grafting a bureaucratic, government-controlled heavy industry upon a semi-feudal agrarian base. In modern Japan, the interlocking of landlordism, banking, and government resulted in highly centralized control by a small ruling oligarchy, and Japan's industrial achievements were accomplished at the cost of an impoverished peasantry, a large surplus agricultural popula-

Commentary on

CHINA'S DESTINY

and

CHINESE ECONOMIC THEORY

By Philip Jaffe

land system, there can be no adequate market for the products of modern factories; no extensive use of power or transport facilities; and no consumers' market in any way commensurate with the size of the Chinese population. To embark on such an ambitious project as the Yangtze River dam in China today, before the land system has been sufficiently modernized to ensure consumers for the proposed output of electric power, is putting the cart before the horse.

This is all the more true in view of the fact that the economic philosophy of the present rulers of China openly calls for the preservation of the existing agrarian system as the basis of China's future economic structure. Although spokesmen for China's ruling bureaucracy are constantly emphasizing that their country would be a profitable field for American capital investment, the cold facts of the case indicate that these landed gentry have no real interest in promoting Chinese industrialization. How else can we explain their reluctance to invest their own wealth in their own country? Reliable estimates place the total of Chinese cash deposits in American banks, including both open and hidden accounts, at approximately two billion American dollars. It is also well known in Washington that almost all of the proceeds from wartime and post-war American loans to China have either found their way into the pockets of high-ranking Chinese bureaucrats or have been used to support civil war. These facts suggest that the members of China's ruling clique have no desire to bring peace to China nor to facilitate industrialization, but prefer to keep their wealth abroad, or use it to speculate in land, currency, and commodities.

Harley Stevens, writing in the *Far Eastern Survey* for September 26, 1946, on the basis of a recent trip to China as representative of a major American oil company, points out that the growth of what he describes as "bureaucratic capitalism" in Kuomintang China has already caused "many Chinese businessmen and industrialists to side with the Chinese Communist party in the struggle for the democratization of the National Government." Mr. Stevens reports that "new government corporations have been organized during the past few months at the rate of one or more a week. As soon as they are organized, private interests tend to be either prohibited by law from participation or frozen out by the politicians in control of the purse strings." In his view, "unless present tendencies are checked and Chinese private capital obtains greater influence in government policies through participation in a more widely representative government, peace in China will find bureaucratic capital firmly entrenched in all strategic industries in areas other than Communist. These strategic economic positions will be employed to further the growth of bureaucratic economic interests at the expense of a broad national economy dominated by private enterprise. These developments and their significance appear to be neither appreciated nor understood, except in China, by those who insist on all out support of the Kuomintang."

As noted previously in this commentary, the Chinese landed gentry gained their dominant political power as a result of Japan's capture of the industrial centers along the Chinese coast and the Chinese Government's forced retreat into the backward, rural areas of the interior. With the end of the war and the re-establishment of Chinese control over the coastal areas, one might have expected a resurgence of the power and political influence of the native industrialists and bankers that would lead the Government to adopt a more realistic approach to China's economic problems. As of the autumn of 1946, however, the native industrial-banking group had not made much headway in breaking the monopoly of power acquired by the landed gentry during the war years. The latter had been quick to move in on the coastal areas and take over Japanese and puppet-controlled enterprises, and those native industrialists that managed to salvage some of their pre-war properties found themselves confronted with the competition of Government-subsidized concerns, controlled by the landed gentry and the comprador class or their representatives.

Whether or not these landed gentry and compradors will be able to keep the upper hand over the native industrialists and financiers of the coastal cities remains an open question. But it is certain that if they do, it will constitute a serious setback for China. Only a decisive change in the Chinese political and economic structure that will remove the landed gentry and compradors from political power can open the sluice gates for large-scale investment in the industrialization of China, in which all native as well as friendly foreign capital can play a progressive role. It is surprising that American business does not see through the deception behind the constant appeals of China's ruling bureaucracy for American capital investment in China. For even the die-hards in American business circles must be aware that they cannot sell much to a poorhouse, regardless of the extensive privileges granted them in the new China-America trade treaty.

If *China's Destiny* and *Chinese Economic Theory* were merely academic exercises in writing Chinese history, they would be no more of a menace than thousands of Ph.D. theses, now gathering dust in the libraries of the world. But the fact is that these books are being taught in the key political training centers of China; that thousands of Chinese students are being examined and tested for their acceptance of this ideology; and that *China's Destiny* specifically states that anyone that does not accept these theories must be destroyed. The statement in *China's Destiny* that if the opposition forces do not submit to Kuomintang control, "no reasonable solution can be found," is a very thinly veiled threat of civil war.

As a matter of fact, the Central Government of China began its war against all opposition forces immediately after V-J Day; against Communist-led forces by military operations, and against opposition in Kuomintang areas by terrorism and assassination. Prior to the Japanese surrender, the vast majority of foreign civilian and military observers in China were of the opinion that, left entirely on its own, the Chinese Government would be compelled to yield to the overwhelming demand for the institution of a democratic coalition government, and that there would be no civil war because the Kuomintang regime could not command sufficient popular support for such a project. But the leading militarists of the Chinese Government, together with a few high-ranking American generals, thought otherwise. They felt confident that the Central Government armies were strong enough militarily and had sufficient popular support to win quickly in a civil war.

The events of the first few months after V-J Day proved the fallacy of this belief. In the province of Shansi, the Japanese surrendered their forces to General Yen Hsi-shan, whose troops had actually been under Japanese direction since February, 1944. General Yen then launched an attack against the Communist-led Eighth Route Army and suffered a severe defeat, losing about four thousand killed and eleven thousand captured. In the Hopei-Honan area, the Kuomintang armies also attacked Communist-led forces and captured considerable territory with Japanese assistance, but the Eighth Route Army counterattacked and surrounded three Kuomintang armies—the New 8th, the 13th and the 14th. The New 8th Army, including both officers and troops, promptly went over to the Communists, and the 13th and 14th armies surrendered. It is estimated that the Kuomintang lost fifty thousand troops in this Honan battle (October 30, 1945). Kuomintang forces and Mongolian puppet troops under General Fu Tso-yi were also badly defeated in the North Shansi-Suiyuan-Chahar campaign, and were forced back from Kalgan, which the Communist-led Eighth Route Army had captured from the Japanese on August 17th. In fact, on all occasions when the Kuomintang forces fought on their own against the Communist-led troops, whether in Manchuria, Shantung,

Hopei, Suiyuan, or elsewhere, they were defeated. Only when they were supported by American troops, munitions, and transport facilities did they make any headway.

In *China's Destiny*, Chiang Kai-shek criticizes the Manchu Government because when it was "beset internally by popular revolutionary forces and externally by pressure from the foreign powers, it chose to yield to the demands of the foreign nations." He also attacks the Manchus for clinging to the policy that "it is better to give to friends than to one's own slaves." Yet what are he and his followers doing, if not soliciting foreign (i.e., American) aid in suppressing popular opposition to the Kuomintang dictatorship? It may come as a surprise to most Americans to learn that the total American financial aid given or earmarked for China during the first year following V-J Day amounted to approximately three billion American dollars—a sum far greater than the assistance given China during the entire war. This total included an estimated one billion dollars of lend-lease, which China, alone of all our wartime allies, continued to receive on wartime terms. It also included an ear-marked five-hundred-million-dollar Export-Import bank credit, and further loans scheduled to enable the Kuomintang Government to pay for surplus American military equipment and supplies, valued at from seven hundred to eight hundred million dollars, that were to be turned over to the Chinese. This is exclusive of the plan to turn over to the Chinese Government two hundred and seventy-one U. S. Navy combat vessels, with American navy personnel to train Chinese crews to man these vessels, as well as the $800 million worth of surplus military goods on Okinawa. Another example of American support of the Kuomintang regime which has not received sufficient publicity in the United States is the fact that in the first year following V-J Day, the American Government trained and equipped forty Kuomintang divisions, as compared with twenty divisions trained and equipped by the United States during the entire war. It is against the background of such facts that one must evaluate Chiang Kai-shek's criticism of the Manchu dynasty for its supine reliance on foreigners, and his exhortations to the Chinese people to cultivate a spirit of independence and self-reliance.

Any commentary on *China's Destiny* and *Chinese Economic Theory* would not be complete without a very positive statement that the author has completely perverted the teachings of Sun Yat-sen. Both the books under discussion consistently quote Sun Yat-sen out of context, and without reference to one of his two major aims. Sun Yat-sen was determined to free China from foreign domination, but he was equally determined to free the Chinese people from the stranglehold of feudalism that the present Kuomintang leadership is trying desperately to revive, even though in a modernized form. Chiang Kai-shek's effort to picture Sun Yat-sen as a staunch and enthusiastic exponent of the teachings of China's ancient sages has no foundation in fact.

A well-known scholar of the Kuomintang, T. C. Woo, in his book, *The Kuomintang and the Future of the Chinese Revolution*, comments on Dr. Sun's attitude toward the philosophies of Confucius, Mencius, etc., as follows: "He was not in the habit of picking up the doctrine of any great author for discussion. Perhaps their power over him was mainly negative, in affording ground for his attack on the existing social order. . . . His work was to overthrow the then existing government, and he found no support from the philosophers whose views had been adapted to support a regime that he intended to overthrow. To popularize the work of revolution, he needed to have an intellectual basis. It is evident that this new intellectual basis of his must go contrariwise to the old one. As we all know, he was a revolutionist in thought as well as in action."

More recent appraisers of Sun Yat-sen's political views, notably Stephen Chen and Robert Payne in their book, *Sun Yat-sen: A Portrait*, point out that from the beginning, Dr.

Sun "appears to have feared the emergence of a nonrevolutionary group" because "when the revolution is exchanged for politics, the vision perishes." They also note that in Sun Yat-sen's time, the Chinese nationalist movement was based primarily on an appeal to the needs and interests of the peasants and workers, and that its program emphasized economic and social reforms with particular stress on the freeing of peasants from the oppression of their landlords. The implication of this and other appraisals of Sun Yat-sen's aims and beliefs is that if he were alive today, he would have great difficulty in recognizing the Kuomintang as the same party that he founded and led. Certainly the knowledge that the landlords are strongly entrenched in the seats of power, while peasants and workers are harried and oppressed by the Party's secret police would be enough to make the late Father of his Country turn over in his elaborate tomb.

It is also worth noting that nowhere in *China's Destiny* or *Chinese Economic Theory* is there any reference to the "Three Great Policies" which, together with the Three People's Principles, were bequeathed to the Kuomintang by Sun Yat-sen. These three policies were: Alliance with the U.S.S.R. in foreign affairs; a united front with the Chinese Communists in internal affairs; and assistance to the Chinese workers and peasants. At the time Sun Yat-sen advocated these three policies, the Soviet Union was the only power that had renounced its "unequal treaties" and was willing to aid China in her efforts to attain national freedom and a modernized social structure, while the Western powers and Japan were trying desperately to maintain their control over China's economic and political life. Were Sun Yat-sen alive today, when both Great Britain and the United States have joined the Soviet Union in relinquishing their extraterritorial rights, he might well have expanded the first of his three policies to include an alliance with all three powers in foreign policy. The present Kuomintang leadership, however, has chosen to substitute the United States for the Soviet Union as far as its foreign orientation is concerned, and has completely abandoned the second and third of Sun Yat-sen's three policies. Moreover, in seeking exclusive American aid for its own regime, the Kuomintang bureaucracy has promoted the thesis that without such aid, China would overnight become a Communist state.

In this connection, it is pertinent to recall that even during Sun Yat-sen's lifetime, the Soviet Union had no thought of trying to "communize" China. As Borodin, chief Russian adviser to Sun Yat-sen, declared: "The only Communism possible in China today is the Communism of poverty, a lot of people eating rice out of an almost empty bowl. At present and for many years to come, Communists and capitalists alike in China must have the same ideal of a prosperous and much more highly developed industrial China and a general rise in Chinese standards of living. China is neither the producer nor the consumer that she could be. The Chinese Nationalists want an agrarian revolution, but they want it in order to clear the way for China's economic development. Intellectuals used to think that by reminding the world of China's long civilized history, they would get her a place in the family of nations. China has learned, since Versailles, that that family tolerates no poor relations, even with four thousand years of a respectable past."

Honest students of the Chinese political and social scene recognize that Communism is not the issue in China and that no human power can convert today's backward Chinese economy into the basis for a Communist state. A prominent Chinese Communist spokesman recently stated that he did not foresee Communism as an issue in China for a long time. And just twenty years after Borodin's statement, a similar appraisal of China's economic needs was made by the leader of the Chinese Communist Party, Mao Tse-tung, in his book, *On Coalition Government*, published just prior to V-J Day. In this book, Mao explains the Chinese Communist attitude toward the development of private capital in China as follows: "Some people do not understand why Chinese Communists do not fear capitalism, but on the contrary promote its development. Our answer is simple: to replace foreign imperialist and native feudalist oppression with capitalistic development is not only progress but also an inevitable course, for it benefits the capitalist class as well as the proletariat. What is superfluous in present-day China is foreign imperialism and native feudalism, and not native capitalism. On the contrary, our capitalism is indeed too little."

Mao also emphasizes that the Chinese Communists will not only "struggle for the independence, freedom, democracy and unity of China, but will also struggle for the industrialization of China and the modernization of her agriculture. . . . To develop industry, enormous capital is needed. Where will it come from? It can only come from two sources, namely the capital accumulated by the Chinese people themselves and from foreign loans. On condition that they abide by the laws of China and are of advantage to the economy of China, foreign investments are welcome."

Today, when all the major powers have renounced their unequal treaties, the Chinese people, if permitted to speak freely, would undoubtedly seek and welcome the co-operation and assistance of all friendly powers, but only on condition that such foreign aid would have as its main purpose the building of a politically democratic and economically independent China. As a matter of fact, President Truman himself, in his statement of December 15, 1945, outlined accurately those conditions. In that statement, the President declared that the United States would give economic assistance only if China took steps to solve her internal conflicts through the institution of a "broadly representative government" that would give "all major political elements in the country . . . a fair and effective representation in the Chinese National Government." When China had demonstrated that she was advancing toward peace and unity along these lines, the United States would be prepared to consider loans and credits that would "contribute to the development of a healthy economy throughout China and healthy trade relations between China and the United States."

Unfortunately, this stated policy was not observed in practice, as evidenced by the extensive financial aid extended to the Chinese Government by the United States before any of the conditions stipulated by the President had been fulfilled. But the American people can still hope that their Government will realize, before it is too late, the dangers inherent in backing a regime that by its own words and actions stands revealed as the proponent of all that is antidemocratic and as the major obstacle to the development of mutually beneficial relations between China and the United States—a regime that is doing everything possible to foment discord between the United States and the Soviet Union, and a regime, moreover, that has aroused the vigorous opposition of all liberal elements in China, and that maintains its power only because it has managed to secure American military and financial support.

It is not easy to forecast the future development of China. But if the Kuomintang regime obtains the necessary aid to continue its undemocratic system of repressive government and its civil war policy for any prolonged period, China can only become once again a football among the powers; her freedom from the bondage of the unequal treaties will be more theoretical than real; and the development of a healthy Chinese economy will once more have received a serious setback. Chiang Kai-shek maintains in all his writings that China's destiny "rests with the Kuomintang." But the truth is that China's destiny rests with all the people of China, who alone can form a genuinely representative government involving the participation of every section of Chinese society, and thus give reality to Sun Yat-sen's dream, which he chose to express in the words of Lincoln—a "government of the people, by the people, and for the people." Only such a government deserves support, and only such a government can fulfill China's real destiny as a major factor in building world peace and prosperity.

GUIDE TO THE PRONUNCIATION OF
CHINESE NAMES

The Chinese differentiate between the following aspirated and unaspirated consonants: p, t, k, ch, ts. For *p* read *b;* for *t* read *d;* for *k* read *g;* for *ch* read *j;* and for *ts* read *dz.* For *p', t', k', ch', ts',* read *p, t, k, ch, ts,* as in normal English pronunciation. For example, for *Ch'ing,* read *ching,* and for *Ching,* read *jing.* Also, read *j* as *r, hs* as *sh, ih* as *ee, eh* as *er, en* as *un, eng* as *ung, ou* as *oh,* and *ei* as *ay.*

CHRONOLOGY OF CHINESE DYNASTIES

Hsia Dynasty (legendary)...................*c.* 2205–*c.* 1523 B.C.

Shang or Yin Kingdom....................*c.* 1523–*c.* 1027 B.C.

Chou Dynasty............................*c.* 1027–221 B.C.
   Ch'un Ch'iu Period 722–481 B.C.

Ch'in Dynasty...............................221–207 B.C.

Han Dynasty..........................207 B.C.–A.D. 221

Three Kingdoms (*San Kuo*).....................221–265

Tsin Dynasty....................................265–316

Northern and Southern Empires (*Nan Pei Chao*).........317–589
   Wei Dynasty 386–556

Sui Dynasty....................................589–618

T'ang Dynasty..................................618–906

Five Dynasty Period (*Wu Tai*)......................907–960

Sung Dynasty..................................960–1127

Chin and Southern Sung Dynasties.................1127–1280

Yuan (Mongol) Dynasty...........................1280–1368

Ming Dynasty..................................1368–1644

Ch'ing (Manchu) Dynasty........................1644–1911

Republic.......................................1911–

335

INDEX

(*Because of the numerous Chinese names, this index is strictly alphabetical, with the chief section of each entry regarded as a unit. Thus hyphens, apostrophes, and spaces between parts of names have been disregarded in deciding alphabetization.*)

Printed in the United States
By Bookmasters